ISAAC BASHEVIS SINGER

ISAAC BASHEVIS SINGER

———◆———

A LIFE

Janet Hadda

The University of Wisconsin Press

The University of Wisconsin Press
1930 Monroe Street
Madison, Wisconsin 53711

www.wisc.edu/wisconsinpress/

3 Henrietta Street
London WC2E 8LU, England

1   3   5   4   2

Printed in the United States of America

A cataloging-in-publication record for this book is available from the Library of Congress
ISBN 0-299-18694-6

CONTENTS

DEDICATION

DURING my years of study at Columbia University, I was also a student at the YIVO Institute for Jewish Research (Yidisher visnshaftlekher institut). In addition to my professors and teachers, I was privileged to meet and get to know people at YIVO who represented Eastern European Jewish culture at its finest and most vibrant: Bolek Ellenbogen, Hannah Fryshdorf, Moyshe Kligsberg, Shmuel Lapin, Shloyme Noble, Borekh Tshubinsky, ז"ל, as well as Dina Abramowicz and Bine Weinreich. As informal instructors, they enriched me with books, stories, vocabulary, gentle introductions to YIVO etiquette—and sometimes with criticisms that stung but nonetheless revealed engagement and concern. As a newcomer to Yiddish, I drank in the world they transmitted and am still nourished by it today. Without them, I could not have written this book, and so I dedicate it to them.

ACKNOWLEDGMENTS

AS I thought about and prepared this book, many people gave freely of their insights, their time, and their knowledge. I would like to thank them all here: Ellen Dirksen, Professor of Cell Biology at UCLA, who first suggested that I write a biography of Singer; Singer's translators, Mirra Ginsburg, Aliza Shevrin, Elizabeth Shub, and Dorothea Straus, who explained what it was like to work with him; Nobel laureate Saul Bellow, who fostered my understanding of Singer's role as a Yiddish writer in America; author and translator Cynthia Ozick, who answered my candid questions; members of Singer's family, including Alma Singer, Israel Zamir, Eleanor Foa Dienstag, and Meirav Hen, who revealed aspects of his mercurial nature to me; Singer's friends, colleagues, and people who thought deeply about his writing, including Ophra Alyagon, Rabbi Ben-Zion Gold, Itche Goldberg, Ida Haendel, Paul Mazursky, Avrom Shulman, Roger Simon, Roger Straus—all allowed me to interview them and all provided me with thought-provoking information; Morris Schappes, editor of *Jewish Currents*, who kindly supplied me with his Singer clipping files, saving me countless hours and exposing me to unusual and valuable sources; Edith Shackell, who offered detailed and discerning comments about the characters in Singer's life; my agent, Jane Dystel, and my editor, Nancy Lane, who assisted me with everything from the conception of the book to the final details—their standards are high and I admire them both.

Michael and Irene Ross and UCLA provided generous sponsorship of my research, for which I am most grateful.

Two people read every word of my manuscript as it unfolded. Kenneth Turan, film critic of *The Los Angeles Times*, and great friend of Yiddish, aided and inspired me every step of the way, from advice about tone to details about Singer on film. He has my deepest appreciation for his encouragement, intelligent perspective, and savvy understanding. The other, my husband, Allan J. Tobin, challenged me to tell the story and helped me find my voice. His support never wavers and his creativity continues to amaze me. As always, I feel blessed to share his presence—*nokh a yor, nokh a yor*.

INTRODUCTION

Mameloshn faces a situation as grotesque as it is excruciating. For hundreds of years, Yiddish thrived as the language of Ashkenaz, the pre-Shoah locus—geographic, cultural, and psychological—of Eastern European Jewish existence. But now, not even sixty years after the end of World War II, the language of Ashkenaz faces extinction. On the one hand, historians, filmmakers, and anthropologists rush to document the last witnesses of that civilization before they and their memories are forever lost. On the other hand, legions of Yiddish-lovers eagerly embrace the music, foods, and ritual behaviors that they view as central to pre-Shoah Eastern European Jewish life. Like admirers of some exotic bird, they celebrate the parts of Ashkenaz that are most foreign to their quotidian existence.

For as long as I have been involved with Yiddish and *yidishkeyt*—since 1969—I have been both disconcerted and angered by the persistent stereotyping of Ashkenaz. The stereotypes, perpetuated by Jews and non-Jews alike, fall into two basic categories: the first suggests that Eastern European Jewish life was monolithic, and the second suggests that the Jews themselves were uniformly simple. According to these notions, all Eastern European Jews were orthodox in their religious observance, lived in quaint *shtetlekh,* had little contact with their non-Jewish neighbors, and remained distant from secular pursuits.

The reality could not have been more different. During the last election before the Germans marched into Poland in 1939, the Bund (the Jewish Socialist party) emerged as the favorite among Poland's 3.3 million Jews. These secular Jews believed in physical self-defense and, like other socialists, considered themselves citizens of the world. On the eve of World War II, nearly half of Polish Jews lived in towns and cities of more than ten thousand Jews. Some Eastern European Jews were indeed rabbis, scholars, apprentices, porters, peddlers, and beggars. But others were physicians, demographers, linguists, entrepreneurs, librarians, and gangsters.

Two goals propelled my writing. First, I wanted to chronicle Bashevis's life and creative development. I sought to show his origins as the lonely child of brilliant but ill-matched parents, who were themselves overwhelmed by the roles that their era and their social environment had carved out for them. By studying the internal psychological dimension of his personality and character, I wanted to shed light on the struggles that Bashevis was compelled to endure. As a keen observer, Bashevis might have been describing conflicts and miseries that he himself had not experienced. But that was not the case. Like his protagonists, Bashevis was intimately acquainted with despair, depression, envy, hopelessness, and confusion.

While Bashevis's inner life was my central concern, my second goal was to depict the cultural milieu from which he emerged. I was determined to show the richness of his heritage and the vibrancy of modern Jewish life in Poland. I was certain that readers would welcome and appreciate my efforts to dispel the stereotypes surrounding *yidishkeyt* and Ashkenaz.

I was completely unprepared to discover that a segment of my audience neither welcomed nor appreciated such information. These readers considered my book unsympathetic, even hostile. Certain critics inferred that I hated Bashevis; they denigrated what they saw as my cavalier attitude towards his *oeuvre;* they complained that my discussions of his personality and family dynamics were intrusive and reductive. For some, my psychoanalytic training—and perhaps my California address—were evidence enough that I had engaged in distortion and psychobabble.

To my dismay, these readers objected to the suggestion that Bashevis was anything but a pigeon-feeding old man who frequented dairy restaurants and shabby coffee shops on New York's Upper West Side. They did not want to know that he had abandoned his only child when the boy was five and did not see him again for twenty five years, that he regularly violated contracts he had insisted on signing, that he was a registered Republican who was thrilled to speak at West Point.

What would cause such readers to hide from the truth? My guess is that, as an understandable response to the annihilation of the culture itself, they needed to idealize Ashkenaz, and its most famous representative.

Before the Shoah, American Jews tended to flee from Ashkenaz. For many immigrants and, especially, for their children, the realm of *yidishkeyt* was an impediment to success in the New World. In their pursuit of Americanization, the Yiddish language was a burdensome reminder of another time and place. The label *griner,* "greenhorn," was never a compliment.

Abraham Cahan, the long-time editor of *Der Forverts* (*The Jewish Daily Forward*) the most popular Yiddish newspaper in New York, had the explicit mission of educating his huge readership to become Americanized. Under a banner head that read "Workers of the World Unite," Cahan epitomized the virtue of *oysgrinen zikh,* or shedding greenhorn qualities. Cahan's quest was largely successful, in part because there were other cultural forces encouraging assimilation into an English-speaking milieu. But in the course of providing entertainment for his readers, Cahan also made possible the publication of Yiddish *belles lettres,* including the work of Bashevis, who—although he and Cahan detested one another—contributed to the paper for decades. Thus, even as he was promoting distance from Yiddish, Cahan strengthened the existence of Yiddish literature in an easily available form. Yet, ever increasing numbers of Yiddish speakers turned to English as their main vehicle of communication.

Even after the Shoah, when survivors of Hitler brought a fresh influx of Yiddish speakers to the United States, their experiences and their pre-War lives excited little interest. It took a generation—until the children of these survivors began to ask questions—for widespread discussion to begin. By then, however, the existence of Ashkenaz had suffered irreversibly. And there could be no regeneration from the old source, since that source had been reduced to rubble.

The result of this situation was a race to recapture as much of that culture as possible, before it disappeared forever. The last thirty years have been marked by the ever growing emergence of celebratory recognition of the riches that *yidishkeyt* has to offer. Anyone who observes Jewish culture is aware of the Yiddish festivals, camps, concerts, and courses that have sprung up all over the United States and Europe. These events appear to have reached an all-time high. At the same time, seemingly paradoxically, the number of Yiddish enthusiasts who have any familiarity with Ashkenaz has dwindled drastically.

These celebrations may be welcome, but, sadly, they do not recapture the essence of pre-Shoah Eastern European Jewish culture. That culture was a dizzying collision of religious tradition, political foment, urbanization, secularization, immigration, and modernization.

The epitome of the attempt to reinvent Ashkenaz is Ariel, a so-called Jewish restaurant in Kasimierz, which was the pre-Shoah center of the Krakow Jewish community—hence, it is actually located in the heart of what was Ashkenaz. The food features Eastern European Jewish delicacies, such as *heldzlekh,* stuffed chicken necks, but also, inexplicably, Sephardic specialties that may be Jewish but that have no connection to Poland. The music is a bizarre mix of secular and religious melodies, juxtaposed randomly. But among the musicians and restaurant employees, there is not a Jew in sight. And, when the musicians take their breaks, the rosy lights disappear and the restaurant reverts to what it really is—a Polish, non-Jewish, lure for tourists.

What does Bashevis have to do with this scene? As "Mr. Ashkenaz," he was both privileged and cursed to be seen by English speakers as the quintessential Eastern European Jew. While many Yiddish speakers saw Bashevis as perverse and disreputable, his English readers have the opposite view. Had his works not appeared in English, he probably would not have achieved significance on the world literary stage. Almost certainly, he would not have become the only Yiddish author ever to win the Nobel Prize.

Speakers of Yiddish have sometimes bemoaned Bashevis's jaundiced portrayals of Jewish types, but a careful reader will find almost every sort of Eastern European Jew in the pages of his work—especially his early work. Nonetheless, his English audience is more likely to recall *The Slave,* which depicts a seventeenth-century Jew cleaving to his faith against enormous odds, than *The Family Moskat,* which recounts, with impressive complexity, the shifting and often contradictory fortunes of Poland's Jews in the twentieth century.

In short, the general public valued Bashevis's work for its folkloric richness far more than for its precise rendering of the exciting diversity that was Ashkenaz. Readers who delight in the portrayal of an unfamiliar environment do not ask themselves an essential question: Why would an artist who spent more than half his life in the United States continually seek to recapture Ashkenaz in time and space?

For Bashevis, this impulse was born out of a dual need. He had to mourn a world that he knew no longer existed. At the same time, he had to create a sense of continuity for himself. The two goals were irreconcilable, because essential to Bashevis's sense of personal cohesiveness was the acceptance that Ashkenaz had been destroyed. It was not possible for Bashevis to return to Ashkenaz in order to reconnect with his origins. Nor could he grieve over the loss of his heritage by traditional means—there were no funerals to attend, no graves to visit. Only the attempt to make memory concrete could serve this function.

Imagine the heartrending position in which Bashevis found himself. As a consummate artist, he was forced—if he wanted the fame and recognition he craved—continuously to reconstruct Ashkenaz in its most traditional form, even as he grew increasingly distant from that aspect of his past. At the same time, his audiences—including the Swedish Academy — were not interested in his literary sophistication, his psychological perspicacity, his professional ambition, and his personal malaise. These characteristics would have burst the image of an unchanging and perfectly contained world that they, and not Bashevis, needed to preserve. In the end, Bashevis benefited from the bargain financially and, to a lesser extent, personally, but he was caught in a perpetual vise, from which he never freed himself.

During the writing of *Isaac Bashevis Singer: A Life,* I was often overwhelmed by the immense challenge inherent in the project. I was documenting the inner life of a man who could only have emerged out of the clashes between secularism and orthodoxy, modernism and tradition, concrete poverty and intellectual plenty as they managed to co-exist in him and in pre-Shoah Poland. Simultaneously, I had to place that man and his work into a context that would reveal his unique artistic sensibility. The task was further complicated by my powerful desire to set the record straight with respect to Ashkenaz and *yidishkeyt.*

Now, five years later, the plight of Yiddish and of *yidishkeyt* is graver than ever. By writing explicitly about the denial of this reality, I hope to make still more explicit just what intricate treasures lie in the universe of Ashkenaz. But, to the extent that I succeed, the loss of those treasures becomes all the more painful to me and to my readers. I am consoled by my trust that the profound and vibrant culture of Yiddish and *yidishkeyt,* even in its present diminished state, can be forever enriching, and even transforming.

ISAAC BASHEVIS SINGER

Prologue

Initially, it was no more than an inkling, something about the way my interviews were going. For example, there was the day my attempt to meet one of Bashevis's translators was thwarted by a parade. Stranded on one side of Sixth Avenue for half an hour, I fumed, but I reminded myself that such occurrences are common in New York City. I am not superstitious.

During the first months of work on Bashevis's biography, I had many occasions to reiterate my confidence in normal coincidence. Listening to strange stories of demonic microphones, uncanny encounters with birds, doors mysteriously swinging open and shut, I was fascinated, but I remained convinced that each occurrence could be explained as random. But when my suitcase vanished on a trip to Miami, never to be seen again, I had to wonder. Was I becoming a character in Bashevis's crazy world? And if so, what did that say about him and about me? I think I have found an answer to these questions; but first I want to back up and explain how I came to write about Bashevis in the first place.

It all started on a bleak, snowy day in 1968. I was a miserable graduate student of Germanic linguistics at Cornell. Bored and disaffected, I left my carrel in the library and wandered around the stacks. Apparently by accident, I found myself in the Jewish literature section. I picked up a fat volume by someone called Isaac Bashevis Singer. One paragraph in, and I was already hooked. I now recall reading the novel in one sitting, although I know I remember incorrectly as *The Family Moskat* is over 600 pages long. By the time I finished, I had decided to get my hands on that culture, that world, that language. The thought of trying to meet the author who had turned my complacent if unhappy world upside down never occurred to me.

I first encountered Bashevis several years later, in 1971. By now I was a graduate student of Yiddish literature at Columbia and the YIVO. The occasion was a *Yugntruf* (Youth for Yiddish) convention, held at the Atran House on Madison Avenue, home of several Yiddish cultural organizations. Bashevis was to be the guest speaker. As it happened, just as the tiny, creaky, and grotesquely slow elevator was about to take off on its seemingly endless journey up to the fourth floor, Bashevis slipped aboard. I had never before seen him in person. He was slight of build and frail, even fragile. Although he was still in his sixties, he appeared ancient to me. Above all, he was extraordinarily pale, and the veins shone through his translucent skin to an alarming degree. I worried that he might die while the elevator strained its way to our destination.

On that occasion, I think the audience grumbled about his being unprepared, but I was enthralled. The phenomenon of "The Yiddish Reading," or *vort-kontsert* (concert of words) was still new to me: the black glasses whipped out with a fanfare, the sonorous rendition, certainly by heart, because no one wearing those glasses could possibly see, the inevitable dissatisfaction of an insatiable audience, starving for more words, even as the language was drying up before its eyes.

By the next time I saw Bashevis, in 1974, I was an assistant professor at UCLA, and, as it turned out, he was less than four years away from winning the Nobel prize. To my surprise, he filled Ackerman Ballroom, a huge space in the Student Union building. He gave a talk that was full of quips, one-liners, and bon mots. I was disgruntled, and my reaction soon turned to dismay. A member of the audience asked him to say something in Yiddish. "No one will understand me," he replied. "Yes, we will," a chorus chanted from the floor. "No one will understand me," Bashevis repeated. Then, from the back of the hall, came words in a clear *galitsyaner* dialect: "Why won't you talk Yiddish to us?" It was a student of mine, the daughter of immigrants. She spoke with the rich pronunciation of her parents, who had come from Galicia, an area north of the Eastern Carpathian mountains. Traditionally, *galitsyaner*, Jews from Galicia, were considered less educated and less sophisticated than their *litvak* counterparts (Jews from the area corresponding to Lithuania, Belorussia, and Latvia).

Bashevis knew that the members of his audience would recognize the *galitsyaner-litvak* stereotype, even if they were hazy about the geography. He replied in English, "I'll tell you a joke. Why doesn't God speak to us anymore? Why? Because He doesn't want us to know He's a Galitsyaner." The members of the audience howled with delight, not realizing, or not caring, that Bashevis had seduced them out of the desire to hear Yiddish. I was incensed, furious that my student had been the butt of a joke, and that no one understood the sly maneuver except for the perpetrator and me. I decided then and there that those in the Yiddish world who hated Bashevis had a point. He was manipulative, nasty, opportunistic, and cynical. Furthermore, he was a sell-out; he had sacrificed his Yiddish soul for money and fame in America. I wrote an angry article explaining the betrayal, but no one wanted to publish it.

Years passed. Bashevis was coming back to UCLA for another visit. As I recall, it was 1981. This time, I was to introduce him. The award of the Nobel prize had made me feel slightly more benign toward him. I told myself that he had, despite himself, managed to resuscitate Yiddish, at least temporarily, and for that I was thankful. I still thought of him as a cagey and calculating operator who happened to be serving the culture. And I scoffed at my friend, Deborah Lipstadt, who urged me to understand that Bashevis was not as wily as I believed. "I've stood behind him at the bank," she explained. "He gets flustered and confused."

I was apprehensive. Bashevis was no longer relegated to a makeshift lecture hall in the student union. This time the address was being held in the posh auditorium of Royce Hall, UCLA's elegant signature building. We were to gather in the Green Room, and then I was to escort the author to the auditorium. When I arrived, Bashevis was already there. He looked as I remembered him from times past, before I uncovered his chicanery: delicate, parchment-skinned with bright blue, slightly bulging eyes that shone with humor and intelligence—an old man, completely unlikely to receive the kind of sexual advances he so often described in his stories. In fact, I wondered whether he was strong enough to walk unaided through the solidly constructed corridors. The sight of him looking so small, even next to me, reminded me of the first time I had seen him in the elevator of the Atran House. Now, because I was still mistrustful of him, I suspected that his infirmity was just part of the hype.

Out of nowhere, a fortyish woman with dazzling red hair appeared on the scene. She approached Bashevis, grabbed his hands, gazed into his eyes, and breathed: "Isaac! Your karma is my karma. We must have dinner tonight." My mouth fell open. Had he arranged this? But Bashevis clearly did not know the woman. With a gracious smile, he gently disengaged himself from her grasp. "Maybe next time," he murmured.

Although Bashevis was to deliver a written lecture, he told me that there was a slight complication. He had forgotten his spectacles and had with him only his deep black sunglasses. I took this difficulty in stride, wavering between dismissing the oversight as another trick and viewing it as an indication of some abiding loyalty to The Yiddish Reading.

We proceeded slowly to the darkened backstage area. The auditorium was packed. The representative of the student organization that had invited Bashevis was introducing me. In about forty-five seconds I would go on stage to give my introduction. Suddenly, at my elbow, I heard a little moan and then: "Oy, please help me." The student representative was announcing me. Unnerved, I whirled to face Bashevis. Was he having a heart attack? "Please help," he repeated, and shoved a sheaf of aging yellow ruled paper into my hands. I looked at the pages, immediately recognizing the problem. On top was page five, followed by page eleven, then page two, etc. "I can't see," he said, pointing to his eyes. "I only have these sunglasses." The audience was applauding the student representative. I was due on stage. Bashevis looked at me with the expression of that helpless little boy he had so often described in his stories, the little boy I was prepared to dismiss as a fake. "I guess the audience won't mind waiting a second while I fix this," I told him. He smiled gratefully, unaware that, in that moment, he had healed a wound in me. I now understood that Bashevis was both sharp and naive, that he could be both cruel and charming. But he had falsified neither his characters nor his culture. Knowing that, I could accept his considerable imperfections.

After that, I had a couple of pleasant contacts with Bashevis. During the last one, in Los Angeles, we sat by the swimming pool of the simple but gracious Del Capri Hotel in Westwood and spoke Yiddish. Bashevis talked with bemusement about the usefulness of such neologisms as *shvim-baseyn*, swimming pool. Then his imagination took off. Looking up at the tall apartment buildings that surrounded the two-floor hotel, he began an elaborate and, for some reason, hilarious story about all the millionaires who might spit into the *shvim-baseyn* from their penthouses. For the first time, I understood the power of his ageless charm.

Bashevis's death in 1991 saddened me greatly, reminding me how much his existence had influenced my life and the course of my career. With these thoughts in mind, I wrote an obituary essay for the *Los Angeles Jewish Journal.* In response to the piece, I received a note from an acquaintance, urging that I write a biography of Bashevis. The back of my neck tingled: I realized instantly that this was the project for me. Little did I know that I was embarking on an adventure.

I do not believe in demons, sprites, *dybbukim* (souls of the dead who seek refuge in the bodies of living individuals), or other forms of supernatural existence. So I am not about to relate that I have been visited by Bashevis's ghost, soul, or spirit. I am convinced, however, that at times I have been part of his fictional world. I take what happened to me as an illustration of the fuzzy boundary between imagination and experience that Bashevis maintained in his life and transmitted through his writing.

Until I began work on the biography, my encounters with colorful characters were easy to assimilate within a context that generally made sense to me. Once I started my research, however, I met, in quick succession, a collection of oddballs and difficult personalities—*kantike mentshn,* people with square edges—the likes of whom I had previously found only in Bashevis's fiction. Moreover, as I have already indicated, Singeresque things started happening to me.

My first meeting with Alma Singer, Bashevis's widow, was a good introduction to the world of my subject. Even though I later discovered that she was mild compared with the other characters I would come across, she provided a benchmark for the contradictions and conflicts that epitomized Bashevis's life. In late 1992, Alma was eighty-five years old, dainty, and impeccably attired for our lunch. I had heard that she was hard and thoughtless, yet her manner seemed wistful and vulnerable, almost naive. Her apartment in Surfside, just north of Miami Beach, was simple and not especially well equipped for entertaining. The dining room table served as a repository for the accumulated mail that continued to arrive despite the death of Isaac, as Alma referred to her late husband. The kitchen was cramped, clearly not the domain of an eager cook. In a corner of the living room, however, stood a little marble table, and this was Alma's pride, for it was here that she had set up her own nook for receiving guests. As she proudly proclaimed, she had designed the space herself—meaning that it was not part of the furniture that had come with the apartment. She explained that she had moved herself and the ailing Isaac at short notice some years earlier, when it had become clear that he needed around-the-clock care. Although she had not liked the apartment's furnishings, there had been no time for quibbling. She had bought the table afterwards as a reward.

Alma's taste in dining out had evidently been honed by years of living with the frugal and gustatorially challenged Isaac: she favored Denny's (where she consumed clam chowder, a double taboo for Isaac), as well as Danny's and Sheldon's—all three establishments of the luncheonette/coffee shop variety. And, although her manner was sweet and friendly, there was also something withholding and nearly mocking about the way she served coffee: in cups that she was pleased to announce came from a local bank.

As we drank our coffee, Alma put forward a surprising proposal: perhaps I could help her with the sale of Isaac's archives. She quickly revealed herself to be anxious about money; moreover, it seemed that she was being manipulated by someone who had insinuated himself into the venture of selling Bashevis's literary estate. She didn't want him to be involved. What should she do? I felt myself pulled into her drama. I would help, I would get involved. Maybe UCLA could buy the collection.

In the end, the undertaking came to nought, and the papers eventually found a safe home at the University of Texas, Austin. But I had had my first lesson in Bashevis madness—the panicky mix of emergency and pettiness that epitomizes the struggles his characters must regularly face.

I knew beforehand that Bashevis had led a bifurcated existence: there was his Yiddish self and his American persona, his Warsaw milieu and his New York environment, even his New York and his Miami homes, with different friends and events in each. But the split goes further, extending to the people who surrounded him.

They divide into those who hate him and can say nothing good about him, and those who love him and will lie to protect him. The former are mainly men, the latter almost exclusively women.

From the men, I learned that Bashevis was unscrupulous, ungenerous, and unreliable. Two of the men who could have been closest to him, his two nephews, Joseph Singer and Maurice Carr, refused to be interviewed at all. Carr, whose mother was Bashevis's sister, the writer Esther Kreitman, even threatened to sue me. He was concerned lest I repeat Alma Singer's claim that Esther had once been hospitalized in a Paris clinic and that Bashevis had footed the bill. From the women, I learned that Bashevis was capricious, captivating, and childlike. They encouraged me to accept a fascinating but implausible fact: that Bashevis had slept with all his translators, except for the one who happened to be telling me about all the others. Indeed, his womanizing was problematic to pursue. Everyone acknowledged it, but, during conversations that began to resemble an intelligence mission in Wonderland, no one had any idea who the women might have been.

It was the process of investigating, not the results themselves, that first gave me the sense of living inside fiction. Early on, I learned that writing Bashevis's biography would be an entirely different enterprise than anything I had previously endeavored. Unlike the quiet and solitary work with texts that had occupied me in the past, I was going to be conducting many interviews and talking to a variety of people about Bashevis. The prospect was intriguing, but I had no idea that it would turn out to be so complicated. In my psychoanalytic practice, I am accustomed to asking questions, fielding sensitive emotional terrain, and figuring out hidden dynamics. But neither my academic nor my psychoanalytic training prepared me for the intricate negotiations through which I would have to tiptoe just to arrange something as simple as a meeting or a telephone consultation.

Take Shaloma, for instance. I first heard about Shaloma from Bashevis's granddaughter, Meirav Hen. "She's difficult, but you'll learn a lot from her," Meirav told me. Meirav didn't have Shaloma's phone number, so she suggested I contact her father, Israel Zamir, an Israeli journalist and Bashevis's only child. I placed a call to Zamir's home on Kibbutz Beit Alpha and reached his wife. We had recently met at a conference in London, and she was cordial. But when I stated my business, her tone changed. As she called her husband to the phone, I could hear her alerting him: "You don't have Shaloma's number, do you?" He caught on immediately. "I don't have Shaloma's number," he told me, "and in any case, you don't want to talk to her." "Oh, but I do," I insisted, feeling challenged now, although I had no idea myself why I might want to talk to Shaloma. Who was she anyway? To his credit, Zamir is not much of a liar. With a minimum of prodding, a long-forgotten address book turned up, and I was off and running.

Right into a brick wall. The number I tried was disconnected. I learned later that Shaloma had moved to temporary quarters after her home in Miami was devastated by Hurricane Hugo. I also eventually found out that Zamir had mispronounced and misspelled her last name. At the time, however, all I knew was that she was not listed anywhere in the greater Miami area. Frustrated, I started playing with the sounds of the name I had been given, using an old technique familiar to me from analyzing modernist Yiddish poetry. From there, I compiled a list of possible alternatives and picked up the phone. After at least thirty wrong numbers, a friendly female voice answered. "Shaloma? No, there's no Shaloma here—but she's my roommate's mother." I felt exhilarated, sleuth-like, and efficient. Little did I know that my difficulties were only beginning.

During the first of several protracted phone conversations devoted to planning the interview, Shaloma told me that she had made a documentary film about Bashevis. She assured me that her work would answer all my questions, revealing the very essence of the man and his fiction. Shaloma wanted to collaborate with me; she was writing a play that would consist solely of dialogue between Bashevis and a psychiatrist. We could work a deal, she explained. She would let me view the film, and in return I would serve as clinical consultant for the play. Of course, it all depended on her lawyer. In the meantime, though, why didn't I come to Miami?

The time and place of our rendezvous necessitated additional lengthy conversations once I got to Florida. By the end of each deliberation, my head was spinning. During one call, the interview would take place in Miami. By the next time, Miami was out; it was Key Largo or nothing. Arranging the hour was unfathomably complex as well. I was beginning to get discouraged. Finally, we hammered out an agreement to meet that afternoon in the lobby of a Coral Gables hotel. "I'll be wearing a little beanie," she told me in the broad Boston accent that was now familiar to me, after all our bargaining.

Weary but once again optimistic, I set out. Somewhere along the way, though, I took a wrong turn. Suddenly, the road narrowed dramatically and began to twist. At first, I was not distressed. Nonetheless, I started thinking about the narrator in Bashevis's "Hanka," who unexpectedly finds himself adrift in a world that, just moments before, had seemed safe and predictable: "There was an air of curfew and Black Sabbath.... Unseen dogs were barking; unseen cats mewed and yowled."[1] As I drove along the palm-lined streets of what I hoped was Coral Gables, I remembered the hapless narrator of "One Night in Brazil," reacting with uneasiness and bewilderment to the alien tropical setting where he has landed: "Crickets sawed unseen trees with invisible saws. Frogs croaked with human voices. From the banana trees, the wild flowers, and thickets of grass and leaves rose a scorching heat...."[2]

Forty minutes later, I was distressed. I had forfeited my chance to meet Shaloma. Surely, she would not be likely to sit around waiting for me. The failure of the appointment was bad enough, but, in addition, I was totally lost. Unbelievably, during all the time I was charting my unknown course, searching for some landmark to guide me, I had not seen a single person from whom to ask directions. At long last, I reached an intersection; with relief, I pulled up next to a huge white Cadillac. Although the signal was changing, I rolled down my window and mentioned the name of the hotel. "Follow me," the driver bellowed. "I'm going there." The white boat took off, but not before I had recognized the voice, the Boston accent, the little beanie. I was following Shaloma. Two traffic lights later, she screeched to a stop and jumped out of her car into the middle of the street. "Are you Hadda?" she yelled.

I never saw Shaloma's film. Although I was disappointed at the time, I had begun to realize by then that my interactions with the people in Bashevis's orbit were going to be unusual at best. I would have to play it by ear, grab every opportunity, take things as they came. Above all, I would have to develop a tolerance for frustration and unexpected adversity. The loss of my suitcase is an example.

Like most frequent fliers, I have more than once arrived at a destination, only to find that my suitcase has been misplaced. Once, my luggage was lost for a couple of weeks. What was odd about this experience was my utter conviction that I would never see my luggage again. Even as I was walking towards the baggage claim area at the Miami airport, something told me that the case wouldn't be there. I was right. Then I began to sense that I would never get it back. As it turned out, I was right about this, too. I don't know how long I stood there, mesmerized, collecting my thoughts and worrying about the next day. I was taking Alma to lunch. She would no doubt be wearing some elegant dress, possibly linen. How could I show up in blue jeans and a tee shirt?

The empty carousel went round and round. Everyone else had gone home. Suddenly, I remembered Bashevis's story "The Lecture," in which the narrator loses his briefcase and, with it, his emotional integrity, his sense of self. At that moment I understood beyond any doubt that I had entered Bashevis's realm, a place where exotic, unexplained things happen, and where occurrences that would not appear unusual in any other context take on a peculiar and spooky twist. If I was going to write about Bashevis's life and his fiction, I would have to accept the existence of that domain.

Having made the leap, I was now free to embark on adventures that would have been impossible before the night at the airport. One such escapade involved Bashevis's old friend, the Israeli journalist Ophra Alyagon. Ophra happened to be staying at our house in Los Angeles for a week. Towards the end of her stay, she told me that I really should come to New York while she would be there, because then I would have the opportunity to meet Avrom Shulman, who had known Bashevis well and who had even written a book about him. Deciding to seize the day, I cancelled my plans for the weekend and flew to New York.

Ophra was staying at the Mayflower Hotel, at Columbus Circle. Although she had been in fine health the day before when she had left Los Angeles, I arrived to find her lying in bed, felled by a sudden upper-respiratory infection. With her was a short, compact man, obviously Avrom Shulman, arguing with her in loud tones about some failure on her part to help him get published in Israel. He would talk to me soon about Bashevis, he promised me with a wave of the hand. But before I knew it, he and I were on our way to visit Genye, a friend of Ophra's from Israel, now residing in New York. Genye had made some chicken soup; Shulman and I were to fetch it and bring it back to the hotel in a taxi. "Don't be afraid of what you will see," Ophra warned me, her voice a dark mixture of foreboding and incipient laryngitis. We set out; on the way, Shulman complained nonstop about Bashevis, whom he described in an excited voice as devious, unscrupulous, and heartless. In particular, he was enraged about a 1971 contract, authorizing him to adapt Bashevis's "Teibele and Her Demon" for the stage. Bashevis had insisted on the written agreement, only to violate it subsequently.

Genye did not live far from the hotel, but I was exhausted by the time we reached her apartment. We rang the bell, and the door opened. Although we were still in Manhattan and not in Brooklyn, I could have sworn I had walked in on Bashevis's story, "Sam Palka and David Vishkover": "...I saw a room that looked exactly like one in the old country. If I hadn't known that I was in Brownsville, I would have thought that I was in Konskowola.... Even the smells were from Konskowola—fried onions, chicory, moldy bread. On the sofa sat a girl as beautiful as Queen Esther.... She was dressed like a greenhorn who had just arrived: a long skirt and shoes with buttons."[3] True, Genye was no longer a girl, but she exuded an Old Country warmth and grace. Surely there was nothing ominous about this cheerful and efficient woman, bustling about packing up soup and other specialties for her languishing friend.

Then I saw what Ophra had meant. Sitting at a table in the dining area was a woman who looked about seventy, although she may have been considerably younger. Wearing a faded housedress over stockings rolled at the ankles, she was rhythmically shoveling corn flakes into her sagging mouth. She swallowed without chewing. Her eyes blank pools of depression, her body completely slack, except for the robotic movement of hand to mouth, the woman did not respond to Shulman's greetings. Indeed, she seemed oblivious to our presence. Shulman beckoned to me. Reluctantly, I edged closer, curious but uneasy, afraid to intrude. With one word, spoken *sotto voce* in his rich Yiddish accent, Shulman summarized the scene: "Drogs," he solemnly intoned.

The door to Genye's apartment finally closed behind us; Shulman and I were on our way back to the Mayflower, armed with enough food to sustain Ophra for a week. As we got into the elevator, I felt an incomprehensible surge of relief. It was only when the taxi was whizzing downtown, and Shulman's complaints were once again ringing in my ears, that I understood my apparently absurd reaction: I had just emerged from inside one of Bashevis's short stories, and I had escaped the fate of having to stay there forever, trapped in a timeless and tragically unchanging plot.

Far from being a fluke, the episode at Genye's was familiar to me, once I was able to place it in the context of my psychoanalytic work. As a clinician, I am privileged and challenged to experience the world from the perspective of others. At times, I have had the illusion that I am literally looking out from behind someone else's eyes. But I do not lose myself in the process. Rather, I bring my own reality to every encounter, even as I become fleetingly merged with perceptions, fantasies, and memories that are not my own. During the process of writing Bashevis's biography, I gradually entered a similar relationship with him, largely through imagining myself into his fiction and resonating with the emotional truths he presented there.

I am not convinced that Bashevis fully believed in otherworldly phenomena, because he often spoke of the supernatural as a manifestation of psychological phenomena. However, as a profoundly religious man, he tried to find meaning in the random incidents that more practical types attribute to chance. At the same time, his work made the zaniest human beings approach and admire him. In his fiction, he invented and depicted characters who attracted real people. Those meetings inspired more fiction. The cycle was never-ending during his lifetime and it endures after his death. His survivors continue to bicker and act out, worrying about money and fame, competing over how much he loved them.

In a sense, the people I interviewed were Bashevis's raw material. They are no less eccentric now that he is not around to describe them.

Witnessing aspects of Bashevis's life has made his fiction, even at its most bizarre, authentic and believable to me. Once inside that reality, it was perhaps inevitable that I would come to view my own activities concerning him as part of the very life I had set out to document.

1

———◆———

WARSAW, 1911. Seven-year-old Yitskhok, or Itshele, as he is called—all fiery red hair, translucent, milk-white skin and brilliant blue eyes—sits in his family's apartment at No. 10 Krochmalna Street. He is intent on his efforts: "Taking sheets of paper from my father's drawer, I covered them with scribbles and freakish sketches."[1]

Krochmalna Street, in a poor section of the city, is bustling as usual, overflowing with life of all kinds: in the courtyard of No. 10, peddlers cry out their hot cakes and offer to buy rags and mend windows;[2] pickpockets are on the job, lottery sales are brisk;[3] the sounds of children shrieking in play merges with the strains of gramophones blaring arias, marches, waltzes,[4] and Yiddish songs:

> *Hot a yid a vaybele,*
> *Hot er fun ir tsores;*
> *Hot a yid a vaybele,*
> *Toyg zi af kapores.*
>
> Give a Jew a little wife,
> She'll only cause him trouble;
> Give a Jew a little wife,
> She'll only cost him double.[5]

No trees beautify this scene.[6] The staircase leading to the apartment at No. 10, lit only by tiny kerosene lamps, is dingy, dirty, rat-infested, and foul-smelling—perhaps from the outhouse in the courtyard. Cats lurk in the stairwells. The apartment upstairs is poor and meager: a study empty except for two books, a bedroom with two bedsteads, a larder containing only the day's provisions.[7] The potted plants that cheer the misery of other apartments in the courtyard are absent here, for this is a deeply religious home, and pagan customs are forbidden.[8] The boy notices nothing but his scribbling.[9]

Itshele's family includes his father, Pinkhos Menakhem, his mother, Basheve, his older sister, Hinde Esther, nicknamed Hindele, his older brother, Yisroel Yehoshue, known at home as Shiye, and his baby brother Moyshe—Moyshele to those who can find the time to address him.

Pinkhos Menakhem, a fresh-faced, softly formed man, is the unofficial rabbi of Krochmalna Street. He has refused to learn Russian and to take the exam that would grant him government recognition. As the informal authority of his neighborhood, he is responsible for deciding on matters of ritual purity, granting divorces, and settling disputes; Basheve, the *rebetsin*, is a tall, spare, highly educated woman who barely endures her life in Warsaw. Cooking and housework do not come naturally to her; she would rather spend her time reading. Shiye is a brilliant student who has nonetheless embarked on a life of rebellion against his parents' orthodox ways—he has begun to paint, to study Russian, and to read secular Yiddish literature; little blond Moyshele makes scant impression on Itshele.

Itshele's sudden artistic debut coincides exactly with an imminent transformation in the structure of his family: Hindele, the eldest child and thirteen years Itshele's senior, has finally gotten engaged—at age twenty, she is almost past her prime. The union has been arranged by her parents, as is the custom, but it was no easy task, for Hindele is difficult and willful. She is about to depart Warsaw for Antwerp.

Within three years, Itshele's family will be dissolved, the victim of war, modernity, and domestic conflict. Itshele will one day call himself Bashevis and become a great writer—the only Yiddish author ever to win the Nobel prize. But on this day, he is a small and lonely child, soon to lose perhaps the most important figure in his world, a person whose dramatic eccentricity will remain a source of fear and fascination to him for the rest of his life. Not knowing what to do in the face of such monumental change, Itshele turns inward—far from the torments of his household—and scribbles.

*   *   *

Isaac Bashevis Singer, the man who commemorated Eastern-European–Jewish life for an English-reading public, combined the zaniness of individual characterizations with an unerring ability to convince his readers that he embodied the essence of traditional *yidishkeyt*: the world of Torah—or *toyre*—of *shtetl*, of Jewish law and ritual. And, in a way, he could describe the scene from inside out, for he was raised in a home filled with piety and learning, as well as with the grinding poverty that epitomized Polish Jewry. Much later, in his famous memoir, *In My Father's Court,* Singer labored to depict his family as superficially typical: parents who were always present and who fulfilled the prescribed duties of an orthodox Jewish existence, lively siblings, quotidian trials—a fairly happy, fairly ordinary family.

This retrospective portrayal notwithstanding, nothing could be further from the truth. Singer's home was truly unusual in every possible way: both parents were brilliant, immature, and irresponsible; Hindele was strange, given to wild mood swings; Shiye tended towards cynicism and was fiercely nonconformist. Everyone in the family also experienced considerable confusion over gender roles—a problem that subsequently absorbed Singer in many of his works.

By the time Itshele was born, on July 14, 1904, the family was established in its routines and habits; but the story starts with Pinkhos Menakhem and Basheve.

> *My father was a saint.... My mother was even more of a saint than my father because for him it was natural and she had to make an effort. I loved my parents. Whoo! They made my life a misery but I loved them very much.*—I. B. S., 1972[10]

BORN and raised in Tomaszow, Itshele's father, Pinkhos Menakhem Singer, had been coddled and pampered by his energetic and admiring mother. The youngest of five children, he was a quintessential mama's boy who is reputed to have appeared at his wedding in a woolen muffler, although it was the middle of summer, because he had a chill and his mother was worried about him.[11] Such unfashionable attire was not uncharacteristic, for Pinkhos Menakhem shunned modern trends. They smacked to him of secularism, the very thought of which filled him with alarm and contempt.[12]

Pinkhos Menakhem was warm and gentle, a man who was not afraid to show his feelings—or perhaps he was incapable of containing them. His congregants loved his mildness and the erudition he never flaunted before them. Such was Pinkhos Menakhem's tenderness that he found room to pity his neighbor's hogs, even though they were, of course, unclean according to Jewish law. Their owner was a pig butcher, "squat, fair, his little eyes, snub nose, and bristly hair lending him a close resemblance to his animals"—whose cruelty caused his victims to howl in pain. Pinkhos Menakhem suffered on their behalf, walking about "ashen-faced, his heart filled with compassion for the anguished beasts that, even though they were impure, were still creatures of God."[13] Many years later, when he was already an old man, Pinkhos Menakhem's grandson described him: "Never before have I seen, nor shall I ever see again, such a childlike lovingness in a grown man, or such a look of innocence but also wisdom in those gentle blue eyes."[14]

Pinkhos Menakhem was a *khosid*, an adherent of the Hasidic tenets originally developed by Israel Baal Shem Tov at the end of the seventeenth century and elaborated throughout the eighteenth and nineteenth centuries. A major religious force in Eastern-European-Jewish life, Hasidism was ecstatic, mystical, and hierarchical, resting its authority in the figure of the *rebbe*. Each Hasidic dynasty had its own rebbe, whose holiness was unquestioned. Followers would undertake pilgrimages to their chosen rebbe's, where they would hang on his every word and delight in eating the leftovers of his meals. By the time of Itshele's birth, Pinkhos Menakhem was deeply involved with the Radzymin rebbe, a coarse and all too worldly man whom Pinkhos Menakhem nonetheless trusted even as he was being cheated and exploited. The situation—especially because the maltreatment involved failure to pay wages for Pinkhos Menakhem's work as head of the yeshiva—did not sit well with his wife, Basheve.

And who was Basheve Singer, née Zylberman? She was, above all, a powerful intellect. She knew much more about scholarly matters than other women of similar background and standing. Perhaps most important for the family dynamic, since it served to create endless conflicts between her and her husband, she was a rationalist. Basheve was the daughter of the Bilgoray rabbi, who ruled as undisputed leader of his community and who was a *misnaged*—a strict opponent of Hasidism. In her approach to life and religion, Basheve resembled her father far more than her husband, and she had no time for Pinkhos Menakhem's emotional and anti-intellectual pursuits. Nonetheless, she also admired Pinkhos Menakhem—and had agreed to marry him—for his formidable mind.

As opposed to her preternaturally optimistic and serene husband, Basheve was blunt and dour. Her treatment of others could be brusque and cold. Hindele believed that her mother cared only for herself, that she was simply oblivious to her daughter's obvious struggles and miseries.[15] Shiye, who enjoyed sparring with his mother on philosophical and religious matters, viewed her self-absorption as stemming from depression rather than from insensitivity or narcissism. For Shiye, his mother's tragedy was her utter unsuitability to the role of *rebetsin*. She could not serve as the female role model for the women of Krochmalna Street because she was like an alien plant among them: she was unable to socialize with them, to gossip, to find satisfaction in the housewifely tasks that filled their lives. They, in turn, could not enter her realm of erudition and refinement; consequently, they saw her as snobbish. Basheve was stuck: an educated woman in an environment where her learning could have no outlet. She soon realized that she was an inappropriate consort for her husband.[16]

Basheve was frequently withdrawn and morose, and her melancholy endured throughout the growth of her children, whom she bore over a span of more than thirteen years. She was an avid reader, but her involvement, far from functioning as a pleasurable escape, served rather as a grim exercise in moral training. She would lose herself in the didactic books that were standard fare for educated Jewish women, who—like Eastern-European-Jewish women in general—were traditionally raised to view themselves as the sinful descendants of Eve. For Basheve, these works, such as *The Duty of the Heart* or *The Beginning of Wisdom* had direct meaning. They guided her in her attempts to recover from her sense that she had offended the other women of Krochmalna Street, those women to whom she bore so little resemblance, either physically or temperamentally. By both character and upbringing, she was woefully out of her element as the wife of a local leader who secretly wished he could achieve the status of a charismatic figure.[17]

Try as she might, Basheve could not acquire the tone necessary to communicate with Krochmalna Street. Many years later, Isaac Bashevis Singer told the story of a woman who came to see Pinkhos Menakhem because, years before, she had given birth to an illegitimate child and had abandoned him in front of a church. Subsequently, she had begun to realize that her son must have been raised as a non-Jew, and she was plagued by the idea that her offspring might be an anti-Semite and that she had caused this evil in the world. At first, the woman confessed to Basheve—an indication of the fluid line separating Pinkhos Menakhem's authority from that of his wife: "My mother was pale; her lips were clenched. The fact that she did not immediately attempt to comfort the woman was an indication to me of how grievous was the sin that she had committed."[18]

The two women decided that the penitent should talk to Pinkhos Menakhem: "Mother entered Father's study. It was not long before he was sighing....The holy books described the atonement for such a sin, but would the woman be prepared to undertake such a penance? And would it not be beyond the limits of her strength? The generation of today was weak. Father was afraid he might go too far, might cause the woman to become ill. Then he would have committed a sin greater than hers...."[19] Pinkhos Menakhem began to question and comfort the woman: "Father's words melted the woman's heart like wax, as the saying goes. Her weeping became even more intense, yet now there was in it something of joy. She looked upon Father with shining eyes. In essence he had told her exactly what my mother had already said, but somehow his words seemed warmer, more intimate."[20]

To say that Basheve and Pinkhos Menakhem were singularly mismatched is an understatement. Years later, I. J. Singer underscored the magnitude of their incompatibility: "They would have been a well-mated couple if she had been the husband and he the wife. Even externally each seemed better suited for the other's role. Father was short and round, with a soft, fine, delicate face; warm blue eyes; full rosy cheeks; a small, chiseled nose, and plump, feminine hands. If not for the great reddish-brown beard and corkscrew-like sidelocks, he would have resembled a woman. Mother, on the other hand, was tall and somewhat stooped, with large, piercing, cold-grey eyes, a sharp nose, and a jutting pointed chin like a man's."[21] Each was locked in a separate world. Pinkhos Menakhem lived in a realm of easy emotion and empathy for strangers, but one of less compassion and certainly less energy when it came to his own family. Basheve's domain was isolated; she was aloof, dispirited, and unwilling to perform the duties of a rabbi's wife. At the same time, she longed for a piece of her husband's authority.

To add to the weight of their burdens, neither Pinkhos Menakhem nor Basheve were able to fully separate from their own parents, and each would periodically run home to procure what was not available in the marriage. Pinkhos Menakhem basked in his mother's admiration and approval; in her eyes, he was perfect, whereas his wife considered him a perpetual disappointment. Basheve, in turn, found reinforcement for her rationalist views. She relished the atmosphere of Bilgoray, which was ruled with an iron hand by her father, the rabbi. In their parental homes, both Pinkhos Menakhem and Basheve could gain respite from the needling responsibilities of adult family life.

These "rest cures" at the parental source were not the only reasons for the frequent visits and intermediate contact. Many problems, including frequent financial difficulties, drove Pinkhos Menakhem and Basheve to their parents; seldom did they attempt to find a solution together. The pattern was consistent: Pinkhos Menakhem would proclaim his faith in God's providence and Basheve would sink deeper into her dissatisfied melancholy. Then each would write home for money—Pinkhos Menakhem to his mother, Basheve to her father—and aid would arrive.[22] In each case, succor came from the parent of the opposite sex.

Pinkhos Menakhem's parents in Tomaszow and Basheve's parents in Bilgoray exerted an influence that went beyond their children to touch the next generation as well, the generation of Hindele, Shiye, Itshele, and Moyshele. Basheve's father, in particular, wielded a powerful moral and religious force that his grandchildren felt throughout their lives. Against the radiance of that imposing figure, the more retiring presence of Pinkhos Menakhem's father, Shmuel, faded into the background. Although also a rabbi, Shmuel could not compete with the Bilgoray lion. Nonetheless, his eccentricity would one day provide literary material for his famous grandson. A man with ascetic tendencies, Shmuel would pray with such intensity that he had to change his shirt afterwards. He once undertook a vow of silence and for years would not even address his wife. He loved to fast and periodically refused to eat meat because it brought too much pleasure to the body. This last self-mortification sometimes had to be performed in secret, lest his wife and mother-in-law learn of it. Lacking the personality and verve of a rabbinic leader, Shmuel preferred to expend his energies on the secrets of Torah.[23]

Shmuel's wife, Teme Blume, or Temerl, was a cheerful, active woman who supported the family as a jewelry merchant. The couple seemed to get along, evidently because of Temerl's great good nature and forbearance. She was respectful and patient—"all sweetness and biblical quotations"[24]—and she allowed her husband his silence. This is not to say that Temerl had come from a completely ordinary and traditionally common background. Far from it: Temerl's mother, Hindele, was such a remarkable woman, that "the famous Rabbi Shalom of Belz [the Belzer rebbe] had offered [her] a chair when she came to visit him"[25] —an unheard-of honor for a woman. Moreover, family lore had it that Hindele "wore ritual fringes just like a man."[26] Pinkhos Menakhem, therefore, emerged from a family where gender lines were blurred, only to find himself married into another such household.

Temerl adored her Pinkhos Menakhem. Although she had other children, the ones who managed not to die prematurely were a disappointment to her. She was particularly exasperated with her eldest son, Yeshaye. Although clever enough to have become a scholar, Yeshaye had instead turned to business, married into a rich home and moved to Rohatyn. Temerl was ashamed of him. She put all her hopes in Pinkhos Menakhem, who had inherited his father's passion for study. Whereas Yeshaye reveled in the talk of commerce, his younger brother knew only the language of Torah. According to the custom of *kest*—room and board provided for the new husband by the wife's family—Pinkhos Menakhem would be supported for several years, so that he might continue his learning, unimpeded by financial concerns. When the time came for him to enter the home of his bride, Basheve, Pinkhos Menakhem welcomed the chance of studying with his famous father-in-law.

If Pinkhos Menakhem had hoped to join a family where the warmth and indulgence of his mother's home would be perpetuated, he was to be harshly let down. The Bilgoray rabbi's household illustrated how much unhappiness can result from forcing pubescent youngsters to marry. The problem had been set in motion a generation earlier. Basheve's maternal grandfather, Reb Itshe (after whom Itshele was named), was a merchant who had struck it rich with the changeover from candles to kerosene—in which he happened to deal. He had one surviving daughter, Khane, and, as was the custom for a man of means, he betrothed her to a scholar. In arranging this match, Itshe used his wealth to buy *yikhes*, or the status normally reserved for those of pedigree. The groom, Yankev Mordkhe Zylberman, from the shtetl Mezeritch, had delivered a *drash*, a learned religious speech, when he was only nine. Like his future bride, Yankev Mordkhe was the precious child of parents whose other offspring had died. Khane was somewhere between nine and fourteen years old when the couple married, and Yankev Mordkhe was a year older.[27]

Yankev Mordkhe's parents were poor—so poor, in fact, that the young scholar could not study with his peers because he lacked the money for a candle to read by in the communal study house. In the evenings, Yankev Mordkhe pored over his books by the light of the single candle the family possessed. Should his mother, Fradl, need the candle to do some household chore like salting meat, Yankev Mordkhe would follow her and keep studying. The constraint does not appear to have concerned the boy, for—like his daughter, Basheve—Yankev Mordkhe tended to separate himself from others.[28]

As conditions of his betrothal to Khane, Yankev Mordkhe received a generous dowry and moved into his father-in-law's household in Matshev, near Kovle. By now he was tall, broad-boned, with a full head of hair, and strong teeth.[29] Yankev Mordkhe soon became known as "The *Matshev Iluye*—The Young Genius of Matshev."[30] By enhancing his esteem in the eyes of the community, Yankev Mordkhe was also increasing the position of his father-in-law. While the future Bilgoray rabbi was astonishing the Jews of Matshev with his erudition and acumen, his new bride was playing with her rag dolls—much to the chagrin of her mother, who expected her to conduct herself as a mature adult.[31] However, Khane paid scant attention to her mother or to anyone else; she was spoiled and prone to tantrums if she failed to get what she wanted. Like her famous grandson, she had fiery red hair and blue eyes. Her moods were mercurial and her movements swift.

Despite their different levels of intellectual sophistication, Khane and Yankev Mordkhe were a fruitful couple. Khane was pregnant by the time she was thirteen or fourteen.[32] This young family was not unusual: in other homes people started bearing children even earlier. Children were sometimes betrothed at birth, married off before puberty, and then became parents as soon as it was physically possible. Jews felt that early childbearing was good for the health of the community.[33] Soon, there were five Zylberman children: Yoysef (the eldest—who would become a widower before the age of eighteen), Itshe (the youngest child), Sore [pronounced Soreh], Toybe, and Basheve, the youngest daughter. Basheve was born in Prisk, where her father had become rabbi after some years of *kest*.

Yankev Mordkhe was about thirty-three when he became rabbi in Bilgoray. Attaining this position was a major achievement, because the town had a scholarly reputation and was even mentioned in learned books. The environs and the religious ferment of the centuries before Yankev Mordkhe brought his family to Bilgoray would figure importantly in the future writer Isaac Bashevis Singer's repertoire. At the time of the Chmielnicki pogroms (in 1648), Bilgoray—as well as Zamoshtsh, Goray, and Tomaszow, where Pinkhos Menakhem was raised—was attacked and many Jews killed. The town had disciples of the false messiah, Shabbtai Zvi, and there were later followers of the cult leader Jacob Frank as well.

At the time Yankev Mordkhe brought his family to Bilgoray, the town was so old that only one illegible gravestone remained standing in the old cemetery, the other stones having sunk into the earth. It was a pretty place, circled with pine forests and fields, but isolated, since it was far from the railway. Nonetheless, it boasted a *shul* that had supposedly been built by an Italian architect. (Years later, Isaac Bashevis Singer found old books and half-erased manuscripts in the attic of the shul and also of the *besmedresh*—the house of study.)

The new rabbi was leader of the town's 10,000 or so Jews. Bilgoray had its own industry—sieves woven from horsehair. Some of those who sold the sieves became rich, but the workers were desperately poor. Nearby was the river San which separated Russian Poland from Austrian Galicia. Because of its position near the Austrian border, Bilgoray was inhabited by Russian soldiers stationed there, and the Jews did commerce with them. Yankev Mordkhe never left Bilgoray, although he was subsequently offered other positions. Once, representatives from Apt came to offer him the job of rabbi there. He asked them: "Do people die there?" When they admitted that they did, Yankev Mordkhe is reputed to have said: "Then why should I move?" To their rejoinder: "You'll get more money," he made a modest reply: "I have enough." Khane, angry at this exchange, remarked tartly: "What about your children and grandchildren?"—to which Yankev Mordkhe countered, thereby ending the matter: "I didn't promise to make you a wealthy woman."[34]

The argument about money and status was illustrative of the relationship between the Bilgoray rabbi and Khane, for they were in frequent strife with one another. Khane had grown into "a bitter, skeptical woman who, without detracting from her piety, could wound profoundly."[35] In particular, she was insubordinate and impudent concerning her husband. "'Who do you think he is, the Tsar?' she berated her eldest son [Yoysef] as he paced back and forth working up his nerve to face his father. 'Go on in, he won't spank you....'"[36] Khane and her husband had nothing to say to one another. Instead, they turned to their favorite children for conversation and spiritual sustenance. Khane favored her youngest child, Itshe, and she doted on him even when he was an adult and a married man. Basheve harbored a lifelong grudge against her brother, because she herself could not win her mother's love.[37]

Basheve was virtually raised by her older sisters, Toybe (five years

her senior) and Sore. Although she could not get her mother's attention, Basheve was singled out for notice by her father, the rabbi.
This regard meant that he deigned to talk to her where he declined
to speak to the other females in the family—including his wife.
"She was the only female in the family with intellectual tendencies, and grandfather often decried the fact that she hadn't been
born a man." Nonetheless, "[h]e still did not take her into his confidence; she was, after all, only a woman."[38]

Basheve was pretty in an unconventional way: thin, red-haired,
flat-chested, with sunken cheeks. Women said that she did not eat
enough. They also criticized her for avoiding her peers. The girls of
Bilgoray would get together and dance, make pickles, chop cab-
bage, bake cookies. Some were good at sewing, knitting, embroi-
dery. They followed fashions. These girls wanted to befriend the
rabbi's youngest daughter, but Basheve told her mother she had
nothing to say to them. Instead, Basheve, a true daughter of her
father, immersed herself in scholarly pursuits.

During the years of Yankev Mordkhe's leadership in Bilgoray,
the Enlightenment, which had begun in Western Europe in the
eighteenth century, had made its way east and had reached Poland.
For Jews, the Enlightenment meant a thirst for intellectual and cultural commonality with the non-Jewish world. Although most
Enlightenment Jews did not at first seek assimilation, they did want
to expand beyond what they considered to be the narrow confines
of a strictly orthodox intellectual life. They did not want to be limited to speaking Yiddish, which was a vernacular language, a vehicle of daily communication, but—until the latter part of the nineteenth century—not one where literary and aesthetic thoughts
could be expressed. Instead, adherents to Enlightenment ideals
strove to revive the historical Jewish language of study and contemplation, Hebrew, as a modern tongue. Alternatively, they
sought to master Polish or Russian. Once Basheve reached an age
where she could read, she found that she was interested in secular
as well as religious matters. She read about the Dreyfus case, and—
through studying this famous account of anti-Semitism in the
French military—learned about European politics. There was also a
Hebrew newspaper that came from St. Petersburg, and there she
discovered Russian and French literature.[39]

As Basheve approached the age of sixteen, her parents began to suggest matches for her. There were two potential husbands who appealed to her parents: one was a wealthy man from Lublin, the other was Pinkhos Menakhem, who had already authored a book of religious commentary. Basheve was impressed by Pinkhos Menakhem's scholarly achievements and by his ostensible maturity, for he was already twenty-one years of age, rather older than usual for betrothal. The reason for the delay was that he had been drafted into the military, and his mother, Temerl, refused to think about arranging a marriage for her precious youngest son until he had finished his service.[40]

Basheve chose Pinkhos Menakhem. Yet, she was trapped by her gender, because marriage implied that she must now devote herself to her husband and to the children that the entire community hoped would promptly materialize. The option of not marrying simply did not exist.

The marriage was doomed from the start. Despite the nonconformist stance of his grandmother, Hinde Esther, Pinkhos Menakhem wanted a wife who would resemble his beloved mother—loyal, long-suffering, admiring, and indulgent. Basheve, however, had as her only role model for spousal behavior the disrespectful and pithy attitude and language of her mother. And Basheve's idea of a husband, based as it was on what she had seen with her father, was a strong, stern figure, long on silence and short on effusiveness—in other words, the antithesis of the soft and malleable Pinkhos Menakhem. Basheve steadfastly deflated her husband, even as he came to her for admiration. Pinkhos Menakhem "spent his days setting down his innovations and interpretations. Each time he uncovered some fresh nuance in the Torah or Gemara his cheeks would flush, his blue eyes sparkle, and he would bask in the glow of discovery and revelation. Having no one else with whom to share his joy, he confided in [Basheve]. The eternal enthusiast and seeker of warmth and approbation, he couldn't cope with her resentments. 'Will you feed your wife and family with revelations?' she asked."[41]

Whatever his disappointments with the union, Pinkhos Menakhem still enjoyed the respect and scholarly absorption that came to him legitimately because of his calling. Basheve, however, was diminished by her new position. She was more than a mere woman, but she could never be a man. The Bilgoray rabbi's disappointment with Basheve for not being a man may have contributed to her stern and "unfeminine" appearance and demeanor. "Pale, thin, and with those large grey eyes of hers, she looked like a Talmudist who spends his days and nights and years in study, rather than a woman. Even the black dress and velvet jacket she had on scarcely betrayed her."[42] Basheve's sense of futility about the prospects for an intelligent, scholarly girl almost certainly lay behind her powerful rejection of her own daughter, Hindele. Such was her inability to bond with the infant—her first child—that Basheve sent Hindele away to a wet nurse immediately after the baby's birth. What could be less prestigious, more useless, than a girl? As it transpired, Hindele was not worth touching or visiting more than once a week. Basheve did not reclaim her until Hindele was three years old and Shiye was on the scene.[43]

What was it that held Pinkhos Menakhem and Basheve together? Why did this miserable couple decide not to separate, since divorce was always an option? Perhaps it was the combination of optimism on the part of Pinkhos Menakhem and stubbornness on Basheve's part that glued the pair to one another. They provided a balance for one another that caused them both to function more effectively within the framework of responsible adult life. Neither one was fully competent in traditional terms; however, what might each have been like without the counterbalancing weight of the other? Pinkhos Menakhem was forever having money problems—and his gullibility did not help matters. As the head of the yeshiva in Radzymin, he had failed to demand timely and adequate payment for his services. In Warsaw, where his remuneration came from donations by the residents of Krochmalna Street, he shied away from insisting that he receive his due. Were it not for Basheve and her insistence on the needs of her family, Pinkhos Menakhem would probably have lost himself in his studies and his writing, happily oblivious to the mundane requirements of earning a living. Basheve, for her part, since she was completely without friends, relied on her husband for companionship and intellectual stimulation, even though she deprecated his flights of fervor. Later, Basheve would repeat the same pattern of companionship and rejection with Shiye.

During the couple's periodic separations from one another, when the balance was undermined, Pinkhos Menakhem and Basheve revealed what they were like when left to their own devices. As might be expected from a man used to being affirmed and cherished, Pinkhos Menakhem basked in the deference offered by others. In the years before Warsaw, for example, when Basheve went home to Bilgoray for the summer, "the women...were only too glad to cook for their rabbi and to keep his house clean....He was also quite willing to attend every party to which he was invited, even at the most socially unacceptable homes. Women especially were drawn to his sweet nature, to his innocence and childlike trust, and they pampered and coddled him when his wife went away."[44] In sharp and painful contrast, Basheve's general depressed mood intensified when her husband was gone. Rather than reaching out for the company of others, as Pinkhos Menakhem was used to doing, she tended to sink further into herself and to become even less capable of attending to her daily tasks. During one of Pinkhos Menakhem's extended absences, Basheve sank into a depression so disconsolate that she stopped functioning altogether: "A mood of despair settled over [the] household. [She] stopped doing her household chores. She only wept and cajoled the German mailman...." Of course, when Pinkhos Menakhem finally did return, Basheve greeted him with anger and complaint, because he had not considered her or the children, so intent was he on receiving the attentions of his mother and his friends.[45]

One hint that the bond between the couple was not merely one of mutual dependence and regulation is the suggestion that they enjoyed a satisfying sexual rapport. Basheve's brothers were evidently lusty lovers. Her elder brother, Yoysef, when he remarried, chose a simple woman of whom his parents did not approve; he was insistent, however, and passionate. Yoysef's new wife complained that he kept her up at night and that he wanted her to violate the commandment of the *mikve*—the ritual bath. Attendance at the mikve would signify that it was now permitted to resume sexual relations after the monthly menstrual period, during which time Jewish women are traditionally considered unclean and unapproachable. Khane was scandalized, but Yoysef was unflappable.[46]

Apparently, Basheve's youngest brother, Itshe, was a rogue as well. Although he was instructed by his stern father-in-law to reserve sexual relations for purposes of procreation only, Itshe was too playful for such restrictions; moreover, he was caught touching his wife in public—an activity forbidden in traditional circles. The young couple was taking turns each trying to open the other's closed fist.[47]

Years later, Pinkhos Menakhem gave his daughter Hindele the advice that she should enjoy her sexual relationship with her future husband just as he had done with Basheve.[48] Later still, Isaac Bashevis Singer's widow, Alma, saw nothing incongruous or unlikely in this rendition of the family history. (Alma's observation, made during a discussion about the longevity of her own marriage, implicitly suggested that high sexual energy and interest were strong components of the lineage.)

Despite the pockets of harmony, respect, and sexual contentment, however, the Singer household was grim and cheerless. The atmosphere was not lost on the three children who would later use the literary word to express their reactions to an atmosphere both stultifying and painfully lacking in contact: "Our house was gloomy.... One cause of this gloom was the Torah, which filled every cranny of our house and weighed heavily on the spirits of those living there. Ours was more a study house than a home, a House of God rather than one of man...."[49] or: "Absentmindedly the family drank their tea.... And yet, though they all seemed to be unaware of each other's presence, every one breathed a breath of gentle disapproval on his neighbor."[50]

Itshele was ten years younger than Shiye, and thirteen years younger than Hindele. In the scheme of Eastern–European–Jewish families, his siblings were virtually old enough to be his parents. Moreover, with a father who was a public figure and a mother who was depressed—with two parents who were often lost in their own books, thoughts, or conflict with one another—the small child would naturally have turned to his older brother and sister for company, advice, stimulation, and education. On the day that little Itshele began to "scribble," then, he was about to lose not only a sister but a surrogate mother as well. While each Singer child had to accommodate to the family style, with its deprivations and heartaches, Itshele incorporated—as a child and later as a writer—the disparate influences of four powerful and distinct parental personalities.

2

---·•·---

"He was to me not as a brother; I regarded him as my master, my teacher."—I. B. S.*

ISRAEL Joshua Singer (1893–1944) was Yitskhok's (Isaac's) acknowledged hero: his mentor, literary role model, the one whose example he imitated, from choice of career to rejection of orthodoxy. Israel Joshua was a hard act to follow—but an irresistible magnet as well—all the more so because Basheve, who openly disdained her husband, treated her eldest son with respect. Moreover, Israel Joshua's exciting new views frequently turned to his small brother's future: "...my brother would have long talks with my mother, and often, in my presence, they would discuss me. "'What's to become of him?' my brother would argue. 'Must he marry and open a store or become a teacher in a heder?'"[1] The whimsical Pinkhos Menakhem—who was also a Yiddish writer of sorts (he had translated the *Selection of Pearls*, a collection of sayings, from Hebrew[2]—no doubt inspired aspects of Yitskhok's moral and religious development. But it was clearly Israel Joshua, with his modern ideas and practices, his stalwart energy, and his eventual access to the Warsaw Yiddish literary scene, who exercised the major life influence on Yitskhok. Early on, the stage was set for an unfolding scene of brotherly admiration, emulation, and grati-

31

tude—especially since Israel Joshua ultimately saved Yitskhok from the Nazis by facilitating his immigration to the United States.

Israel Joshua was the only member of Yitskhok's immediate family who was not helpless. He could be relied upon where the others faltered. While all three writer-siblings experienced the same parental neglect, Israel Joshua, as the eldest male, understood that he was required to take over. Even when a task seemed equally possible for anyone in the family, it was Israel Joshua who somehow came through. The visa for Bilgoray that Basheve needed in order to leave Warsaw during World War I is a case in point. Three members of the family took turns standing in line: Basheve, Israel Joshua, and Yitskhok. The youngest child, Moyshe, was evidently too small, and Pinkhos Menakhem was presumably too occupied with his rabbinic work. In any case, because of corruption and anti-Semitism, the family failed to advance in the line, until the day that Israel Joshua—who was not even planning to travel to Bilgoray—somehow managed to procure the money for a bribe, returning home with visas for Basheve, Yitskhok, and Moyshe.

Israel Joshua's independence of mind and behavior, his responsibility to mother and siblings, grew out of a profound and pervasive sense that no one was really concerned with him, no one would protect him. Unlike Yitskhok, who could look to *him*—Israel Joshua had the doubly unfortunate experience of an emotionally absent father and a mother who actively diminished that father. All the children, but especially Israel Joshua, therefore grew up with the perception, fostered by Basheve herself, that Pinkhos Menakhem was not someone to be admired.

One of Israel Joshua's early memories was a feeling of shame about his father. The incident occurred in the little village of Leoncin, where Pinkhos Menakhem was a rabbi in the years between his stay in Bilgoray and his move to Radzymin. A local non-Jew made a traditional, but nonetheless inflammatory blood-libel accusation, claiming that Jews had murdered a Christian child in order to use its blood for baking Passover matzos. In the ensuing fracas, a Russian official became aware that Pinkhos Menakhem was acting as rabbi when he was not legally permitted to do so. After it emerged that one of the wealthier Leoncin townspeople would be willing to influence the matter with a bribe, the official agreed that Pinkhos Menakhem might perform unofficial tasks:

"'You can study your Jewish Torah all you like...but don't perform any official acts or things will go hard with you. Get me?'" Israel Joshua was mortified: "My father seemed to have turned to jelly. Never in my childhood was I so ashamed of him and his servility as at that time."[3]

Indeed, such was Israel Joshua's failure to honor and identify with his father that he actively wished he were not a boy. Recognizing the differences in roles already as a small child in *kheyder*, he reviled his fate: "At noon, the melamed [teacher] occasionally released his pupils for a half hour. But he didn't grant that respite often, and insisted that lunch be brought to the heder. Only the girls were allowed to leave after a few hours, and I recall envying them and resenting God for having made me a boy."[4] The desire to be like someone who has privileges one covets is not necessarily a sign of gender confusion—but Israel Joshua did conclude later that his parents were trapped in the wrong gender roles.

The failure to identify firmly with his father influenced Israel Joshua's literary themes: his writings are replete with characters whose personalities are either split or doubled. In one of his first stories, a photographer's reflection blends with the face of a woman whose portrait he is developing; in his last novel, *The Family Carnovsky*, Gregor completely repudiates his father and sympathizes with his mother. His famous novel, *Yoshe kalb*, concerns a man who disappears and returns home to find that others mistrust his identity. And there are the twins of *The Brothers Ashkenazi*, whose conflicting traits finally resemble two sides of a single disposition.

Who would want to be male if it meant associating with a father who was impossible to appreciate?

Basheve openly criticized her husband as weak and unmasculine, and she encouraged her son to be more stouthearted. On one occasion, Israel Joshua excitedly pitched in with some manual labor to help with the building of a new house for the family in Leoncin. He was under thirteen years of age. "Father—soft, delicate, and so inept he couldn't drive a nail into the wall—was aghast. 'Fie, it's not for you,' he said. 'We must ask someone to do it for us.' But Mother encouraged me to keep on....Don't *you* grow up a helpless dreamer too.' There was no doubt to whom she was referring—nor would she allow father to wrap a kerchief around my neck in cold weather, a precaution to which he strongly subscribed. 'Your mother ruined you with the kerchief around your neck,' she said to him with bitterness. 'On account of that kerchief the children and I suffer all our lives....'"[5] Basheve's seemingly trivial reference to the kerchief had an ominous, larger intimation—the scarf Pinkhos Menakhem had worn to his wedding.

Instead of reaching out to Pinkhos Menakhem, Israel Joshua turned his deference to his maternal grandfather in Bilgoray: "A kind of implacable force seemed to emanate from the tall, stern, imposing man who appeared to have been born for his role as shepherd of a community. He ruled the city with wisdom and justice, feared nothing and no one...."[6] In his veneration, Israel Joshua not only distanced himself from his father, but also drew closer to his mother, who shared the view of her father as a holy man.

Despite the harsh view of his father that Israel Joshua absorbed from Basheve, he was nonetheless disappointed to find that Pinkhos Menakhem had no time for him. There were a few things that the son could esteem in his father: his compassion for others, his warmth and openness, his willingness to understand the problems and pains of his charges. How hard, then, to realize that the same solicitude and attention were not forthcoming from Pinkhos Menakhem for Israel Joshua—his eldest, and for many years, his only son.

When it came to Israel Joshua's education, for instance, Pinkhos Menakhem chose tutors regardless of their compatibility with his son. While notions of education were different then from now, Israel Joshua was deeply hurt. Even when he explicitly disliked a prospective instructor, he could not convince Pinkhos Menakhem to change his mind. Pinkhos Menakhem was delighted with his choice and turned a deaf ear to his son's pleas: "'Reb Berishl is a God-fearing Jew and a scholar. You should be thankful he wants you for his pupil.'" But Israel Joshua was not at all thankful.[7]

Israel Joshua's antipathy to his tutors may have stemmed from his disinterest in religious studies or he may have grown disaffected with the subject matter because he was badly taught. Whichever came first, Pinkhos Menakhem, who could empathize with his flock and even with the neighborhood hogs, could not understand his son; instead, he simply removed himself from Israel Joshua's intellectual and spiritual existence—not to speak of his company.

Israel Joshua was able to engage his mother with his quick wit and sassy rebellion against traditional orthodoxy, which thrilled even as it appalled. Nonetheless, he had also learned at an early age that he could not count on her to take proper care of him. One story reveals the characteristic situation. Israel Joshua was traveling by train with his mother and Hinde Esther on one of their periodic trips to Bilgoray. At one of the stations, Israel Joshua became aware of a commotion. Suddenly he and his sister were on a moving train—without Basheve. "My sister began to cry. Although I was younger, I did not—crying is something I have never done, not even in the worst crisis."[8] Eventually—but not at all immediately— the three were reunited when a policeman located Basheve on another train. Such an oversight may be possible in any family. However, its occurrence in the Singer household, where no one ever seemed to be in charge except the children, is shockingly unsurprising. Moreover, already at that delicate age, Israel Joshua had learned to rely on himself, not on his older sister and definitely not on Basheve.

A measure of how much Israel Joshua longed for connection is obvious in the effect Pinkhos Menakhem's story-telling had on his son. Like a sponge, the boy soaked up his father's tales. Indeed, Israel Joshua's early and highly successful *Yoshe Kalb* was inspired by a story he heard when he was still a small boy in Leoncin: "Among the many stories told that day was one Father told about a rabbi's son named Moshe Haim Kaminker, who deserted his wife, the Sieniawa rabbi's daughter. When the husband, Moshe, came back years later, people accused him of being someone else, a beggar named Yoshe Kalb who had deserted his own wife, a woman of low origin. My father had personally known this man and he told the fantastic story in a most engaging way. The guests sat agape, listening to the mystery no one had been able to solve. I was positively entranced by it."[9] And it can hardly be an accident that Israel Joshua entitled his first volume of short stories *Pearls*, when his father had translated *A Selection of Pearls* from Hebrew into Yiddish.

How was Israel Joshua to deal with the familial conflicts and deprivations? Intellectually, he took the path of escape—first to the street, then to bohemianism and secularism. This route inevitably estranged him from his father: Pinkhos Menakhem could not bear to watch his son stray from religious observance and orthodox thought. It evidently did not occur to Pinkhos Menakhem that he had made little effort to encourage a traditional life. Israel Joshua defended his worldly philosophy and behavior with analytic arguments; he was fearless in challenging his parents. When it came to his emotional maturation, however, he developed a profound, albeit initially unconscious, compulsion to protect himself.

Early on, Israel Joshua effected an "I don't care" front. He presented a breezy nonchalance that hid his anguish over his mother's depression, over the friction between his parents, and over the resultant disinterest in him. This behavior was his way of assuring himself that he did not share Basheve's despondency, or Pinkhos Menakhem's impotence. He would be aggressively male, invulnerable to the easy compassion that mobilized his father and to the existential pain that ground his mother to a halt. He would be outraged at the injustices of life, expressing his indignation towards the world instead of towards his parents. The more anxious, stressful, or unhappy the domestic scene, the more Israel Joshua engaged in hyperkinetic activity, in reckless and immoderate play.

A childhood example of Israel Joshua's self-protective insouciance indicates both how powerful it was and how much it represented a response to pain. The Singer family had two daughters between Israel Joshua and Yitskhok. One Sabbath, while Pinkhos Menakhem and Israel Joshua were at morning prayers (Yitskhok was not yet born), a neighbor came running to get Pinkhos Menakhem, announcing with alarm that the little girls were dying. Although travel is normally forbidden on the Sabbath, Pinkhos Menakhem and Basheve hoped that a specialist in the town of Nowidwor could rescue the girls. They immediately set out on their journey—a permissible decision dictated by *pikuekh nefesh*, the saving of a soul. In the midst of this crisis, Israel Joshua suddenly found himself abandoned. "A neighbor took charge of me and my sister [Hindele] and fed us good things from her Sabbath table. 'Eat, children,' she urged us, 'your mama and papa will soon be back and everything will be the same as always....' Her kind words made me forget. Freed from all supervision, I spent the time playing wildly with my friends."[10] Even at such a tender age, however, Israel Joshua's realization of the true situation was just below the surface. When his parents returned home alone, the girls having succumbed to scarlet fever, he was quick to grasp the tragedy and to deal with it by cursing God: "I raged against God so persistently that pious people stopped up their ears and warned me I would pay for my arrogance."[11]

Israel Joshua used the same stratagems to cope with anxiety and the awareness of possible loss. His behavior at the time his brother Yitskhok was born provides an illustration. The story concerns a stray dog, with whom Israel Joshua had become friends and to whom he had given the name Briton. The mere fact of this camaraderie deserves mention, because it represented Israel Joshua's victory over a fear of dogs that was ubiquitous among Eastern European Jews; in Pinkhos Menakhem, this trepidation had reached the proportions of terror.

The development of Israel Joshua's relationship with Briton coincided with the impending birth of the new baby, whose arrival naturally aroused family memories of the two little girls and their tragic deaths. The delivery was difficult, and everyone feared for Basheve and the infant. The moment was complex and bewildering for Israel Joshua. He had reclaimed the position of youngest child through the death of his sisters, and this privilege, although it may have been a source of guilt and confusion for him, was not one that he was necessarily eager to relinquish. At the same time, he faced the potential of losing his mother, an eventuality that, young as he was, he could well envision. To remove himself from the immediate situation, Israel Joshua turned to the dog he had befriended: "When Mother went into labor, Briton planted himself outside the door and howled to come in. I grew so unnerved by this howling that I led him inside the hall. I don't remember how long Mother writhed in pain, but I do recall that I never spent such happy hours in my entire childhood."[12] The idyll was rudely interrupted by the appearance of Pinkhos Menakhem, who was, first of all, petrified by the dog and, secondly, enraged at his son's "un-Jewish" behavior, rebuking him with uncharacteristic harshness.

Israel Joshua's response to his humiliation reveals that somewhere—at least inchoately—he realized that his happiness with the dog had been an avoidance of the family's crisis, a manifestation of irresponsibility for which he must now pay a price. Although he attributed his behavior to stupidity, it seems more likely that Israel Joshua was exacting from himself the punishment that he believed his disloyalty warranted. He had angered his father and disregarded his mother. To make matters worse, he risked increased separation from his parents, now that there was a new baby on the scene. Yet even as he attempted to do penance, he reacted with familiar composure. At the time, he was only eleven years old, but his behavior was already characteristic. Israel Joshua acted with defiance. He challenged himself to prove that he was invincible, that he would succumb neither to melancholy nor to mortification: "Briton howled in shame and disappointment after I was forced to kick him out of the house.... But soon I brought something even worse into the house. One of my friends came down with smallpox and I was stupid enough to go to his bedside and play a game of buttons with him. Soon afterward I developed a high fever; then my sister and my little brother—at that time an infant—became infected too."[13]

Even when he got older, Israel Joshua's tendency for impetuosity and rashness remained in evidence, but he later understood the connection between his perception of incipient depression and his need to avoid it. In his adolescence, for instance—during one of Pinkhos Menakhem's long and silent absences—Israel Joshua responded with frantic activity and seeming abandon when Basheve collapsed and withdrew into her incapacitating despondency. Despite his outward joviality and vivacity, however, he knew that he was attempting to dispel his own underlying melancholy: "Mother's eternal praying depressed me and my only consolation was the fact that I was now relieved of studying and could run wild through the countryside with my friends."[14] The effort never fully succeeded. Years later, his nephew described Israel Joshua's eyes: "... that indifferent faraway gaze has given way to a strange, a very strange, glitter in the whites of the eyes conveying absolute authority and absolute melancholy.... a daunting melancholy that seems innate and inborn."[15]

By the time Yitskhok had grown beyond his earliest childhood, Israel Joshua was already a free thinker, a feisty rebel, and consequently somewhat of a stranger in the family. The real influence around the household during the years before World War I was his sister, Hinde Esther, whose effect on young Yitskhok was both powerful and indelible, much as he might later attempt to ignore her formative impact.

* * *

Hers was a life of holidays, hymns, hope, and exultation. She was a Hasid in skirts, but she suffered from hysteria and had mild attacks of epilepsy. At times, she seemed possessed by a dibbuk.—I.B.S.[16]

Hinde Esther (1891–1954) was the least treasured and most disregarded member of the Singer family. She was, first of all, female, which meant that her clear intelligence and thirst for knowledge were not viewed as assets—Pinkhos Menakhem was incapable of treating her with the regard Yankev Mordkhe had shown Basheve. Secondly, as the eldest child, she was called upon to care for the younger children when her mother and father were overwhelmed with their own concerns. Unlike Israel Joshua, she could not feign an easy-going manner in the face of parental neglect; consequently, she was often criticized, especially by Basheve. Most important, however—largely because it was so misunderstood—was the effect of Hinde Esther's epilepsy on the feelings and behavior of the entire family.

When Yitskhok referred much later in his life to the fact that Hinde Esther was a "Hasid in skirts," he was comparing her to her great-grandmother and namesake. He also correctly implied that, beyond any superficial similarity with the original Hinde Esther, his sister had to confront her own gender difficulties. She wanted the privileges enjoyed by her brothers and she clamored to be treated as their equal. She was surrounded by males and naturally had difficulty tolerating her supposed inferiority. Moreover, her mother, the one woman through whom she could hope to learn acceptance of herself, refused to support her daughter. Since Basheve despised her own position as a woman, she was unable to treat her daughter with sympathy, let alone help smooth her path. Instead, Basheve both chastised Hinde Esther for her ambitions and hated her for her femininity.

Mother and daughter were always at loggerheads with one another. The problems had started at the very outset, with Hinde Esther's birth. Basheve had been so distraught with the birth of a girl that she had completely rejected the infant. Unwilling to care for the newborn child, Basheve had abandoned her for three years to a wet nurse whose poverty dictated that the baby be kept under a table. Understandably, Hinde Esther held a lifelong grudge against her mother—although Basheve was evidently not moved to contrition on that score.

Some of Hinde Esther's difficulty in aligning herself with her mother stemmed from the fact that Basheve prohibited any connection that could foster positive identification. Although she herself had suffered because her aspirations were frustrated, she refused to help her daughter when the time came. Israel Joshua recounts a deflating incident for Hinde Esther, which occurred during a discussion with Basheve concerning his future: "When my sister asked Mother what *she* should be when *she* grew up, Mother answered her question with another: 'What *can* a girl be?'"[17] Israel Joshua saw the interchange as proof of Hinde Esther's inequality and he understood her envy of him: "This was a source of constant friction between us."[18]

Hinde Esther was more reticent about Pinkhos Menakhem than were her brothers, but she clearly preferred him to Basheve. Yet, if she had hoped that her father would be more sympathetic to her than her mother, she was sadly mistaken. Pinkhos Menakhem, for all his intelligence and sensitivity, remained completely traditional when it came to his views about the roles of males and females. When he returned home after a prolonged absence, for instance, he brought gifts—only for Israel Joshua. Israel Joshua was somewhat disappointed, but at least he had received something: "Mother knew better than to ask for a present for herself, but my sister wanted to know what Father had brought *her*. He looked at her in astonishment: 'What can you give a girl?' he asked."[19]

Years later, Hinde Esther, using her married name, Esther Kreitman, thinly fictionalized her experiences in her autobiographical novel, *Der sheydim tants* (literally, *The Demons' Dance*), which later appeared in English as *Deborah*. One episode indicates what it must have been like for Hinde Esther to struggle with her position in the household: when his daughter asks what she can be when she grows up, the father replies: "'What are *you* going to be one day? Nothing, of course!'"[20] Despite discouragement, Hinde Esther refused to be downtrodden—the result, though, was her need to view intellect and erudition as masculine traits: "It was quite true that most girls grew up only to marry and become drudges, but there were exceptions, such as her own mother,... who was highly educated, a real lady, and as wise as any man."[21]

Although her position differed significantly from that of her mother, Hinde Esther was equally trapped. Basheve had been treated as some hybrid between male and female, and consequently she was an awkward and ambivalent woman. Hinde Esther was uncertain of her position, but not because she had enjoyed the ambiguous privilege of identifying with a man. Rather, she was confused because neither her mother nor her father had been willing to serve as her role model and cornerstone of bonding. Hinde Esther's predicament over her primary relationships was explicit: "She did not know whether it was best to look solemn, like her mother, or happy, like her father."[22] The result of her rejection by both parents was a miserable combination of emptiness and anger.

At best, Hinde Esther was equivocal towards Basheve. She agitated for her mother's affection and closeness and at the same time rebuffed her because she herself felt spurned. Most of the time, the relationship between mother and daughter was openly adversarial, with both parties feeling maligned, misunderstood, and mistreated. Hinde Esther described her mother as narcissistic—she thought only of herself and her own struggles, never of her daughter and what the younger female might be enduring. Mother and daughter argued, for example, because Hinde Esther was convinced that her mother wanted to marry her off in order to get rid of her (a scene that Yitskhok subsequently wrote about). She later described the disagreement in her novel, rendering Basheve as an exasperated and impatient woman completely lacking in sympathy for the child who is being sent to a strange country to marry a man she has never even seen: "'It's too bad.... That precious daughter of ours is doing her best to kill me.'"[23] Later, suspecting that her daughter might be unhappy in her new marriage, the mother writes, ostensibly to encourage her daughter's confidences. All too soon, however, the true motive emerges: "'Do not make me suffer, do not keep me in nervous suspense by stinting your correspondence with me. I am your mother and I want you to confide in me. Tell me the truth, tell me if you are happy. I am terribly uneasy about you. Do not make my life unbearable. Believe me, if I have done you an injury, I now have my punishment in full. Do not make things worse for me....'"[24]

However belittled Hinde Esther felt with respect to her parents and her powerful younger brother, Israel Joshua, her irritability and envy do not appear to have extended to her much younger siblings. This does not mean, however, that her position in the family went unnoticed by them. Her younger brother Yitskhok later on described the situation in psychological and dynamic terms: "Although we were not acquainted with Freud in those days, it could be said that a Freudian drama was occurring at home. My sister suspected my mother of not loving her, which was untrue, but actually, they were incompatible."[25] He noticed, furthermore, that—in contrast to Basheve's cool and rational approach to life, which alternated with quiet melancholy and silent depression— Hinde Esther was dramatic, emotional, and subject to noisy highs and lows. Above all, she was the source of warmth and affection for the rest of the family. Having experienced a reserved and undemonstrative mother, it is no wonder that little Yitskhok vividly recalled his sister's uninhibited and passionate displays of feeling. He understood the distinction between her positive responses to Moyshele and himself and the ambivalent ones to Israel Joshua: "In her jealousy of my brother Israel Joshua, she made up numerous accusations, but then, regretting what she had done, she would want to kiss him.... We younger children were always being kissed and fondled by her."[26]

As he developed, Yitskhok came to associate story-telling and sentiment with his excitable sister. The juxtaposition of her imminent departure from Krochmalna Street and his debut as a "writer" initiated a lifetime compulsion to write. He wrote in order to fill the overwhelming void of loss—and fill it he did, with all the vibrant, expansive, crazy and troubling characters who represented Hinde Esther's disturbing but enlivening presence.

Despite the seeming candor of his recollections, there is much that Yitskhok omitted from his depiction of the family. For one thing, Hinde Esther was probably accurate when she claimed that Basheve did not love her. Certainly, their relationship never improved. Years later, after the two had been separated for almost a generation, they met in Warsaw: "...mother and daughter go through the motions of a tepid embrace. Then the mother says to the daughter: 'Why Hindele, you are not at all as ugly as I thought you were!'"[27] Yitskhok is also silent about the fact that Hinde

Esther's interest in Israel Joshua included some sexual demands and that she would coax the younger children into bed with her by promising to tell them stories.[28] Perhaps this is why Israel Joshua would later retreat at the sight of his older sister.[29]

Writing about Hinde Esther from the vantage point of adulthood—and after she was already dead, Yitskhok attributed her spectacular behavior to the fact that she had inherited the extreme emotional make-up of her father's side of the family, the same lineage that had resulted in the famous Hinde Esther, Pinkhos Menakhem's illustrious grandmother. While this connection may be valid, it is more likely that the younger Hinde Esther's extremes of attitude and conduct resulted from her epilepsy. To judge from the descriptions of her behavior set down by her brother Yitskhok, as well as from her own narratives, Hinde Esther probably suffered from the type of epilepsy known as *partial complex seizures*.

Partial complex seizures erupt out of normal behavior and are therefore often not recognized by observers as attacks. These seizures, which differ from the more commonly known *grand mal* and *petit mal* forms of epilepsy, characteristically begin with a blank stare, or a bewildered or frightened look. The next stage, automatism, includes such signs as lip smacking, humming, crude vocalization, laughing, walking, and crying. If interfered with at that point, "patients can groan, moan, or lash out at the disturbance."[30] After the seizure, the affected individual remembers nothing of the event. Generally, the seizures are brief, lasting approximately two minutes at most. However, the situation may be complicated by the appearance of several seizures in sequence, interspersed with variable return to consciousness. Additionally, in the case of *partial complex status epilepticus*, seizures may continue for hours and even days. A further problem is the occurrence of exaggerated—or even invented—attacks, because seizures usually inspire sympathetic attention from others.

Given the intricacy of the condition, and the fact that its symptoms were certainly not well-described in pre–World War I Poland (or anywhere else in that era), the Singer family was understandably baffled by Hinde Esther. On some occasions, she suffered from secondarily generalized seizures—ones that more closely resemble epilepsy as it is traditionally recognized: "...she glazed over her blue eyes and fell into a faint. She lay on the floor, trembled with cramps and tossed as in an epileptic fit.... Pitiful sounds came from her throat. The neighbors heard and came running." People on the scene put a key into her clenched fist, part of the common wisdom about how to deal with a seizure. Afterwards, Basheve—for once available to her daughter—tried to help Hinde Esther by taking her to a doctor. But, of course, the remedies available at that time were neither advanced nor precise. The doctor treated her for "'nerves': he prescribed pills and made electric treatments. He put a machine to her head that sent out electric waves to the brain. The doctor also prescribed massages with alcohol and a medicine that had iron in it. The doctor said she needed fresh air."[31]

Yitskhok's attempts to describe his sister's condition were consistent with an exaggerated or even concocted version of her symptoms. He depicted her as conscious and aware of her surroundings, which would not be the case during an actual seizure. If Hinde Esther suffered multiple brief attacks, however, Yitskhok may not have detected the transition between several—or even many—episodes. As he saw it, Hinde Esther "kept chattering, singing, and laughing all day long, expressing opinions that she should have kept to herself. Whoever she liked was praised excessively, and those she disliked received unrelenting abuse. She tended toward exaggeration, leaping when joyous, crying when unhappy, and sometimes falling into a faint... she always did so in a way that she would not get hurt. She swooned, blinked, and smiled. Yet, even though she seemed to be pretending, it was all terribly real."[32]

Hinde Esther's writing, in contrast, vividly revealed her familiarity with *partial complex status epilepticus*. Curiously, she portrayed the phenomenon indirectly, probably because she had no first-hand recollection of the attacks: "She behaves so unnaturally. All day long she goes about with a vacant stare on her face, as if her mind were blank, or full of queer, faraway thoughts, and then suddenly she will start to cry and then in the midst of her tears she will burst into song like an imbecile.... At the slightest provocation she'll fly into a terrible rage and jump down your throat.'"[33] The family's confusion over the authenticity and severity of Hinde Esther's malady was exacerbated by the fact that she could neither predict an attack nor remember it afterwards. Moreover, she tended to attribute the strange results of her behavior to the mischief of demons—for example, a forbidden Sabbath fire which she had absently started during a seizure.[34] No one knew how to understand this strange girl.

Although the organic problems were sufficient cause for consternation and turmoil, Hinde Esther also suffered throughout her life from illnesses of a psychological origin. The distress had begun even before Yitskhok was born—at the age of twelve, for instance, she had become bloated with a mysterious, seemingly near-fatal illness,[35] possibly an hysterical pregnancy. Yitskhok was therefore raised in constant awareness of bizarre and unexplained behavior. Hinde Esther was the only person who provided him with consistent and exuberant expressions of affection—and she abruptly left him when he was still a small child. The combination of drama, love, madness, and abandonment in a female proved to be a potent influence. Life with Hinde Esther caused lifelong complications for Yitskhok in his associations with women: he forever oscillated between attraction and loathing, fascination and terror, cordiality and aloofness, friendship and rancor.

*   *   *

Even before I learned to read or write, I was obsessed by the paradoxes of time, space, infinity, and moreover I was convinced that only I myself could reason out such enigmas, that no one could help me.—I. B. S.[36]

Anyone who reads enough of Isaac Bashevis Singer (1904–1991) will be struck by the unique blend of sophistication and naivete, loneliness and charismatic charm, helplessness and resilience that pervades his work. These qualities are the direct result of his beginnings in the amazing and mercurial Singer home. True, the exigencies of immigration and the particular trauma of the Holocaust would cast his fate—and his talents—in ways that could not have been foreseen. But the genesis of it all was rooted in Krochmalna Street, Radzymin, and Bilgoray—all the places where the young boy witnessed the clashes between tradition and modernity, male and female, depression and enthusiasm, reason and ecstasy.

Unlike Israel Joshua and Hinde Esther, who wrote their family stories while some or all of the dramatis personae were still alive, Yitskhok began his rendition only after everyone—his siblings included—was dead. His portrayals, perhaps for this reason, lack the bite of the others and are more elegiac. Most of all, Yitskhok seems eager to rehabilitate Pinkhos Menakhem—or perhaps, to create him. He makes much, for example, of his father's warmth, his tender way of dealing with the simple and often tormented people who came to him for advice. And, while refusing to criticize his mother, he manages to disclose a view of her that tallies with the opinion of his siblings; Basheve was simply not able to comfort and provide relief the way Pinkhos Menakhem could.

Nonetheless, despite his attempt to emphasize the beauty of Krochmalna Street and its inhabitants, especially his father, Yitskhok was faced with the same issues that had occupied Israel Joshua and Hinde Esther in their recreations of the past. His problems had been similar to theirs: which parent to choose as a role model, how to get attention in a preoccupied household, where to find intelligent yet sensitive companions, how to tolerate the pain and loneliness of parental neglect. Unlike his siblings, Yitskhok avoided gender issues *per se*, other than to report that, when he started *kheyder*, his first school, he was the youngest child and found himself relegated to playing with the girls. The boys teased him, calling him *khamoyr-eyzl* (jack-ass)—the equivalent of sissy.[37] Yitskhok framed his difficulty in deciding whether to identify with Basheve or Pinkhos Menakhem not as a conflict over expected roles, but rather as a struggle between his mother's rationality and his father's faith.

A single anecdote from early childhood epitomizes Yitskhok's— then Itshele's—dilemma. At stake was a disagreement about whether dead geese can shriek. A local woman had come to Pinkhos Menakhem in his role as the Krochmalna Street rabbi because her geese, even after proper ritual slaughter, continued to emit a plaintive cry when prodded. Any child, hearing such a frightening story, would likely want to be consoled, and Itshele was no exception. However, no help was forthcoming from Pinkhos Menakhem, the supposed authority and hero. Instead, his father was so agitated that he violated one of the principal rules of traditional modesty, the interdiction against looking at a woman: "I wanted to run from the room. But where would I run? My throat constricted with fear. Then I, too, screamed and clung to my mother's skirt, like a child of three. Father forgot that one must avert one's eyes from a woman. He ran to the table. He was no less frightened than I."[38]

In sharp contradiction to Pinkhos Menakhem, Basheve insisted that there could be no supernatural reason for the phenomenon. Itshele hoped that she would be proven wrong, and that he would consequently be able to maintain admiration for his idealized father: "Everything hung in the balance. If the geese shrieked, Mother would have lost all: her rationalist's daring, her skepticism which she had inherited from her intellectual father. And I? Although I was afraid, I prayed inwardly that the geese *would* shriek, shriek so loud that people in the street would hear and come running."[39]

In the end, Basheve's opinion was confirmed, and—adding insult to injury—she went on to pronounce the geese kosher, leaving Pinkhos Menakhem in the humiliating position of echoing his wife's rabbinic judgment. Thus, despite the story's clear attempt to commemorate and beautify Pinkhos Menakhem, he emerges as weak and inept next to the powerful and compelling Basheve. The boy's regard for his father was probably not enhanced by Pinkhos Menakhem's subsequent decision to confide in his son by deprecating Basheve: "Suddenly he began to speak to me as though I were an adult. 'Your mother takes after your grandfather, the Rabbi of Bilgoray. He is a great scholar, but a cold-blooded rationalist. People warned me before our betrothal....' And then Father threw up his hands, as if to say: It is too late to call off the wedding."[40]

Even before the family moved from Radzymin to Krochmalna Street, when he was only four, Itshele had learned that his father would not protect him. Many years later, he recalled an incident from Radzymin which, although superficially amusing, reveals— probably unintentionally—his father's inaccessibility. The wife of the Radzymin Rebbe was so beautiful, educated, and cultured that even the normally indifferent Basheve was jealous.[41] The Rebetsin loved to receive Pinkhos Menakhem when he called on her, and she would shower Itshele with affection. The boy was electrified but overwhelmed by the attention, later even attributing some of his erotic demands to these precocious experiences.

Once, in an attempt to find a way out of his predicament, Itshele tried to appeal to the Rebetsin's religious constraints, having learned that a Hasid like his father was forbidden to look at—let alone touch—a woman. In his confusion, however, he mixed up the syllables of the word *khosid*, and when the Rebetsin reached out to kiss him, he shouted: "Rebetsin, it's forbidden! I am a *sokhid*!" The Rebetsin paid no heed to his agitation, kissing him all the more, even as she humiliated him with her laughter. Pinkhos Menakhem, far from realizing Itshele's plight, subjected him to something even more upsetting: he allowed his son to overhear the Rebetsin confessing her longing for Pinkhos Menakhem and her revelation that the Rebbe, her husband, was impotent.[42] This embarrassing and excessively stimulating episode convinced Itshele that he could not rely on his father to prevent him from being engulfed by emotions that were too powerful for a small child to handle.

Yitskhok's memorial to the beauty of his parents' world, *In My Father's Court,* is filled with one story after another that inadvertently divulges how inadequate his parents were to the task of taking proper care of him. By the time of his birth, Pinkhos Menakhem and Basheve were supposedly experienced parents, having begun their family over a decade earlier and having already produced four older children; nonetheless, they failed to provide the calm and safety necessary to help Itshele manage his childhood crises. Instead, they were in the habit of succumbing to all the same reactions—fear, horror, helplessness, bewilderment—with which he needed assistance.

On one occasion, Pinkhos Menakhem allowed Itshele to see a corpse, and the boy paid for his curiosity with both immediate and long-term trauma. His first response was one of panic: "I suddenly felt a tightness in my head and an icy shudder ran down my spine....A man agreed to go back with me. I was shaking all over and my teeth were chattering." Unable to be of true comfort and emotional availability to him, his parents plied him with food; the normally cool and analytical Basheve showed her superstitious side, which tended to appear at moments when she felt powerless: "When I was led into the house, my mother began to wring her hands. 'Woe is me! Just look at this child!' They warmed me up and blew on me. My mother recited an incantation. I was given tea and preserves and all of the goodies which were in the house. My father paced back and forth in his study. He chewed his beard and rubbed his forehead....For a long, long time afterwards there was talk in our house of this grim episode and for a long period I was afflicted with nightmares."[43]

Itshele's nightmares reveal how unsuccessful his parents' ministrations had been: food, tea, and reliance on magic could not substitute for a firm, protective stance that would reassure the boy of his safety. Above all, the boy needed to know from his parents that he would not find himself all alone, like that poor corpse. Unfortunately, their anxiety-ridden response—perhaps especially Basheve's superstitious reaction—highlighted the extent to which Itshele *was* alone. It was bad enough that he could not count on his parents. Even worse was his realization—forced on him at an extremely early age—that they needed him.

On one occasion, Itshele decided to help out by becoming his father's money collector; the ones his father hired were dishonest, a fact that the idealistic Pinkhos Menakhem refused to accept. The result of Itshele's effort to clear up his father's financial problems was catastrophic. Although things went well at first, and although he was successful in his pursuit—he got the money—the toll on him turned out to be intolerable. As he pushed open the door of an apartment in a dark hallway, the youngster was once again confronted by a corpse. His reaction was swift and dramatic: "My ribs tingling with fright, I slammed the door and backed into the hallway, fiery spots before my eyes, my ears throbbing. I began to run but became entangled in a basket or crate. It was as if someone had clutched my coattail, drawing me backward; bony fingers dug into me. I heard a dreadful scream. In a cold sweat, I ran out, tearing my gabardine. There would be no more collecting for me. I threw up, and shivered. The coins burdened me as I walked. It seemed to me that I had grown old in that one day."[44]

Itshele certainly had his moments of naughtiness and protest against his parents for the premature load they placed on his shoulders, but those moments were rare and he always wound up paying for his freedom. Having once received a ruble in return for running an errand, he determined not to divulge his windfall to his parents: "I knew that if I stayed home my parents would ruin that ruble. They would buy me something to wear which I would have got in any case, or they would borrow the ruble from me and, though they would never deny the debt, I would never see it again."[45] But, having squandered the money on droshky (horse-drawn cab) rides and candy, the boy felt defiled, miserably sinful, on the verge of sinking into eternal perfidy. His self-condemnation was the only punishment he needed.

Whenever he was defiant, Itshele wound up bitterly regretting his insurrection. On one occasion that the mature Yitskhok never forgot, he and a friend entered an orchard and, although they knew perfectly well that it was forbidden, they picked some unripe pears. Suddenly, Basheve appeared out of nowhere, confiscated the fruit, and threw it into a nearby dung heap. As soon as she left, however, the boys—in a fit of childish anarchy—approached the heap and reclaimed the fruit. But Basheve, not trusting the boys, returned to the scene, this time accompanied by Israel Joshua and Hinde Esther. They stripped Itshele on the spot and dragged him home naked, whereupon they added to his shame by scrubbing him and—since he had ingested some of the dirt—forcing him to vomit.[46] Such inordinate retaliations for small acts of mischief help explain Yitskhok's vast sensitivity to sin and punishment.

Yitskhok, like his siblings, was required to find his own way of reacting to the stresses, prohibitions, and conflicts of the Singer home. His solutions, however, were different from theirs and absolutely his own—produced by the particular interaction of constitution and environment that characterizes every individual's growth. Israel Joshua dealt with the problems in the household by avoidance and reckless rebellion; Hinde Esther clamored and fainted in her efforts to gain the attention she could never inspire in any other way. Yitskhok became a loner, a solitary observer of the world, a balcony enthusiast who loved to watch from a safe distance. Above all, he turned to fiction as a way of life.

Pinkhos Menakhem's inability to be as intimate with his children as he was with the assorted characters of Krochmalna Street signified to Itshele that his father cared for him as he would for any creature of God. Love was another matter. The occasion of Itshele's bitter realization began with a suicide. A neighborhood youth had killed himself out of despair over a woman. Since, according to Jewish law, a suicide cannot be buried within the walls of the cemetery, his mother, extremely upset, had approached Pinkhos Menakhem hoping that he would intercede on her behalf to obtain a ritual burial for the boy. "'If this thing could happen, there is no

God!' screamed the woman in an inhuman voice." Pinkhos Menakhem, as empathic as ever, realized that the woman's blasphemous
expletives required his compassion, even though she was desecrat-
ing the Sabbath. "'*No man is judged in his hour of grief*,' murmured
my father, perhaps to me, perhaps to no one."[47] Later, Pinkhos
Menakhem, who usually lay down with a book after the Sabbath
lunch, remained in his study with Itshele. The boy had already
been musing over the mysteries of love, and his parents had dis-
missed him with the assurance that he would comprehend the matter when he got older. But the events he had witnessed in his
father's study, combined with the gossip about the suicide that was
swirling in the street, so inflamed his curiosity that he felt compelled to ask questions. Before he could even contemplate romantic and sexual love, he had to ascertain whether or not his father
loved him.

Knowing Pinkhos Menakhem's reticence and general preoccupation, Itshele had initiated his inquiry indirectly: "'Father, do you
know the Cabala?'"—to which his father answered: "'You speak
like a child.'"[48] Pinkhos Menakhem had started to explain the
impossibility of comprehending God's essence, but Itshele, unable
to contain himself, interrupted: "Father, what is love?" Oblivious
to the boy's urgent reason for asking, his father had responded that
one must first of all love God: "'See, I love you because you are my
child. But who created you? The Creator of the Universe. If I love
you, obviously I must love the Creator, for without Him neither
you nor I would exist.'"[49] The lesson was clear: God was more
important to Pinkhos Menakhem than his own son. Unlike the
young suicide, he would never sacrifice himself for love. Unlike the
mother of the youth, he would never protest against God for the
sake of his son.

Although Pinkhos Menakhem had been unusually available on
that particular Sabbath afternoon, Itshele learned from the episode
that he should not imagine himself uniquely lovable. If his own
father regarded him as merely generically valuable, what could he
hope for from others? The effects of his sad realization were swift
and astonishing: while he was in the midst of playing with his companions, Itshele underwent a mysterious and negative change of
mood: "Suddenly the game bored me, and I walked off alone
towards Gnoyna Street...."[50] On that day, Yitskhok began his life-

long experience—which was only partially hidden by his consummate charm—of profound, friendless isolation.

The burden of discerning that his most heartfelt questions about life and love would be answered with moral comments and homilies—that is, if he could get his parents' attention at all—led to Itshele's lonely conclusion that he would have to bear everything on his own. Israel Joshua spent as little time at home as possible, Hinde Esther treated him like an adorable toy, and his parents were constantly squabbling and worrying. He was unhappy, but no one must know it: "Even though I was only a boy then and did not have the courage to comment, I was filled with questions, which I would take out to the balcony to ponder.... Even before I learned to read or write, I was obsessed by the paradoxes of time, space, infinity, and moreover I was convinced that only I myself could reason out such enigmas, that no one could help me."[51] An event as routine as going to school was fraught with misery, since he could not safely confide that he was being bullied. Itshele expected his parents to tell him that if he was unique, it was his own fault and nothing to feel good about. Rather, it rendered him odd and made him deserve his persecution:[52] "The trip to heder each morning was agonizing, but I couldn't complain to my parents—they had their own troubles. Besides, they'd probably say: 'That's what you get for being different from everyone else....'"[53]

Life in a household filled with complex and arduous prohibitions, combined with the perception of himself as fundamentally unlovable, led Itshele to develop a belief that he was sinful. In any case, how—and why—would he be more special than his imperfect siblings, who were themselves continually criticized for being human? Yitskhok did not generally expose his natural desire for acknowledgment. On the rare occasions when he did, the outcome seemed to remind him that he should never seek recognition for his looks, his apparel, his prosperity. His grim conclusion—fostered by the gloomy disapproval radiated throughout the home by his parents—remained with him throughout his long and eventually successful life.

One Passover season in his early adolescence, for example, a grateful Krochmalna Street tailor decided to thank Pinkhos Menakhem by sewing a new outfit for Yitskhok. At first, the lad was uninterested in the new wardrobe, but he soon conceived a fascination with the possibility of acquisition. His reason was simple: "I had visions of entering the study house triumphantly on Passover Eve, and amazing all the boys there. Previously, my clothes had made me feel inferior to them, even though I was more informed than they.... But now they would see that I could also have a new outfit for the holiday."[54]

As pleased as he was with his fantasy, however, he was plagued as well by the haunting conviction that, if he hoped for admiration and attention, fate would subvert his desire and shatter his dream: "All the same, I felt a premonition of disaster, for how could things go as smoothly as the way I dreamed them?...I knew that the material world was full of snares. I had become too enamored of its pleasures."[55] Sure enough, Yitskhok's fears came true, but in an unexpected manner. The study house was closed due to a gas failure; father and son therefore wound up in another place of prayer, where no one knew them and where his new finery—and he himself—went unnoticed.

In the midst of the stark and lonely realities that burdened his young existence, Itshele discovered one solace that would for a lifetime remove him from immediate pain: fiction. Fiction, in the form of reading and creating, became his salvation. On the surface, he was just like all the other children on Krochmalna Street, but something very different was developing inside: "as I went through the games of tag, hide-and-seek, and cops-and-robbers, my imagination was at work.... My thoughts, which were not the thoughts of other boys, made me both proud and lonely."[56]

His quarrels were not the quarrels of other boys, either. Confronted with a group of peers who ignored him, perhaps out of jealousy—but why?—Itshele responded in the only way he knew how: "There was nothing I could do but wait it out. My kind has to become accustomed to loneliness.... I grew accustomed to being alone and the days no longer seemed interminable. I studied, wrote, read stories. My brother had brought home a two-volume book called *Crime and Punishment*. Although I didn't really comprehend it, it fascinated me. Secluded in the bedroom, I read for hours.... I was in another world. I forgot about my friends."[57] By the time his friends repented, the merger of literature and reality had become full-blown and explicit. Fiction was protection from hurt as well as permission for the expansive fantasies that he ordinarily banished from his thoughts. Approached by a messenger from the group, Itshele was indifferent: "It was like a scene from a novel. My friends wrote that they missed me. 'We wander about in a daze....' I still remember what they said. Despite this great triumph, I was so immersed in my book that it scarcely seemed important any more that they wanted to make amends."

When he finally accepted the sincere remorse of his companions, Itshele invited camaraderie by telling stories, a trick he was to use with exquisite skill for the rest of his professional and private life: "We talked together late and I spoke of my book. 'This is no storybook, this is literature...,' I said. I created for them a fantastic mélange of incidents and my own thoughts, and infected them with my own excitement. Hours passed."[58]

By the end of World War I, the Singer family of Krochmalna Street had been dispersed: Israel Joshua was in the new Soviet Union, Hinde Esther was married and living in England, Basheve and her two young sons had gone to seek refuge in Bilgoray—itself forever altered by the deaths of Basheve's parents. All that remained of that home, and that world, would now live solely through the efforts of the three extraordinary siblings, who took their conflicts and their pain and turned them into the special history that literature alone can create.

3

YITSKOK'S life was going nowhere.

In 1917, Basheve took thirteen-year-old Yitskhok and little Moyshele to Bilgoray, where they spent the remainder of World War I, surrounded by numerous aunts, uncles, and cousins. Despite all the people, however, Yitskhok was lonely. Basheve was absorbed in her age-old sibling rivalries and had no time for him; Pinkhos Menakhem had gone back to Radzymin to assist the Rebbe;[1] Hinde Esther was in England and Israel Joshua was in the Soviet Union. Yitskhok fought the isolation that threatened to envelop him in Bilgoray by avoiding his extended family. He nourished his intellect by studying Zionism and dabbling in secularism; he soothed his loneliness by pursuing romance. To earn a little money, he gave private Hebrew lessons. He read voraciously: "Every Yiddish book was an event for me, every journal or newspaper that found its way to Bilgoray was a discovery for me. All the authors were my relatives in a way, and I had accounts to settle with them."[2] But nothing could conquer the stagnation that eventually wore him down. Yitskhok later realized that, despite its deficiencies, Bilgoray had furnished him with rich emotional and physical impressions—an internal landscape that even half a century of American experience could not diminish. As an adolescent verging on manhood, however, he knew only the desperation to escape its superstition, obscurantism, insularity, and intolerance.

At the conclusion of World War I, Basheve and Moyshele had left Bilgoray for tiny Dzikow Stary, in Galicia,[3] where Pinkhos Menakhem had taken a rabbinic position. In the early 1920s, unable to tolerate life in Bilgoray for another moment, Yitskhok—by then eighteen years old—decided to join his parents. It was a move born of resignation: "I came to this village so broken in spirit that I was ready to give in to my parents, let them arrange a match for me... and become a storekeeper, a teacher, or whatever fate held in store for me. I stopped shaving my beard and let my earlocks grow."[4] Yitskhok's sojourn in the "half-bog, half-village" lasted nine months and, at the end of it, his psychological condition was no better than before. In the meantime, Israel Joshua had come back to Poland from the Soviet Union, where he had grown disillusioned with the socialist experiment. Not knowing what else to do, Yitskhok made his way to Warsaw—and to Israel Joshua.

Still hoping to please his parents, Yitskhok entered a rabbinical seminary; but his heart was not in it.[5] Moreover, although he was now a young adult, he felt completely inadequate to the task of establishing himself in Warsaw. He was unsophisticated, inexperienced, completely unpolished. He was also pitifully bashful: "Of all the problems from which I suffered in my young years, my shyness was perhaps the worst and the most amusing. I felt ashamed and didn't really know what I was ashamed of. Was it my clothing? My fire-red hair? The fact that I couldn't earn a penny, didn't have a metier, a profession, a formal education, that I couldn't speak Polish the way one should?"[6]

As usual when he was in need, Yitskhok turned to his brother.[7] For once, however, Israel Joshua could not be of much material help. He was himself unsettled. Although he had started a family— he now had a wife, Genye, and a small son, Yasha—he had neither a job nor an apartment. Indeed, Israel Joshua had to consider himself fortunate that he was able to live with his in-laws. Nevertheless, during the summers, Israel Joshua rented a dacha in Otwotsk, outside Warsaw, and—ever the generous and devoted brother—he invited Yitskhok to join him there.

As glamorous as renting a dacha might sound, the comforts of such places were meager. The wealthy Warsaw Jews owned their own villas or travelled to spas. The average dacha, in contrast, was frugal and unadorned: "The rented dachas were usually one room with a kitchen in a sandy location, without electricity, without running water (the water had to be fetched from a well), without bed linen, without kitchenware. To be sure, one was living in the forest, but the forest consisted of stunted and sparse pine trees." All day long, the inhabitants of these dachas were exposed to the din of trains traveling between Warsaw and Lemberg (Lvov). Moreover, the non-Jews in the vicinity were inhospitable, if not downright hostile, to the Jewish vacationers. Israel Joshua had rented two rooms and a kitchen, but the space was nonetheless too small to provide comfortable accommodation for a household that included Israel Joshua, Genye, Yasha, Genye's parents, and Yitskhok.

Since Yitskhok was fascinated by literature and was beginning to wonder whether he could ever be a writer, he knew all about a Yiddish writer's club that existed in Warsaw. He longed to visit but did not dare to be a gate-crasher. Then came opportunity, predictably in the form of Israel Joshua. One day in the late summer of 1923, Israel Joshua traveled from Otwotsk to Warsaw, where he was hoping to land a job—and he let his brother tag along. The job failed to materialize, but Yitskhok got his introduction to the Writers' Club. [8]

The Club's location, in a modest courtyard on Tlomackie Street, was enhanced by its proximity to the great Tlomackie synagogue. The synagogue, a landmark of Jewish Warsaw, was later destroyed by the Nazis following the Warsaw Ghetto uprising in 1943. But on that day, its proud and imposing structure lent respectability to the nearby courtyard—and Yitskhok finally found a welcoming home.

Tlomackie 13, the *Literatn-farayn* or Writers' Club, was nicknamed *di bude*, the den, by its members.[9] Bashevis himself dubbed it "the temple of Yiddish literature."[10] The courtyard was barely more impressive than those on Krochmalna Street, and it was equally eclectic: the Club shared its quarters with the youth organization of *mizrakhi*, the religious Zionists, and, for a time, with a brothel. Complaints to the landlord about the impropriety of such an establishment in the proximity of innocent youths and literary lions fell on deaf ears—the pimps paid their rent on time.

Established at the conclusion of World War I, the Club was an immediate success. Every notable Yiddish writer was a member; every would-be writer, every literary enthusiast, connived to be admitted as a guest. Strangely, although it was a secular organization, the Club resembled a *shtibl*, a small Hasidic prayer house. The Hasidim would rent a place, set up bookshelves with holy volumes, install an ark, a table and some chairs, and start holding services; similarly, the writers leased Tlomackie 13, installed a few tables, and proclaimed themselves in business.[11]

At the same time, however, the *Literatn-farayn* was anomalous and even obnoxious by Jewish standards: unlike every other communal setting, whether synagogue or *mikve*, the Club restricted its membership.[12] While it was therefore singularly un-Jewish, the Club was also prototypical of a post-War phenomenon. "As strange as it may seem, together with the creation of a Polish state [after World War I] came the creation of a sort of Jewish spiritual state in Poland—a center of ideas, aspirations, theories, fantasies, dreams."[13]

The scene at the Club mesmerized Yitskhok, and he could describe it in detail years later: a large room, appointed with a sideboard and small tables, it resembled a restaurant but was undefinably different from other eating establishments. Pictures and drawings adorned the walls. The men sitting and eating at the tables were unlike the familiar Warsaw types. They had exotic-looking faces and bewitching expressions;[14] almost all of them wore eyeglasses. As they ate their noodle soup and chicken thighs—noisily sucking out the marrow—they engaged in fervid debate, at the same time gesticulating wildly with their hands. Presiding calmly over the commotion was the Club's mascot, Fifi the cat. Actually, various cats came and went, but they were always called Fifi.[15]

Yitskhok was overwhelmed by the spectacle; he sensed that he knew all the writers assembled there, had seen or heard them all before, yet he knew that his perception was impossible without some supernatural explanation. In his distraction, he even forgot his usual severe shyness, staring with unconcerned abandon at the strange mixture of characters. While he was deep in contemplation, the Club's female bouncer pointed an accusing finger at him: Who was he and what business did he have there? Israel Joshua dashed to the rescue, whereupon the woman laughingly exclaimed that they were "as alike as two drops of water."[16]

Israel Joshua eventually guided his younger brother into another room, larger and more elegant than the restaurant, although it, too, was arranged with little tables. To Yitskhok, this room possessed the qualities of an authentic men's club, "like the kind I imagined from reading novels about England, especially Jules Verne's *Around the World in Eighty Days*." While his brother argued heatedly with the Futurist poet and communist Peretz Markish, Yitskhok surveyed the hall: "Over the stage hung a large picture of Y. L. Peretz. In a way, that picture dominated the entire room. Peretz looked almost alive, and I had the feeling that he was watching over the Writers' Club like a father, like a spiritual leader in case, God forbid, someone betrayed his values, his love of Yiddish, his ideal of cultural autonomy."[17]

Y. L. Peretz (1852–1915) was the undisputed master of modern secular Yiddish literature. Much more than his august predecessors, Sholem Abramovitch (usually referred to as Mendele Moykher Sforim) and Sholem Aleichem, Peretz inspired an entire generation of young writers. He was urbane and passionate, savvy about politics and shrewd about literature. His Warsaw apartment served as a literary salon and place of pilgrimage, where aspiring artists from all over Poland converged to receive his judgement. The young hopefuls awaited his pronouncements: should they write poetry or prose? Were they more talented in Hebrew or in Yiddish? Could they dare to anticipate a literary future?

Peretz's death left a void that no single individual could fill. The Club was created as partial restitution for the monumental loss to Yiddish literature in Warsaw. Nonetheless, the thought of a home for writers without the master's riveting presence was unthinkable. Yitskhok experienced the vitality emanating from Peretz's portrait as a powerful influence, and during his initial spurts of literary growth, he sought the dead sage's approval—not always successfully: "I stole a glance at Peretz's picture, and it seemed to me that he was looking at me and saying, without words, 'How can it be that this never occurred to you before? After all, it's so simple.'"[18]

The Club was filled with characters, some of whom seemed to live there. The members argued constantly, and their positions ranged across a wide spectrum of literary and political philosophies: communism—both Trotskyite and Stalinist, Zionism, secularism, traditional Yiddishkeyt. There were enthusiasts of modernism as well as mourners of a bygone era. All co-existed in uneasy harmony because of their shared love for Yiddish. But they were not always kind, or even civilized, to one another.

One of the most testy members was H. D. Nomberg, an early Peretz disciple and a core member of his salon. On Yitskhok's first day at the Club, even as Peretz gazed down on the scene in the big hall, Nomberg literally turned his back on Peretz Markish and Israel Joshua. Nomberg took a dim view of these young modernists, whom he labeled *grafomanen* (graphomaniacs)—a widely used term of derision for writers who produced too much and whose work mattered too little. Nomberg himself could hardly be accused of excessive productivity. The author of such finely honed psychological short stories as *"Fliglman"* ("Fliglman") and *"Shvayg, Shvester"* ("Be Silent, Sister"), Nomberg seemed to wrench his creativity from an inner source that was difficult to locate and easily depleted.[19]

Nomberg's harshness towards the youthful mavericks was ironic, because he had been a rebel in his own day. Having forsaken not only a wife and small children, but also his Hasidism, he became a writer who virtually lived literature, in his own eccentric manner. Even as a doddering old man, grumpily berating the callow upstarts, he remained bizarre. Yitskhok's first impression of him was that he was "weirdly thin, skin and bones. He was wearing a light suit, a colorful, strangely-knotted necktie, yellow shoes, a straw hat. He looked sick. One of his eyes was large, the other small, half-closed and glassy."[20] Nomberg, who could barely walk, shuffled to the stage, where there was a phonograph. "Soon we could hear music and singing. If I remember correctly, it was a tango.... Nomberg had learned the modern dances: tango, shimmy, foxtrot, Charleston, and whatever else. He often danced in the Writers' Club." Yitskhok watched as Nomberg searched the hall for a dancing partner. "A young woman got up from her table, smiled and winked at her companion, and approached Nomberg. He raised his small head, on which there remained bits of blond and grey hair, and—since he was short and she was tall—struggled to place his hand on her shoulder. The two began to dance; Markish's eyes filled with laughter."[21]

For Yitskhok, the Club was both a home and a university. Lacking any formal secular education, he hungered for knowledge of all kinds. He devoured everything he could lay his hands on: Tolstoy, Spinoza, G. K. Chesterton, Thomas Mann, kabbalah, cosmology, William James, and Plato. Books had been his companions throughout his solitary boyhood, and the relationship strengthened with time. Now, in addition to his private musings, he entered into discussions with others, learning from them the techniques and ploys of literary design and construction. By 1925, he was ready to make his debut as a Yiddish writer.

As he rubbed elbows with the regulars at Tlomackie 13, Yitskhok's difficulties in forming close friendships with men became quickly and painfully apparent. His experience with the males in his family had led him to repudiate his father's ineptitude and delicacy while venerating his brother's competence and stamina. As a result, Yitskhok viewed men, and responded to them, with either contempt or submission. Predictably, they disliked him. His shyness and boyish vulnerability, which attracted women, deterred most men, and his competitive spirit, emerging as it did in veiled—even covert—ways, frightened men who could not defend themselves and repelled men who could. Nonetheless, the friends Yitskhok did make, he made for life, choosing complicated, brilliant, talented, and iconoclastic males who felt as uncomfortable as he did in the maelstrom of a new Jewish world.

One of these remarkable men was Arn Tseytlin (Aaron Zeitlin). Arn was the son of Hillel Tseytlin, a prominent Yiddish writer and philosophical thinker who believed that Jewish existence in an age of worldliness would be endangered if the underlying religious basis of Judaism were lost. Arn, like his father and like Yitskhok, was fascinated by kabbalah and mysticism. He and Yitskhok shared the peculiar space occupied by some members of their generation: born into orthodox homes, they were well-acquainted with the modern world but stood apart from it. Although they rejected staunch tradition, they simultaneously refused to identify with the avant-garde.

In 1932, Yitskhok and Arn Tseytlin joined forces to edit the prestigious, albeit short-lived, Yiddish journal, *Globus*. Tseytlin was five years older than Yitskhok, and he had started writing and publishing early; therefore, he was already a recognized writer when Yitskhok first encountered him at Tlomackie 13. With his greater maturity, his heritage, and his complex mind, Tseytlin was a man to whom Yitskhok could look with admiration and the hope of enlightenment: "It's obvious why I should have been eager to know him, but I can't understand to this day why he should have taken an interest in me." Yitskhok later described their first meeting at the Club: "There was a windowless room there where the lights were always on, one wall always stayed warm. It was connected to the oven of a restaurant that was kept constantly heated."[22] Against that deserted yet comfortable wall, the two men became acquainted. Although their lifestyles were different—Tseytlin was married at a time when Yitskhok was filled with experimental zeal towards women—the two enjoyed a fruitful and enriching relationship. Each found in the other a salve for his sense of solitude.

Another good friend to Yitskhok was the critic and author of memoirs, Y. Y. Trunk. Twenty years Yitskhok's senior, Trunk—like Tseytlin—stemmed from an illustrious family and declined to enter the mainstream of modern Warsaw Yiddish culture. Trunk was the grandson of Reb Shiyele Kutner, the religious leader also known as the Kutner Rov. Reb Shiyele had gained the respect and devotion of both Yitskhok's father and grandfather. Indeed, Israel Joshua—Shiye—was named after Reb Shiyele.[23] Trunk's heritage, however, was not strictly rabbinic; his maternal grandfather was a wealthy landowner and by no means a learned man. Trunk, like Yitskhok, had to contend all his life with the conflicts of his mixed ancestry. While Yitskhok vacillated between clashing religious philosophies—Hasidism versus Enlightenment—Trunk struggled to mediate between competing forms of livelihood: scholarship versus commerce.

Trunk, who came from Lodz where his father owned valuable real estate, "did not fit in to the environment at Tlomackie 13." For one thing, he was rich. He dressed like a wealthy man, went abroad every year, bought paintings by Jewish artists, and took the time to pursue his interest in sculpture and music. He was an infrequent visitor at the Club, possibly because he lived on Bagatela Street, far from the Jewish area of Warsaw. Most peculiar of all, Trunk was a Bundist, a Jewish socialist. Since most affluent Jews were Zionists and most Bundists were poor laborers, his position seemed unusual, even incongruous.

For Yitskhok, Trunk's renegade sensibilities were attractive. Moreover, Trunk combined the sophistication of a wealthy, well-educated secularist with the naivete of a simple Jew, and this contradiction captivated Yitskhok, who later mused that his famous story, "Gimpel the Fool," may have been inspired in part by Trunk. Unfortunately for Trunk—as for Gimpel—Yitskhok's fascination sometimes took the form of teasing and pranks. In his playfulness, Yitskhok had an accomplice, the journalist and social activist Shloyme Mendelson, later a leader of the Bund. The two would take turns playing tricks on Trunk. On one occasion, for instance, Mendelson phoned Trunk and announced that the Bund and the Zionists were amalgamating. To a committed Bundist, the notion of these antithetical political and social visions suddenly merging would have been inconceivable; and so it was. Trunk became so agitated that he could not hear the truth, even after Mendelson had decided that it was time to call off the ruse. Eventually, when Trunk had calmed down, he admonished his jester: "Shloymele, one doesn't joke about such things."[24]

Although his new friendships were essential to Yitskhok as he developed into a writer and man about town in Warsaw, he still had to contend with the shadow of his older brother, which followed him wherever he went. Therefore, as an important element of his schooling, Yitskhok began to avoid Israel Joshua. "You could see them sitting at different tables, and they were visible because of their bald, sharply defined heads.... The two of them were born scoffers, yet they never laughed."[25] Although he esteemed and studied Israel Joshua, Yitskhok was desperate to become independent and self sufficient, to stop feeling childlike and small. His first efforts were external: he moved into a rented room, the first of many, and began an affair—also the first of many.

Even as Yitskhok hastened to grow up, however, he found himself recreating the role of little brother/son with someone else: the writer Meylekh Ravitch. Some ten years older than Yitskhok, Ravitch was Israel Joshua's contemporary and colleague. Yitskhok later judged that the combined literary force of Israel Joshua, Ravitch, Peretz Markish, and Uri Zvi Greenberg had exemplified Yiddish modernism during the mid-1920s. These writers, together with their contemporaries in the United States, were experimenting with Yiddish as a literary language, stretching its limits even as they sought to express the pain, outrage, and confusion stimulated by a violent and increasingly impersonal new era.

Ravitch was comically devoted to order, a trait that had originated—so Yitskhok theorized—during a sojourn in Vienna, where he had worked in a bank and reportedly served in the Austrian army. At Tlomackie 13, where his organizational skills were recognized and appreciated, he was the Club's secretary for many years, performing his role with easy efficiency. When it came to Yitskhok, however, radical measures were necessary: Ravitch took him under his wing, spruced him up, and even invited him to move in while his family was out of town. At the time the two met, Ravitch was already a dedicated vegetarian.

One scene at the Writers' Club both epitomizes Ravitch's obsession with uniformity and reveals the extent of Yitskhok's longing for parental care: "In those years my attire was such that my clothes swam on me. I had not long before discarded the *kapote* [the traditional long coat worn by orthodox Jewish men]... and I was wearing my brother's clothes." Since Israel Joshua was taller than Yitskhok, the borrowed suits were obviously too big. But the problem extended beyond size; Yitskhok simply could not make his clothes look right: they slipped, stuck out in some places, fell down in others. Ravitch looked at Yitskhok with the practiced eye of a sergeant surveying a new recruit. But instead of berating the younger man, which Yitskhok seems almost to have expected, Ravitch set himself the task of literally straightening him out—buttoning his shirt, bending down and retying his shoes, all the while repeating, with military precision, the word *ordnung,* "order."

Yitskhok's response appears strange at first but is explained by his obvious eagerness for attention, so clearly part of his make-up even as an older adult: "I immediately felt for him the sort of friendship which positive criticism always evokes in me. He wanted not to shame me but to help me. I knew very well that he was right."[26]

Ravitch had a younger brother of his own, but that relationship did not undermine his capacity to supervise Yitskhok. Hertz Bergner—Bergner was Ravitch's actual surname—was a year or two younger than Yitskhok and became his good friend. Besides being significantly junior to their powerful brothers, Hertz and Yitskhok had in common the experience of being raised by unusual mothers. (Unlike Basheve, however, who articulated her frustrated wisdom only in private, Hinde Bergner eventually publicized her accumulated intelligence and sensitivity in a seasoned memoir.) Ravitch treated his brother with the same blend of attentiveness and control that he displayed towards Yitskhok. In one of his benevolent interventions, he established a hand-printing workshop for Hertz in the attic of 46 Nowolipki Street—where Ravitch himself lived. Just by watching, Yitskhok learned how to set type during this period.

At the same time, every new experience provided a potential source of zany situations that would one day be transformed into stories, as one incident illustrates. The work completed in small hand-printer shops like Hertz's subsequently had to be transported to a larger, better equipped press and sometimes the move did not go smoothly.[27] A prominent journalist became convinced that he was suffering from hallucinations when an obscure expression he had included in one of his columns appeared instead in the column of a competitor at another newspaper. Having eventually satisfied himself that he was indeed sane—and not the victim of demons— he pursued the matter, discovering the following: the missing line had been deleted from his article and mistakenly placed in an advertisement; the advertisement had then been transported to the rival newspaper, where it was again dropped and inadvertently inserted into the competitor's column.[28]

Later on, Yitskhok freely acknowledged the sibling-like relationship he had enjoyed and rebelled against, not only with Ravitch, but with Israel Joshua's other friends as well: "They were all my literary elder brothers, although I often criticized them."[29] The fate of this diverse group, which functioned as the collective literary guardian for the lost and lonely Yitskhok, represents the whirlwind of interbellum Warsaw and simultaneously underscores how fragile and unstable it all was. Greenberg, who had been forced to flee Warsaw in the 1920s in order to escape a trial for slandering Jesus and Mary in one of his poems, returned for long visits to Poland from his new home in Palestine. In later years, he became a revisionist and turned his talents to writing Hebrew. Markish pursued his communist dream in the Soviet Union—only to be killed by Stalin in 1952. Ravitch eventually wound up in Montreal, where he died in the late 1970s. His brother Hertz immigrated to Australia. Israel Joshua moved to the United States in the mid-1930s, buoyed by the successful American dramatization of his novel, *Yoshe kalb*.

Yitskhok could not have imagined what would become of his role models. Although catastrophe hovered in the distance during the 1920s and early 1930s, he concentrated on his development as a writer and as a lover. He later combined these pursuits in extensive but fictionalized descriptions of his passionate adventures. A major focus of quotidian existence in those days was the Club, which attracted him with its promise of conversation and occasional flirtation. Although at first it must have rankled to be accepted only because he was Israel Joshua's brother, Yitskhok's hunger for the companionship, tutelage, and intellectual stimulation provided by the Club soon outweighed any resentment. He needed the Club because he had discovered that only through writing could he hope to give full expression to his feelings. He was a sensitive young Jew in turbulent interwar Poland, and the urge to produce was as vibrant to him as life itself: "I felt in myself creative powers. They stormed in me together with the lust for love and sex."[30]

The yearning to communicate is natural; for Yitskhok, the form it took was story-telling, above all through writing. Over time, the stories assumed such power that he confused them with reality: "Later on I didn't know myself whether they really happened or I made them up."[31] Eventually, the childhood need to escape painful events and emotions by losing himself in "scribbling" had become so deeply automatic that the line between lived experience and fiction ceased to exist altogether: "In later years the suspense in my life and in my writing fused in such fashion that I often didn't know where one began and the other ended."[32]

Yitskhok understood that his compulsion to write stemmed from misery: "I couldn't be the sort of Jew that my pious parents wanted to make of me; I couldn't be, and didn't want to be, a non-Jew. I could live neither with, nor without, God. I aspired to the big, free world, but I had understood already early on that the world was nowhere near as big and as free as I had envisioned. Ideas attacked me like locusts, emotions stormed within me when I was awake and while I slept. I had only one way to express all of that: with my pen, with my Yiddish language...."[33]

While it was intriguing and fun to take part in the heady atmosphere of Tlomackie 13, Yitskhok viewed his literary development with the utmost seriousness. Eventually, the period of observation and apprenticeship began to produce results, both external and internal. In 1925, two momentous events occurred in Yitskhok's life: his first published work of fiction, a short story entitled "*Af der elter"*("In Old Age"), won a prize from the prestigious Yiddish literary journal, *Literarishe bleter;*[34] and he gave birth to himself as Yitskhok Bashevis.

Like many others in his generation, Yitskhok had experimented with writing Hebrew—an endeavor that never really got off the ground. The immediate success of *"Af der elter"* was a vote of confidence for his deeper and fuller capacities in Yiddish. Once he made the linguistic decision, he never wavered—although his mastery of English was eventually greater than he ever publicly let on.

Yitskhok's choice of the name Bashevis, by which he was thereafter known to his Yiddish readers, contained powerful meaning about his struggles with identity. Bashevis is a matronymic, a surname that Yitskhok created by adding a possessive ending to *Basheve*, his mother's first name. The practice was common in Eastern-European-Jewish history: Malkin, Rivkin, and Dworkin are examples, as are Lees, Bayliss, and Perliss. Assuming his new title, Bashevis proclaimed, in no uncertain terms: Do not associate me with my father or with my brother!

How much of the declaration had to do with gender identification is unclear, although Bashevis admitted that, at times of particular stress, he was embarrassed to notice how closely he resembled Basheve: "They weren't my words and not my *nign* [melody], but rather my mother's. Even my voice sounded to me like her's."[35] Bashevis definitely wished to separate himself from everything that the name Singer represented. On the one hand, it meant his father's rabbinic tradition, ecstatic orthodoxy, helplessness, softness, and poverty, which he feared would cling to him and tie him in knots. On the other hand, the name signified his brother's literary success, upward mobility, competence, maturity, and generosity, which Bashevis coveted but did not want to acquire as a result of Israel Joshua's largesse. The move was autonomous and innovative, yet simultaneously defiant and ungrateful. It epitomized the mix of tradition and originality, piety and impudence, that were the hallmarks of Bashevis at his best.

The issue of gender and sexuality went far beyond the boundaries of a new name. During the 1920s, Bashevis was deeply involved in exploring the female, through romance, lust, and rumination. An inseparable part of the Club's attraction for him was the presence of women. He had long puzzled over the mysteries of love and sex; the chance to scrutinize women in the very environment where he was also receiving his education as a writer was convenient and exciting, but also challenging and dangerous. Beyond the fascination the women provided as individuals, their collective presence exemplified the phenomenal change in Eastern-European-Jewish life that had occurred within a single generation. Where their mothers still wore wigs, went to the *mikve*, spoke only Yiddish, kept the dietary laws, and never looked at a strange man, these young women behaved as if they had just been set free from bondage. They "dressed in the latest styles, danced the shimmy, spoke Polish—often better than non-Jewish women—were interested in literature, theater; they read erotic novels, often said that the institution of marriage was obsolete, preached and practiced free love."[36] They wore make-up.[37]

The new women wanted to experience the same freedoms as their male counterparts—and that included admission to the Writers' Club. Moreover, such entry could scarcely be denied them, for in their unconventional pursuits, they were beginning to emerge as artists: writers, painters, models, and actresses. They were also potential audiences and dancing partners for the male members of the Club, whose wives were up in arms about the unusual situation, fearing that for these modern females, the prospect of an affair was not a sin but rather, "a progressive *mitsve* [commandment]."

Bashevis wanted to associate with the worldly women he was encountering at the Club, especially since he had convinced himself that such contact was necessary for his development as a modern Yiddish writer; but he felt unaccomplished and nervous, discouraged by the fear that they were looking at him with "suppressed laughter."[38] Therefore, he did not approach them. Bashevis was by no means the only one to be intimidated. Like him, many writers at the Club were products of traditional religious schooling, and they had neither the cultural preparation nor the social skills to contend with such exotic and powerful creatures.

The issue of feminism and freedom for women had an amusing if grotesque counterpart at the brothel that thrived for a time in the same courtyard as the Writers' Club. Although the women who frequented the Writers' Club preached free love, the practical details were not so simple. Without a place to go—for privacy was hard to find—and with the threat of pregnancy unmitigated by the possibility of legal abortion, much of the revolutionary pronouncement remained *moyl-melokhe* (verbal handicraft).

As always, there was still a place for prostitutes. One of these, Khela, was a phenomenon whose unusual attributes affected life at the Writers' Club. Although she was beautiful and independent— she scorned the idea of a pimp and worked only in the afternoon— and although she walked about wearing nothing but shoes, black socks, and a schoolgirl's cap, these were not the reasons for her notoriety. Khela was outspoken, claiming that all women were in fact prostitutes for their husbands; she could quote extensively from the Bible to bolster her argument that men were historically adept at exploitation and betrayal. For some reason, she favored Hertz Bergner and, whenever he was around, she would abandon her other customers and concentrate on him, even feeding him chocolate and cookies. Furthermore, Khela was a fountain of rich and juicy Yiddish. She possessed "a treasure trove of jokes, curses, vulgar expressions, anecdotes." With her gift for language, Khela was an attraction to none other than the folklorists of YIVO, the Jewish Scientific Institute (now known as the Institute for Jewish Research), who frequented the Writers' Club: "They came to her with their notebooks and wrote down all her charming adages."[39]

The exciting events at Tlomackie 13 were not merely intellectually interesting—Bashevis burned with conflicted desire. He longed for women but could not settle down, and during his early years in Warsaw, he established a pattern that he maintained throughout his life: the tendency to be involved with more than one woman at a time. An incident from 1926 exemplifies the fraught situations that were apt to flare up: "There in the hall, on the polished parquet floor, stands [Bashevis] suffering what looks to be a crucifixion of sorts. His arms are stretched out to their full length and effectively nailed in place, on the one side, a skinny young woman who has dug her fingernails into the wrist she is clutching and, on the other side, a more buxom one who is doing the same. Each wants him wholly to herself. They wage a desperate tug of war, which bids fair to split him clear down the middle.... His gaunt flushed face is wreathed in the torment of a mock-martyr."[40] One of these women was Rokhl Shapira, or Ronye, who later bore Bashevis's only child, Yisroel, but who never became his wife.

Like Bashevis, Ronye was the daughter of a rabbi, but unlike him, she had been educated in a Polish high school. Ronye was an ardent communist; her passionate political involvement angered and frustrated Bashevis, who never sympathized with the cause. Ronye's arrest in 1932, which resulted in a one-day arrest for Bashevis as well, severely strained the already stormy and unstable relationship.[41]

By 1934, Bashevis had been in Warsaw for over a decade. He was establishing a name for himself with stories, reviews, and provocative essays—such as *"Tsu der frage vegn literatur un politik"* ("On the Question of Literature and Politics") in *Globus*.[42] But despite his burgeoning career, Bashevis's life was filled with torment. He was thirty years old. By that age, his grandfather had been a venerated community leader with children who were about to start their own families. Although himself a father—his son Yisroel had been born in 1930—Bashevis was unable to assume the role of husband and parent. He fought with Ronye, yet he could not bring himself to leave her: "We had eight miserable years."[43]

As Bashevis struggled to master his sexual and emotional longings, he was forced to confront a momentous and baffling question: What constituted a suitable match? His mother had been cool and withdrawn and his sister had been passionate and intrusively affectionate. In addition, he had been teased and coddled by the flirtatious Radzymin Rebetsin. His erotic models clashed wildly. Which type was *his* type? Moreover, no matter how sophisticated he became, Bashevis could not shake the remnants of Itshele that refused to disappear. There were important things he had to figure out. Why was he so lonely and different? Why was his family so unhappy? Even if he unraveled the mystery of love, would he be sufficiently stable to sustain a committed union?

Seeking guidance in his inquiries, Bashevis talked to his friends and observed the families of others. From the time of his years in Bilgoray, he had entertained thoughts of suicide. Now, he contemplated writing a book with Arn Tseytlin about the misogynist philosopher, Otto Weininger, who had committed suicide as a young man.[44] He studied the Bergners: Hertz and Meylekh had had an older brother, a painter, who had gone to Vienna to study and had committed suicide there. Hertz barely remembered this brother, and Meylekh referred to him only rarely, revealing few details. Bashevis did not know the reason for the suicide and was therefore left to his own devices in trying to understand it. "Maybe he was mentally ill? Maybe he suffered from an incurable physical illness?"[45]

Even more than suicide, ruminations about insanity pestered Bashevis. He may have appreciated the companionship of his colleagues at the Writers' Club, but he soon learned that they could not help him decipher the puzzle posed by his own family. The decision to translate Thomas Mann's *Zauberberg* (*The Magic Mountain*) allowed Bashevis to contemplate the intricate connection between physical and emotional illness, an intersection that struck at the core of his existence. He needed to know what was really wrong with his sister. Was she epileptic, mildly hysterical, or just plain crazy? Moreover, he was desperate to find out whether Hindele's ailment ran in the family. After all, one of his Bilgoray cousins was known to cry out "as if possessed."[46] This line of inquiry had ramifications that were potentially profound: what if he were to discover that all his problems with women, all his musings about suicide, were signs that he himself was deranged? He could not deny that he was subject to strange visions—which seemed to have their etiology in the time around his sister's departure from the family: "Closing my eyes, I saw shapes and colors that I had never seen before, which kept shifting into new designs and forms. Sometimes I saw a fiery eye, brighter than the sun and with a weird pupil. To this day, when I try to do so, I can still see this radiant eye. My memory of those days is full of visionary flowers and gems. But at that time the visions were so numerous that sometimes I could not get rid of them."[47]

As he had done since boyhood, Bashevis kept his own counsel—and produced fiction—as he sought to conquer his conflicts and resolve his worries. His emotional preoccupation during the mid-1930s resulted in an elaborate exploration of insanity—the monumental *Sotn in goray* (*Satan in Goray*). First serialized in *Globus*, and then published in book form by the prestigious Pen Club in 1935, the novel—Bashevis's first—appeared on the eve of his emigration from Poland. It was an auspicious beginning: the Pen Club later went on to produce the works of such important Yiddish writers as Itsik Manger, Rokhl Korn, and Reyzl Žykhlinski.

Der sotn in goray is set in seventeenth-century Poland. That era—the period of the Chmielnicki pogroms and the subsequent rise of the false messiah Shabbtai Zvi (or *Shapse tsvi* as he was known in Yiddish)—bore some similarity to the tempestuous times Bashevis was witnessing. The novel describes mass hysteria, political chaos, and the specter of annihilation, which occur in an atmosphere of religious and sexual depravity. At the center of the story is Rekhele, a pathetic young woman who starts her life in the wake of the 1648 massacres and dies convinced that she has been impregnated by Satan. Bashevis clearly intends in this novel to provide a picture of actual demonic possession; nevertheless, Rekhele's sufferings bear an astonishing similarity to Hindele's symptoms and emotional vulnerability. In addition, Bashevis probes the lasting damage caused by inadequate parental care—a subject that both he and his sister knew intimately.

As a tiny baby, Rekhele had been taken from home by her mother to escape Chmielnicki's pogroms. Separated since infancy from her father, she had been abandoned at age five, when her mother died. Thereafter, she had lived with Zaydl Ber, her base and vulgar uncle, and his ancient mother-in-law. In order to keep the child at bay and prevent her from exploring the outside world, the old woman—a grotesquely frightening creature—had goaded and terrified Rekhele into submission. There was as well an apparent sexual component to this unscrupulous chaperone's harassment: "She [the old woman] smelled of burned feathers and mice. Sometimes she would lift the girl's shirt and finger her hot body with dead hands, panting with a kind of impure delight: 'Fire! Fire! The girl's burning up!'"[48]

Like Hindele, Rekhele was subject to seizures, especially at moments of stress. Her first attack occurred immediately after the old woman's death: "Late that night, when Uncle came home, he found Rechele lying with her knees pulled to her chest, her eyes glazed and her teeth clenched. Reb Zeydel Ber screamed and people came running. At length Rechele began to groan, but from that evening on she was never the same.... Eventually Rechele improved and could once more stand, but her left leg continued paralyzed, and she walked with a limp."[49]

Zaydl Ber's wish to wed Rekhele after the demise of his mother-in-law was psychologically devastating for the girl. It meant that her uncle was unwilling to be a parent to her. And things did not improve when, upon Zaydl Ber's death, she was returned to her biological father, Eleazer Babad: "Thenceforth Rechele was one apart. She was beset by mysterious ills. Some said she suffered from the falling sickness, others that she was in the power of demons. In Goray Reb Eleazer left her completely on her own...."[50]

Eventually, Rekhele marries, but the attempt at sexual union with her new husband, Itche Mates, is a disaster. Even before the wedding, Rekhele suffers an attack that echoes her original seizure: "Suddenly, dragging her lame leg, as though to step forward, she pulled herself up and fell to laughing so violently and so loudly that everyone was startled. Before anyone could reach her, she had fallen and she lay choking with sobs. Her eyes glazed, her arms and legs contorted, foam ran from her twisted mouth, as if she were an epileptic."[51]

When Gedalye, the charismatic follower of *Shapse tsvi*, comes to Goray, he provides the town—and Rekhele as well, of course—with a powerful parental presence. Combining both maternal and paternal qualities, he exhibits the capacity to soothe as well as to teach; he is available for children and adults alike, and his influence is great on this account alone, quite beyond the wondrous tidings he brings of the messiah *Shapse tsvi*. For Rekhele, the idea that such a perfect parent sees her as special opens the possibility that she may, after all, be lovable. But her experience with parental figures is that they either abandon her or approach her with erotic intentions. Therefore, although she wants to reach out to Gedalye, Rekhele unconsciously knows that he may respond with unwelcome sexual interest—and she is correct. In response to her new plight, Rekhele's seizures escalate and she begins to experience visions.

In the end, *Shapse tsvi* is revealed as a fake and Rekhele can no longer look to Gedalye as the admirable parent he had once seemed to be. This development represents another loss for Rekhele, even though she had been forced to pay for Gedalye's attention by submitting to his sexual demands. It is at this point that Rekhele's possession by a dybbuk occurs and she is convinced that she has been impregnated by Satan. The spiritual interloper is exorcised, but Rekhele succumbs shortly after her deliverance.

Despite the drama and folkloric resonance of a demonic explanation for Rekhele's fate, Bashevis provides ample evidence of emotional disturbance. Having suffered a debilitating separation from both mother and father in her early childhood, Rekhele had clung to the imperfect and violent caretakers she had managed to secure. The subsequent abandonment through death by Zaydl Ber's mother-in-law had left Rekhele with an overwhelming and insurmountable sense of loss, even though she had been mistreated. Moreover, she had been forced to contend with the guilt of having eliminated her oppressor.

Her uncle's sexual interest had further deprived Rekhele of the kind of care and nurturing that she so desperately needed. Completely lacking a person to look up to, Rekhele had sunk progressively into a state of inner deadness, the result of a deep conviction that she was of no consequence whatsoever except as a sexual plaything. After the deaths of her mother, her cruel caretaker, and Zaydl Ber, Rekhele's futile attempt to forge a connection with her biological father had simply intensified her longing and desperation. Her subsequent marriage to Itche Mates—who was too urgently intent on his own rigid and obsessional struggles to pay attention to his fragile and peculiar wife—had compounded Rekhele's desolation. Her submission to Gedalye had therefore constituted both a last-ditch effort to save herself and a signal that, despite everything, she maintained some vestige of hope that someone could love and protect her.

But Gedalye, far from cherishing and shielding Rekhele the child, had instead required her to be a sexual woman. Rekhele had complied physically, while holding herself apart from the experience by losing herself in seizures and visions. Significantly, when Gedalye's credibility as a leader is shattered and his position as idealized parent destroyed, Rekhele's visions cease. Since Gedalye can no longer demand copulation from her in return for the lure of his patronage, Rekhele no longer needs to protect herself by entering the sanctuary of her inner world.

Rekhele's liberation from Gedalye's clutches does not free her, however; on the contrary, her mental state deteriorates further, as she develops the delusion that she has been impregnated by Satan. Her psychosis is an expression of her overwhelming need to be connected somehow to someone—even if it must be through an hysterical pregnancy. The compelling need for attachment combines with her deep certainty that she must be evil if no one will be involved with her except carnally—hence the satanic union.

Having created such potent psychological material, why did Bashevis insist on shrouding it, favoring an appeal to the domain of literal demons, dybbukim, and superstition? He could not have been afraid of seeming outré: he enjoyed flirting with the role of *enfant terrible*. Moreover, an examination of possession as an internal emotional phenomenon was already well known to Warsaw literati: Max Weinreich, the great Yiddish philologist and founder of YIVO, had discussed the case of a young woman possessed by a dybbuk in his seminal 1928 book, *Bilder fun der yidisher literaturgeshikhte* (*Pictures from Yiddish Literary History*). Bashevis may have been influenced by Weinreich's account, which was based on a printed text from the latter half of the seventeenth century, especially since Weinreich—unlike Bashevis in his novel—makes an explicit connection between so-called possession and the real malaise: epilepsy.

The girl in Weinreich's text has experienced trauma that resembles Rekhele's: "Why did the girl become sick? We hear that her sister died shortly before the evil spirit appeared for the first time. The sister's death certainly made a deep impression on her." While it is difficult to ascertain the exact timing of the events, Weinreich speculates that the tumult of the the Chmielnicki pogroms, combined with the loss of her sister, was simply too much for the young girl: "She evidently got falling sickness and at that time, even children in the cradle knew that falling sickness (epilepsy) comes from a dybbuk. Jews and Christians, high and low born, believed this.... The description of how the evil spirit runs from her head to her thigh, how it pulls her hair and turns her upside down, gives us an exact picture of her convulsions. Not only those around her, but she herself was convinced that an evil spirit was torturing her."

Weinreich, who was a devotee of psychoanalysis—and who visited Tlomackie 13—speculates that the girl's epileptic attacks may have been hysterical, brought on by the stresses of her sister's death and the situation of war and dislocation. Weinreich's reasoning for this speculation does not rest in the symptoms themselves but rather in the girl's ultimate cure. As he puts it: "Maybe the story had a particularly pathological basis as well, and perhaps therein lies the secret of why Reb Borekh succeeded in chasing out the evil spirit precisely on Friday evening when no one was around. Let us leave the question open."[52]

Bashevis leaves the question of Rekhele open as well, by refusing to relinquish his concrete demonic explanation of her malady. At the same time, he includes innuendo connecting Rekhele with Hindele: early childhood abandonment and neglect, symptoms that mimic epilepsy, hysterical traits—including a possible false pregnancy—and inappropriate sexuality. Like Rekhele, Hindele had been abandoned by her mother in infancy and neglected by her father; she had begun suffering seizures in adolescence;[53] she thought of herself as possessed; and she had experienced strange abdominal manifestations in her teens. No evidence exists that there was ever overt incest in the Singer home. Nonetheless, Hindele's passion was powerful, as the accounts of her behavior with her brothers make clear: her affectionate effusions towards little Itshele and Moyshele and her demanding pursuit of the adult Israel Joshua. The figure of Rekhele—the sad, exploited, yet strangely dangerous and forceful girl-woman—suggests that Bashevis's lifelong fascination with deranged carnality emerged from his complex relationship with Hindele.

Perhaps Bashevis was unconscious of his decision to provide psychological reasons for Rekhele's peculiarities even as he denied their significance; perhaps in 1935, he felt a need to protect his sister from any open discussion of her emotional instability. Perhaps—despite his thirst for answers about his own sanity and the mental health of his family—he was afraid to broach that subject directly. In any case, after *Der sotn in goray*, he never again explored the issue of demonic possession with such thorough and detailed attention. His standard (eventually clichéd) comments on the supernatural notwithstanding, Bashevis's insistence on the literal reality of demons and spirits markedly attenuated over time. Instead, his descriptions of possession became more and more psychological. At the same time, his absorption with emotional instability and insanity never wavered. As one of his narrators puts it: "Einstein contends that mass is energy. I say that mass is compressed emotion. Neuroses materialize and take on concrete form. Feelings put on bodies or are themselves bodies. Those are your dybbuks, the sprites, the hobgoblins."[54]

Bashevis came to realize that his world of demons and spirits was a helpful but painfully temporary antidote to the loneliness and depression that continued to plague him. The attempt to externalize his conflicts through writing had led to a brilliant and lasting novel, but it had failed to exorcise his own spooks and miseries. Years later, when Tlomackie 13 was no more than a burned-out memory, when most of his youthful friends and competitors were dead, when he was living in a time and place he could not have envisioned even in 1935—on the eve of his departure from Poland—Bashevis remembered his confusion and inner turbulence. As he told his granddaughter when she asked him why he wrote about supernatural phenomena: "You didn't have to face a lot. You can focus on reality and get enjoyment out of it."[55]

4

BY 1935, Bashevis's professional life seemed to be taking off. He had translated several works from German into Yiddish, including Thomas Mann's extraordinary *Zauberberg* (*The Magic Mountain*); he was co-editor of the literary journal *Globus* with Arn Tseytlin; he had published his novel *Der sotn in goray* in serial form in *Globus*, and the Pen Club had issued it in book form.

Bashevis's personal life, however, was marked more by disruption than by success. He was on bad terms with Ronye, with whom he had a five-year-old child, Yisroel. And he was well on the road to becoming a far more neglectful father than his own father could have even contemplated. Yet any pain he suffered due to the dissolution of his new family was overshadowed by two other debilitating losses. His father, Pinkhos Menakhem, and Israel Joshua's older son, fourteen-year-old Yasha, had both died in the previous few years. "The boy's death drove me into a depression that remains with me to this day. It was my first direct contact with death." About his father's death, Bashevis was speechless.[1]

Israel Joshua had immigrated to the United States and was working for the *Forverts* in New York. Without any parental figure to oversee his life, Bashevis saw no reason to remain in Poland. As always, Israel Joshua engineered the change in Bashevis's life: he sent his younger brother an affidavit for an American tourist visa.

Bashevis later recounted his emigration from Poland in a memoir, *Love and Exile,* but some of the book's details cannot be trusted. Describing the work as a "spiritual autobiography," and announcing that he had written "fiction against a background of truth," Bashevis admitted that he was not always factual.[2] Nonetheless, he did not falsify the essentials of his emotional existence at the time: his terrible depression, his anxiety about setting himself up yet again—in a country whose very essence was alien to him—and his disturbing conflicts with Israel Joshua. While Bashevis later sought to portray his emigration as a visionary act, the truth was at once closer to home and more desperate: he could not live without his older brother.

In fleeing Poland, Bashevis left behind his son Yisroel—from whom he was to be separated for twenty years—as well as Basheve and Moyshe, whom he never saw again. He also abandoned his Warsaw career, including his plans to participate in a new journal together with such Yiddish luminaries as the poet Itsik Manger.

Faced with the prospect of immense upheaval, Bashevis employed a mixture of denial and defiance. In his dealings with Israel Joshua, he was nonchalant, even dismissive: "I corresponded with my brother in New York, but I never complained about my lot. Although my plans depended on my brother sending me an affidavit to come to America on a tourist visa and later helping me to remain there, I seldom answered his letters."[3] Similarly, he shrugged off the importance of his ties in Poland. By the time he boarded the train to leave Warsaw, he had relegated his loved ones to a remote and insignificant corner of his awareness: "Although we were still close to Warsaw and the train ran past little depots of familiar towns, I felt as if I were already abroad. I knew that I would never come this way again and that Warsaw, Poland, the Writers' Club, my mother, my brother Moishe, and the women who were near to me had all passed over into the sphere of memory. The fact is that they had been ghosts even while I was still with them."

But if Bashevis was hoping to achieve a more felicitous, life-affirming view of the world by leaving Poland, he was quickly reminded of the reality. Already on the train, he realized the truth: "There had been moments when I assumed that once I got the visa to America I would be happy. But I felt no happiness now, not even a trace."[4] The trip from Warsaw entailed a frightening, but in fact uneventful journey across Nazi Germany. More harrowing—because it evoked all the insecurity he was trying to squelch—was Bashevis's sojourn in Paris, where he saw a stage adaptation of his brother's novel, *Yoshe kalb*. The play's critical acclaim reminded Bashevis that he would soon be back in the shadow of Israel Joshua, with his fame, his competence—and now, his greater knowledge of American life.[5]

Bashevis set sail from Cherbourg on April 19, 1935, on the day before Hitler's birthday and during the intermediate days of Passover. There was no one to see him off at the pier. The ocean voyage to New York, which lasted eight days, was a miserable time for the shy and lonely young man. He could not fight his despondency with the comforting knowledge of his recent achievements, for he was no longer the sought-after author, lover, and habitué of the famous Warsaw Writers' Club. Now, literally at sea, he was once again a little brother, a lost soul, a frightened refugee. His emotional state reflected his self-perception: "Whenever I became overly excited, irritated, lonesome, the anxieties of my childhood returned to me with all their daydreams, false assumptions, ridiculous suspicions, superstitions." In his attempt to shake off the immobility of depression, Bashevis played tricks on himself: "I knew full well that my nerves required suspense and I had to create it....I lost my sense of direction completely....I made flagrant mistakes in speaking. Some mocking demon began to play games with me and even though I realized it was all sham and nonsense I had to cooperate."[6]

Bashevis's urge to enliven himself conflicted with his need to expiate the guilt he felt over forsaking his loved ones in Poland. Consequently, his sense of dislocation and utter isolation from the normal world blended with the fantasy that he was being singled out for neglect—while the others received wine with their meals, he, the only one seated alone in the entire dining room, was given none. Finally, unable to endure the unhappiness of enforced solitude among a crowd of merrymakers, he requested his meals in the cell-like, stultifying chamber that passed for a cabin: "From that day on I was going to America as if on a prison ship... with food brought by a man who could be a prison guard.... The food he brought me was always the same. In the morning—bread with black coffee. For lunch—some groats with no wine or dessert. For dinner—he threw me a piece of stale bread, some cheese, and a kind of white sausage I had never before seen in Poland."[7] (Significantly, Bashevis's memories, recorded years after the fact and certainly embellished, recall not so much a prison ship as a gentrified version of concentration camp fare and treatment.)

The nightmare trip—eventually somewhat mitigated by flirtation—finally ended on May 1st. Yet, Bashevis's arrival in New York precipitated a crisis of decline and despair that threatened to incapacitate him completely. Israel Joshua met him at the pier and escorted him to Seagate, the Brooklyn enclave of Yiddish writers and intellectuals where he was spending the summer. That night the family ate at the landlord's. After almost two years of separation, Genye had not seen fit to prepare a meal for her brother-in-law. "We finished our meal quickly. My brother told me that he still had some work to do on his novel that day.... I said good night and went to my room.... In my room I lit the ceiling lamp, took a Yiddish book out of the cabinet, and tried to read, but I quickly became bored. I glanced into my notebooks, where I had jotted down various themes for short stories. None of them appealed to me at the moment. A deep gloom came over me, the likes of which I had never before experienced, or at least I thought so.... I had managed it so that I would arrive [in America] all alone in a dark cabin, and stay with a family of strict individualists who were as isolated and withdrawn as I myself."[8]

The rejection by Israel Joshua and his family caused Bashevis to sink into a leaden state of depression. Seeking to revive himself, he went out for a walk, promptly becoming disoriented and losing his way. A wave of panic invigorated him and helped him remember how to return home. Calmer now, his first foray into the wilds of Seagate finally behind him, Bashevis stood outside his brother's house. Israel Joshua was visible in a lighted window: "A renewed surge of love for my brother coursed through me. He was not only my brother but my father and master as well."

But Bashevis's relief from inner torpor was short-lived. Despite this welling-up of devotion and respect, he was neither strengthened nor comforted. Instead, he entered a period of intense regression. He felt infantilized and undermined next to his brother: "I could never address him first. I always had to wait for him to make the first overture." Israel Joshua's power consumed Bashevis. He felt dead.[9] He wanted his brother's help, but he sensed that he was a burden. Perhaps he was right, for Israel Joshua was contending with his own melancholy, even without the additional onus of a perpetually depleted brother. On May 1, 1935, Bashevis and Israel Joshua appeared in the rotogravure section of the *Forverts*, with the caption "Two Brothers and Both Writers."[10] Both men stare blankly into the camera, Bashevis's spectacles only enhancing the empty expression in his eyes.

Rising above his own distress, Israel Joshua dutifully arranged work for Bashevis at the *Forverts*. He also introduced him to other writers at the Cafe Royal on the Lower East Side, and exposed him to the animated world of Seagate: "From morning till night the intellectuals sat on the porch and discussed Jewishness, Zionism, Socialism, English and Russian literature, as well as the works of Hebrew and Yiddish writers. Once in a while they were joined by such visitors as B. Charney Vladek, who as a member of the City Council had bridged the gap into the Gentile world, and by his brother, S. Niger, who was considered the outstanding Yiddish literary critic.... As a rule, I seldom swam in the ocean, but on the rare occasions when I did go into the water, I always encountered some Yiddish writer discussing literature or reciting poetry by rote."[11]

Still, nothing seemed to reverse Bashevis's demolished sense of himself as a virile man and a potent artist. Later recollecting his feelings, his clarity is absolute: "In the presence of my brother, I had remained a shy little boy."[12] When his brother introduced him at the Cafe Royal, he failed to act the role of sophisticated and worldly-wise young writer that he had rehearsed in Poland. Instead, he reverted to the timorous and flustered behavior of years earlier, when Israel Joshua had first brought him to the Writers' Club in Warsaw.

In reaction, Bashevis turned against the very person who had done so much for him. Outwardly tongue-tied and shame-faced, Bashevis exploded inwardly with helpless fury: "My brother fully realized what I was enduring and he tried to help me, but this only exacerbated my embarrassment....A rage filled me against America, against my brother for bringing me here, and against myself and my accursed nature. The enemy reposing within me had scored a smashing victory. In my anxiety, I resolved to book a return trip to Poland as quickly as possible and to jump overboard en route there."[13]

Bashevis's malaise turned into a serious writer's block and he felt compelled to avoid his brother. The situation was delicate: through Israel Joshua's influence, he had been hired to write a novel in installments for the *Forverts*. The paper's imperious editor, Abe Cahan, had made the unusual allowance of waiving the requirement that the novel be completed before publication began. This was a huge gift for Bashevis, and it might have worked out well. Given his mood and his inhibition, however, the result was a disaster. He could not produce.

In his despair, Bashevis lost his temper at the offices of the *Forverts*: "Don't try to teach me Yiddish!" he shouted, rejecting some editorial advice, "I know how to write Yiddish!"[14] In addition to all the other emotions rumbling within him, Bashevis felt shame at what Israel Joshua would think of him if he knew: "I was afraid that my brother would ask me how I was progressing with my novel. I neither wanted to deceive him nor could I tell him the truth. He would demand to see what I had written and I knew that he would be shocked. I had but one urge—to hide myself from everyone."[15]

To make matters worse, Israel Joshua was sometimes intimidating and rough during this period. Finally cornering his younger brother, he confirmed precisely what Bashevis feared most: that the deal with the *Forverts* had been a special favor to him, Israel Joshua, and that Bashevis *would* disappoint everyone if he failed to deliver.[16] His brother's subsequent offer to look at the manuscript and perhaps advise Bashevis caused searing humiliation in the already cowering and mortified young immigrant.

Desperate to shore up his sagging spirits, Bashevis searched for female comfort. At Seagate, he turned to an older woman, a widow who ran a boarding house for Yiddish writers, perhaps the widow of a sculptor named Morris Dykaar. Bashevis later described her as "...a beautiful woman, herself a painter who wrote poetry."[17] At the same time, however, his letters to Meylekh Ravitch reveal that, despite his strenuous efforts to lose himself in romantic and sexual pursuits, his soul was anguished by what he perceived to be the demise of Yiddish literature in America. Despite his block, Bashevis remained passionately involved with work.

About three months after his arrival, Bashevis wrote to Ravitch about his new life.[18] The letter starts out jovially enough. Bashevis shows off some of his newly acquired English: he now knows how to say "all right" and "well"; he reports his attendance at the prestigious Cafe Royal. He is working on "a new thing, and it's possible that it will be printed in the *Forverts*. I am also learning a little English. In short, I am doing everything that a human being has to do." Bashevis's tone quickly turns more obviously dark, however: "In spite of everything, it's sad, and it's sad because here in New York I see even more clearly than in Poland that there is no Yiddish literature, that there is no one to work for. There is a crazy Jewish people here which keeps slightly kosher and peddles... and awaits Marxism for the people of the world. But it doesn't need Yiddish literature. We built on a paper bridge." Abruptly changing to a more cheerful tone, Bashevis continues: "I am happy that you are coming to New York. I feel close to you. We will be able, as before, to chat and make plans. If you want, we can try to do something here. We could still do something for Yiddish literature before it perishes.... I am thinking of a journal or a publishing house, or both together." The letter to Ravitch reveals Bashevis's desperation, no matter how hard he attempted to convey a light and humorous tone. Moreover, as an antidote to his hopelessness, he entertained aspirations to rescue all of Yiddish literature in America—if only temporarily.

Within the next year, Bashevis finished *Der zindiker meshiekh* (*The Sinful Messiah*), a novel about Jacob Frank, the eighteenth-century false messiah who claimed to be *Shapse tsvi* reincarnated. He also managed to move out of Israel Joshua's apartment and into his own place. Despite external appearances, however, the new improvements were mainly cosmetic. Bashevis remained at the *Forverts*, but his novel was a huge flop and his productivity continued to shrink alarmingly. Although he now lived on his own, the fourth-floor apartment on East Nineteenth Street off Fourth Avenue was a meager and roach-infested hovel.[19] The distance from his brother allowed him more privacy in which to hide from others and surrender to his depression.

He was too ashamed and disgraced to consider himself a staff member in good standing at the *Forverts*: "Following my fiasco with the novel, I avoided showing my face to the *Forward*

[*Forverts*] writers and I always dropped off my copy late in the evenings when all the staff members were gone. . . . The night elevator man at the *Forward* already knew me. He always made the same joke—that I dropped off my column like an unmarried mother disposed of a bastard."[20]

In mortifying continuation of his position as little brother, Bashevis did not even have his own mailbox at the paper: "There was a box for received mail . . . with separate compartments for the various staff members. My brother had his own box where letters to me were deposited as well."[21]

Almost a year after his arrival on American soil,[22] Bashevis wrote to Ravitch, once again putting on a display of bravado, mixed with his easy wit: "Here in New York, I am just barely all right. I have finished the novel in the *Forverts*. Now I am writing articles about literature. That represents great trust on the part of Cahan, but it doesn't constitute a living. At the *Forverts*, they have mastered the craft of paying badly." Gliding away from a more detailed description of his painful current position, Bashevis turns to a happier discussion of his distinguished past and his hopeful future: "My book *Der sotn in goray* has received positive reviews in almost all the Yiddish newspapers: in the *Forverts*, in the *Tog*, in *Haynt*, *Moment*, *Express*, etc. . . . Leyvik and Opatoshu are putting out a literary collection. It goes without saying that yours truly will have a story there."

Bashevis was pleased that he would be included in a new compendium of fiction, that his career was not entirely dried up, but he could not disguise his continuing unhappiness and his nostalgia: "Why travel all the time? Why not come to New York instead and put out a journal with me? . . . I think New York would be the best place for you. . . . I long for the time when you sat in the Writers' Club and we both visualized a bit of travel. Because what is a journey compared with the longing for a journey? Absolutely nothing. Do you remember that we wanted to write a comedy?"

Four months later,[23] after more than a year in the United States, Bashevis was still wistfully begging Ravitch to come to New York: "I hope, Ravitch, that we will meet in New York and chat in the old way. I will talk to them at the *Forverts* in the next days, although I don't have a great influence there. Not a small one either." Bashevis hoped that Ravitch could awaken in him the sense of artistic purpose he had enjoyed at the Writers' Club, especially since the fate of Yiddish seemed more precarious than ever: "Maybe I will start publishing something new. I am writing it at the moment. I have read one of your poems, a very good one. I am happy that you have gone back to literature, although I know perfectly well how unnecessary it is. Since Yiddish literature is the most unnecessary of all...we are absolutely free. We have no readers. We can say the deepest things. Nobody will say that he doesn't understand."

Bashevis tries not to complain: "Did you know that a literary collection has just appeared in New York? I have a story there....I don't live as well here in New York as in Warsaw. But I have learned one thing: that even a writer must work his eight hours a day. I have taken to my work with energy and I hope the results won't be too long in coming. By the way, I already have my own typewriter."

But much as he wants to appear like the mature and self-contained colleague, Bashevis cannot refrain from revealing his miserable relationship with Israel Joshua; obviously, he still longed for the fatherly solicitude he had received from Ravitch in Warsaw: "I see my brother very little. Somehow we are at loggerheads here, although I can't begin to know why."

Clearly, Bashevis was unhappy in his new home. Moreover, since he was still on a tourist visa, he knew he might have to leave the United States. What would he do then? He confided in Ravitch[24] that he would never go back to Poland: "I read English already and I speak. I have just extended my visa again for six months. But the thought that one can't keep extending forever makes me tremble and flutter. To go back to Poland means to go back to hell. As long as I live I will not return there!" Four months later, he had been thinking further about his future: "I take seriously your advice about Australia, although I hope I won't need it....Yes, Ravitch, we are dragging ourselves around, but you are right. Never again back to Poland. Better to jump into the ocean. Even though Jews are sitting in Poland and are quite happy....Write to me more specifically how I can get to Australia if (God forbid) I can't stay here. One has to know such things...."

In order to solve his visa problem, Bashevis contemplated marrying the widow he had met in Seagate, but the very thought aroused qualms in him: "I was most of all ashamed before my brother. Our parents had raised us to have an aversion toward any kind of sham or swindle."[25] In any case, he was afraid that the woman would not want him, even though his sexual prowess had somehow escaped the lethargy of depression; she had no sympathy for his dejection, criticizing him for what she saw as cringing behavior: "I had told her at the very outset of our affair that I didn't believe in the institution of marriage. Nor did she have any desire to give her son a stepfather such as I, a pauper, a Bohemian who was ten years younger than she. I knew that she had lost faith in me and in my future as a writer."...She often scolded me for neglecting to visit my brother, who had rented a large apartment on Riverside Drive, and for staying away from the Cafe Royal and the writers' gatherings and banquets. A young man my age had no right becoming a hermit. Such conduct could lead to madness."[26]

Bashevis was in wretched straits. He was desperate to remain in the United States, but he didn't know exactly why. The *Forverts*, literary home of sorts that it was, clearly did not value him the way it valued his older brother. It was fine to have a story published in someone else's collection, but a story here and there did not amount to a career. His connection to Israel Joshua, at whose behest he had come to New York, was frayed almost to the breaking point. Would his brother even care if he left? And did he want to stay in the orbit of the man who caused him to feel reduced to childish rage, hatred, and vulnerability when juxtaposed with his distant competence?

Worst of all, underlying everything that had to do with his career in Yiddish letters was the haunting notion that it was all for naught. There was no real audience for him in America and what audience remained in Poland seemed doomed.

In the meantime, as he tried to sort out his tangled emotions, Bashevis studied English. His efforts to master the new language were sometimes comical, as he recalled later: "I came here and saw that everybody speaks English. I mean, there was a Hadassah meeting, and so I went and expected to hear Yiddish. But I came in and there was sitting about two hundred women, and I heard one word, 'delicious, delicious, delicious.' I didn't know what it was, but it wasn't Yiddish. I don't know what they gave them there to eat, but two hundred women were sitting and saying 'delicious.' By the way, this was the first English word I learned."[27]

But speaking English and appearing in English—or even writing about his new environment—were completely different matters. After he won the Nobel prize, Bashevis could look back and announce: "I was prepared actually never to be translated, never to be known, to remain a Yiddish writer."[28] In 1936, mired in depression and writer's block, as he contemplated the possible demise of Yiddish and broke his teeth over the language of his desired homeland, Bashevis thought, as always, of Israel Joshua. "My brother has been and is—a success. His *Brider ashkenazi* (*Brothers Ashkenazi*) is now appearing in English through Knopf publishers," he wrote to Ravitch.[29] In addition to being published in translation—something Bashevis could not even dream of—Israel Joshua had already considered the problems and potentials of writing about his new home: "There are hundreds of objects here for which there are no words in Yiddish. They may not even have names in English," he told Bashevis.

The complications were substantive, reaching beyond vocabulary to encompass all that the Singer brothers had lost by their abandonment of their Polish Jewish context: "I get an occasional urge to write about America," Israel Joshua continued, "but how can you describe character when everything around is rootless? Among the immigrants the father speaks one language and the son another. Often the father has already half-forgotten his. There are a few Yiddish writers here who write about America, but they lack flavor."[30] Any influence or unacknowledgeable competition that Israel Joshua's early and unusual success with English may have aroused in Bashevis, the future Nobel laureate kept to himself.

In the face of his confusion, discomfort, shame, rage, and uncertainty about his possible future direction, Bashevis consoled himself with fantasies of monumental, sometimes God-like, achievements: "I had a harem of beauties. I possessed a magnetism that no woman could resist. I found the means of freeing mankind from the Hitlers, the Stalins, from all sorts of exploiters and criminals, and gave the Land of Israel back to the Jews. I cured all the sick, extended the life of man and of beast for hundreds of years, and brought the dead back to life."[31]

Through these ruminations, Bashevis attempted to believe in

himself, to tell himself that he was not worthless. Nonetheless, he was haunted by the suspicion that his lost parents, his girlfriend, Israel Joshua, even Abe Cahan, saw him as undeserving of respect. In addition, underneath Bashevis's preoccupation with saving the Jews of the world lay his impotence to help his mother and his brother Moyshe, as well as all his compatriots and colleagues who remained in Poland. The unspoken question—which he would attempt to confront in his later writings—chafed at him: did he merit life while others were in danger of dying and, if so, why?

The moment arrived when Bashevis had to stop daydreaming. He had managed to extend his tourist visa twice, but now he learned that he would have to leave within three months. Immediate action was imperative if he wanted to remain in the United States. Like one of the hapless characters in the stories he would later write, however, he kept discovering that he needed additional documents. The immigrant lawyer he had hired was incompetent. Then the managing editor at the *Forverts*, who had learned of Bashevis's plight from—of course—Israel Joshua, recommended a lawyer who specialized in visa problems. The lawyer, an American Jew, was self-assured and efficient. He also demanded more money than Bashevis had at his disposal, "but I knew that my brother would help me out."[32]

The process was simple but terrifying: he would take a bus to Detroit and then, with the help of a guide, smuggle himself into Canada by crossing a bridge at Windsor. From there he would proceed by bus to Toronto, where the American consul would grant him a permanent visa for the United States.

As Bashevis later related the story, his visa adventure was complicated by the appearance of a young woman he had met during the miserable voyage from Europe to the United States. Suddenly showing up in New York, she had impulsively agreed to accompany him to Toronto. From there, they would proceed to Montreal. Bashevis juxtaposes the adventure of smuggling himself over the border with a sexual escapade of deflowerment. The former enterprise was a success, the latter a failure.[33]

Bashevis knew that, however much he may have liked his companion, he had become a "sudden daredevil" and engineered the complex excursion predominantly out of "a hunger for suspense."[34] As exciting as the prospect of his trip may have been, it

was also a gamble that involved temporary isolation and dislocation. And what if he failed to accomplish his mission? Moreover, he
was forced to face the depressing reality that he was still dependent
on the forbearance of Israel Joshua and his connections, that he
lacked the capacity to keep himself afloat on his own. By creating
an aura of erotic uncertainty and potential exhilaration, he could
elude—at least for a while—the gnawing understanding that his
career was on hold, that his Seagate girlfriend was disappointed in
him, that his brother viewed him as irresponsible.

Bashevis got his visa. In the end, though, his manufactured elation and apprehension could not prevent him from feeling empty
and discouraged. He realized, not really to his surprise, that permanent residency in the United States did not provide contentment. "I asked my inner I, my ego, superego, id, or whatever it
should be called if I was finally happy. But they kept diplomatically
silent. It seemed that I had a great talent for suffering, but no positive achievement could ever satisfy me."[35] Returning to his lonely
and ugly room, he called his lover in Seagate—who was cool to
him—and his brother, who was nowhere to be found. Even his
lawyer was unreachable. Left to his own devices, Bashevis lost himself in the heavy sleep of depression.

A year later, Bashevis was still forlorn and depressed. Moreover,
he was now plagued by unpleasant psychosomatic symptoms.
Already at the time of his trip to Canada, he had suffered from
constipation and from the fantasy that his stomach could swell
from drinking the tap water in his room.[36] While he might have
attributed his difficulties to the uncertainty of his immediate
future, his physical condition did not improve. Now it was clear
that the disturbance was emotional.

Bashevis's preoccupation with bodily functions paralleled his sister's hysterical symptoms as well as the manifestations he created
for Rekhele in *Der sotn in goray*. Plagued by hidden terrors, all
three signaled their distress through symbolic expressions of disin-
tegration. The combination of anxiety and depression debilitated
Bashevis: "My state of mind had robbed me of the appetite to write
to such an extent that I had to make an effort each week to complete my brief column.... My hand cramped. My eyes took part in
the sabotage, too. I had heard of hay fever while still in Poland, but
I had never suffered from it there. All of a sudden, I started sneez-

ing in August of that year. My nose became stuffed up, my throat grew scratchy, my ears filled with water and developed a ringing and a whistling. I took a daily bath and kept myself clean, but I suffered from an itch and had constantly to scratch. No pills helped my constipation. I spent whole days in bed...."[37] Bashevis later confirmed his overwhelming malaise at the time, revealing to his friend, Israeli journalist Ophra Alyagon, that he had sometimes been too depressed to get out of bed all day.

In a vain attempt at overcoming his emotional stupor, Bashevis continued to regale himself with elaborate fantasies of amazing feats. The plans and ideas that he harbored at that time were clearly unfulfillable by any mere mortal: "Neither god nor nature could hide forever. Sooner or later must come the revelation. Maybe it was I who was destined to receive it....Somewhere there was a truth that explained Chmielnicki's outrages, Hitler's madness, Stalin's megalomania, the exaltation of a Baal Shem, every vibration of light, every tremor of the nerves. There were nights when I awoke with the feeling that I saw the formula in my dream, or at least some part of it and I stayed awake for hours trying to recollect what I saw."[38]

Later, as he became famous and recognized, Bashevis was noted for his modesty and the freedom with which he articulated his fears. His openness aroused suspicion in the minds of some detractors that he was more self-assured than he implied. But it was only then, when he was more settled, that he could risk divulging his insecurity without the fear that his shame and weakness would overwhelm him.

Bashevis's longings for greatness expressed themselves in terms that were intimately tied to the Jewish fate, past and present. However secular his behavior had become, he had brought with him to America the religious sensibility of his home, as evidenced even by his language, which he suffused with the flavor of liturgy and scholarship. However reluctant his attachment, Bashevis nonetheless accepted the centrality of the Jewish people and the Jewish God. Moreover, even as he was absorbed in his personal drama of incapacity and wretchedness, he could not forget that he was safe, while others, including his mother and younger brother, were not. He understood that human, and especially Jewish, existence was fragile and precarious; he recognized that the only real connection he possessed in the United States was his brother—his father was dead, his sister Hinde Esther was in England, and his mother and younger brother Moyshe remained in Poland. Despite all this, Bashevis continued to be estranged from Israel Joshua and the literary world he represented. "I had surrendered myself to melancholy and it had taken me prisoner.... I knew full well that I should have called my brother but I had lost his phone number—an excuse for me to avoid seeing him and having to justify my lazy existence. It was quite possible that the editorial office wanted to tell me to stop sending in the weekly article, or maybe they had more work for me, but I hid from them in any case."[39]

Bashevis concludes his "spiritual autobiography" of this period with the description of a summer in the Catskills, where he worked on an ambitious but ultimately failed theater project. The year was 1937. But something far more important happened to Bashevis in the Catskills that summer, about which he is curiously silent in his memoirs: he met his future wife, Alma.

5

BASHEVIS could not have found a woman with whom he had less in common than Alma Haimann Wassermann, the German-born fellow-refugee to whom he was married for over fifty years. To begin with, she had nothing to do with his Eastern European heritage: she did not know a word of Yiddish, she came from a completely assimilated home in Munich—in short, she was ignorant of the very issues and conflicts that confounded and animated Bashevis. Moreover, she had grown up in a wealthy mercantile family and was blind to the poverty that had forever encumbered his existence. While she had received a good upper-middle-class education, which allowed her to develop and maintain a taste for literature, she was far from inhabiting the literary realm that Bashevis lived for. By all accounts, she did not provide a model home for him either: she was an uninspired cook and an uninterested housekeeper. Yet, the couple remained together from the time of their marriage in 1940 until Bashevis's death in 1991.

Alma's family was cosmopolitan: "My father was a business man, with two connections: a big retail outlet in Munich and a wholesale and factory outlet in Milan, Italy. He was in the silk and velvet business. My mother was an heiress and only daughter of an important men's clothing manufacturer, in Munich and in Nurenberg. When I was little I was completely in the care of my nanny, an Austrian girl. Luckily she was a wonderful person, gay by nature and very devoted to the family.

"My father was an educated man who spoke seven languages, and my mother was a pretty woman with lots of dark hair, big blue eyes. (My parents were an ill matched pair.) My mother really wanted the high life, which my father could not give her. My father wanted a more intellectual type of companion, which my mother could not be. But still they were a devoted couple.

"I was lucky to have two sets of loving grandparents....My maternal grandmother Bach was all kindness and gave my sister and me all the love and attention and also the little things we did not get at home, like expensive exercise pants for gymnastics, special candy that my parents did not approve of, etc. She took me to concerts and plays, etc. My paternal grandmother, who was French born, was a much more difficult person. She was the gourmet cook, spoke with a heavy French accent that got more pronounced as the years went by. She made the most beautiful needlepoint, was a real student of geography and history. But she was also irascible and moody. The two factions, I mean the two families, were mostly at odds about the way to live, about the way to raise children, and at times it came to a real blow up."[1]

While Alma's days were not precisely frivolous, she was being trained to assume a particular station in society, just as Yitskhok, far away on Krochmalna Street, was learning how to follow in the footsteps of his parents. She was supposed to become an upper-middle-class Western European Jewish woman, prosperous and well-educated in secular culture. He was to be an orthodox Jew, perhaps a rabbi, saturated with traditional *yidishkeyt* and probably poor. While Yitskhok labored to integrate the conflicting influences of his parents, his siblings, his studies, and his neighborhood, Alma was experiencing something quite different: "I began to dance at all the house parties until early in the morning and then we all walked home together and had lots of fun. It was a lovely carefree youth and we had none of the complications that go today with courtship and flirtation because we all knew our place and limitations, boys as well as girls." Whereas Yitskhok's relatives in Bilgoray were even more old-fashioned than his parents in Warsaw, Alma had sophisticated family in Geneva, whom she visited while spending her post-gymnasium months in Switzerland: "They lived at the Quai du Mont Blanc right at the lake in a large and comfortable apartment. They took me by car up the mountains for lunch and also to some *thés dansants* at the big hotels in Geneva which I loved of course, being nineteen and crazy about dancing."

Later, in the 1920s, while Yitskhok moved from furnished room to furnished room in Warsaw, struggling to make ends meet, Alma established herself back in Munich: "It did not take very long before I was resettled and took a job in the Disconto Bank, with whom my father was connected in business and I got a spot in the confidential information bureau where all the business information data were stored. It was not a difficult job. I had access to all the files and could read up on all the inside information of all the clients of our bank. After hours I was sometimes picked up by my friends or sometimes my grandmother who took me out. I think I was the only or first girl in the family who had a job. Soon after, on a blind date with some young people I met on a Sunday hike my first husband. He was tall and good-looking and a doctor of chemistry, a pupil of Dr. Willstatter Chlorophyll [sic]. We were attracted to one another and it did not take more than a few weeks before he proposed to me." Perhaps the 1927 marriage between Alma and Dr. Walter Wassermann was ill-advised from the first: "It was a whirlwind courtship and I really was married almost before I knew what happened. We went to Belgium to Maria Kirke, a very cold place near Ostende on our honeymoon." Still, the match appealed to Alma's parents, especially since Wassermann was a distant relative and wealthy as well. That his money was earned through business rather than through chemistry was irrelevant to them.

Bashevis and Alma continued to live vastly different lives even after each of them reached New York, although both quit Europe at around the same time—Bashevis in 1935 and Alma in 1936. Bashevis landed in the United States without friends, money, or knowledge of the English language. He had left a hopeless and dangerous place only to encounter new insecurity and humiliation. Alma appears to have had none of these problems, although she, like Bashevis, never saw her parents again: 'My parents sent us out ahead; they wanted to wait a little longer.... They waited too long and never got out.'"[2] It was also difficult for her to assume the role of homemaker, since she had never had to keep house or cook before. In addition, she now had two children, Inge and Klaus.

Still, the young family managed to establish a trust in Switzerland a year prior to their departure from Germany, which occurred after taking the "time and courage to come to a definite decision."

The move entailed leaving behind a lucrative business and all other material goods and heading for Switzerland, without knowing what the future would bring. But the young family was fortunate and managed to procure visas to America with astonishing speed. "...and in August of 1936, after a nerve-wracking stay in Paris, we embarked from Boulogne sur Mer for the United States. Some relatives were alerted and promised to take us from the boat. We took the Rotterdam and had a beautiful crossing with all the convenience of a Dutch boat, first class, and we arrived after six days in Hoboken....We applied that same week for first papers because we knew that this was going to be our permanent home. At first it was not easy to adjust. My husband was unacquainted with the way business and finance was handled here." The family set up housekeeping in Washington Heights, then a haven for German-Jewish refugees. Their new home was—psychologically if not geographically—unimaginably far from Coney Island or the *Forverts*.

As it turned out, Alma and Bashevis did not have to accomplish a logistic feat to meet one another: it happened at a Catskill resort in 1937. Alma later recalled: "After our first fall and winter we decided to take a summer vacation and a family in our building suggested a farm in Mountaindale, in New York State. It was as primitive a place as can only be. But nature was beautiful, there was a little brook running through the property, some very old trees were on the lawn, a porch very ramshackle ran around the house, and the food that went with the rent was very simple. The farmer's wife was not a good cook, so an old man took over and it was mostly a thrown together hodge-podge. But nobody complained. There were a few families with children there, many visitors as well and nearby was an artists' colony of Jewish writers and poets.

"Into this milieu stepped one evening a man who was also recommended to this farm. He was young, slim, blond, almost bald, had very blue eyes and seemed completely lost or disoriented as far as finding the dining room, his room or even the road outside, into the village or away from the village was concerned. We learned that he was a budding writer, that he had so far written one book and that it was a good book. This man was Isaac Bashevis Singer...."

Alma, her children and Bashevis were all at the farm—or *kokha-leyn*, "cook alone" as it was known in Yiddish, because it contained a kitchenette downstairs[3]—for the entire summer. A friendship developed between them. There were talks and walks: "Mr. Singer carried the small children through the muddy spots when we went for walks and only occasionally he disappeared for a few days to New York and we missed him." Dr. Wassermann seems not to have been much in evidence.

Elizabeth Shub, who met Bashevis shortly after his arrival in the United States, clearly remembers the summer of 1937. She and her family used to stay at the nearby artists' colony, which was called *Grine felder* (Green Fields) after a novel by the Yiddish writer Peretz Hirshbeyn. The colony was a gathering place for many Yiddish writers, including Ms. Shub's father, the noted Yiddish literary critic S. Niger, and Hirshbeyn himself. That summer, Israel Joshua had rented a room in a boarding house about a mile away, and Ms. Shub would ride her horse to visit. As usual, Bashevis benefitted from his brother's generosity; this time, he stayed in the room and met Alma.[4]

But Bashevis remained curiously silent in his writings about his meeting with Alma. Instead, he later talked about a girlfriend in New York and a girlfriend at *Grine felder*. The *kokhaleyn* was like another world: "'How cheap it was, this farm, I'll tell you. I paid $12 a week for a large room with food. And when I went to New York to meet my girl friend...they didn't charge me anything although I left my valise and everything....'"[5] The colony was both familiar and exotic: "'Every bungalow had a name of a celebrity. Emma Goldman Bungalow. Karl Marx Bungalow. There were many Yiddishists. And there I had also a girl friend, she taught me English.'" Where he does refer to Alma, in his *Fun der alter un nayer heym* (*From the Old and New Home*),[6] he calls her "Louisa": "We always had something to talk about, to share opinions, and Louisa would complain to me: —Too bad that you write in Hebrew; who understands Hebrew? I have the feeling that you are a gifted writer. I reminded her for the umpteenth time that I wrote Yiddish, not Hebrew. But soon she forgot again."[7]

Back in New York, the relationship continued: "He told me that he worked sometimes in the Public Library on 42 Street, in the room of uneven numbers, and so one day I went there to look for him without any previous appointment, and believe it or not, there he was sitting. We both got a kick out of it and we both said this is a clear case of telepathy." Alma is vague concerning the progress of her relationship with Bashevis: "Well, when I met him, he began... We started in a summer home where we got acquainted and then we continued to meet in New York City, first in the public library and then we took walks, and from a friendship it developed into a romance and it got to the point where I just felt that I had to spend the rest of my life with him and therefore I had to give up my marriage and my children which was a very difficult and, really, a very terrible decision to make. But sometimes you have to do things and I never regretted it."[8]

Bashevis, writing years later, has a much more negative, even cynical, description of the relationship. According to him, "Louisa" developed a passion for him that he enjoyed but did not feel in return: "Our conversations were strangely choppy and almost incomprehensible. During that time, Louisa never finished a sentence.... She was always feeling a combination of fear and wonderment....What was happening to her was more powerful than she was, and she didn't know how to master the situation. As for me, I was unscrupulous and wild enough then that the whole thing was a game to me."[9] To make matters worse, Bashevis was still involved with his Seagate lover—whom he was not above torturing with the knowledge of his liaison with Alma.

Alma was divorced in 1939, all attempts by her husband for a reconciliation having failed. Yet, Bashevis was in no hurry to marry: "Isaac was really—through misguided early philosophical reading and practical experience—opposed to the legal tying of the marriage knot. Maybe far ahead of his time he felt exactly like the young people of today. However, how could I, a child of such conservative parents, consent to go and just live with a man? This was, of course, out of the question."

Again, Bashevis tells the story differently. He and Alma had separated, at Alma's insistence; but she was unable to stay away from him. The affair continued but was not leading anywhere. One night, Bashevis had a spat with his Seagate lover and stormed out of her house. Seeking to make up the next day, he had planned to phone her, but somehow—without his conscious awareness— he had dialed Alma instead: "She said: 'What is the matter with you? Where have you been hiding?' 'Do you still want to come to me?' my mouth asked, as if of its own accord. 'Yes, I still do.' 'So, come.' 'Forever?' 'Yes, forever.' 'Well, good. I'll come to you this evening'"[10]

Finally, on February 14, 1940, Alma and Bashevis were married in a civil ceremony at Brooklyn City Hall "in the midst of a real snowstorm." The newlyweds—who together developed a notorious taste for stinginess—started their new life with a bargain: "The kindly old judge, who had no customers that day because of the awful storm outside, consented to give us a little speech for free."[11]

The couple set up house on Ocean Avenue in Brooklyn. (The move to Manhattan occurred a year later—first to 103rd Street and Central Park West, then to 72nd Street, and finally to an apartment on 86th Street.) There was no money for a honeymoon, since Bashevis was still destitute. Still, Alma loved the new apartment, finding it "very empty, clean, and beautiful."

She soon discovered, however, if she did not already know, that life would hardly be as cushy with Bashevis as it had been with Dr. Wassermann: "The very first thing I found out after we were settled in our new home was that we had no money at all for furniture and curtains, for linens and all the other appurtenances." The couple's first acquisition was a desk for Bashevis. Alma had favored a kidney-shaped writing table that she had seen at Wanamaker's, but Bashevis refused to accept what to him looked like "a woman's desk." Some time later, they were walking near Union Square and found the perfect desk in a used furniture store. Although Alma had wanted to spend no more than fifteen or twenty dollars for a desk, this piece amounted to fifty dollars. They bought it anyway, Bashevis assuring his wife that "On this desk I will write great things."[12]

The couple managed to afford the new purchase by spending every penny of their negligible ready cash; in addition, Bashevis wrote some radio commercials for a coffee company.[13] The desk remained with Bashevis until his death, and he did write great things on it. Nonetheless, it was an extravagance that he and Alma could scarcely justify. Moreover, it represented the dominance of Bashevis's aspirations and endeavors over those of his wife, an imbalance that lasted for their entire life together. Alma finally got a little table of her own—but it took half a century until she indulged herself in that marble version of the "woman's desk." She was fast learning that life with Bashevis on Ocean Avenue would not correspond to the romantic fantasy she had envisioned during her happy dancing days in Munich and Geneva. Life with this Eastern European Jew, even though he had fled the constraints of orthodoxy, would always lack the creature comforts and material frivolities she had been educated to expect.

Alma received another nasty surprise as soon as she was married. Bashevis became ill, and the couple had to survive on $2.50 for the entire week. Since her husband was sick, Alma undertook to collect his badly needed check at the *Forverts*: "I was rather disappointed by the place. The building was not kept up at all, and the people were constantly running in and out. I had imagined it would be more impressive."[14] The lack of elegance and order were a sharp reminder to Alma that Bashevis was not only a starving writer, but a starving *Yiddish* writer, whose literary environment had little in common with German-Jewish concepts of art and culture.

In addition to her disillusionment with her husband's unrefined milieu, Alma had to endure the smugness of Bashevis's journalist colleagues, who were convinced that the new marriage would not last: "I believe the friends that Isaac had in the *Jewish Daily Forward* all waited for this adventure to be soon over. All his cronies did not credit him with much marital talent. He was known as a Don Juan and a free-wheeling bachelor." The early notion of the marriage as an escapade gone awry may have prompted Sylvia Weber, widow of the *Forverts* editor, to recall the start of the relationship between Alma and Bashevis as a casual fling that might have gone no further. But Walter Wassermann—motivated, perhaps, by suspicion or cunning—had left a message for Alma one weekend, stating that he was not coming to Mountaindale as planned. He had then appeared and, upon encountering Alma with Bashevis, had locked her out of his home and refused to let her see her children. According to Ms. Weber, speaking over fifty years after the fact, Bashevis had been trapped by honor. Bashevis's longtime translator, Mirra Ginsburg, agreed, commenting that the marriage had occurred only because Alma had left a husband and children, and it was "the knightly thing to do."[15]

And Bashevis himself, even with the perspective of time, fed the notion that he was always a reluctant spouse: "The truth is that even marriage didn't help me. I remained, I can say, a married bachelor. . . . I never planned to marry Louisa. Why must love have a contract?"[16]

As it turned out, Alma had the last laugh, at least as far as the endurance of the marriage. She knew how little Bashevis's cronies understood him. They viewed the sexual escapades as a sign of Bohemian insouciance, while Alma recognized that ". . . they underestimated his conservative streak and also his ambition to succeed as a writer. He knew it was now or never as far as settling down to do some serious work. Also his brother . . . was strongly in favor of his getting married, feeling that [Bashevis] needed a home to succeed in his career."

Nonetheless, despite Alma's fond reminiscences, the union was stormy and often problematic. Why did they stay married? Was it the same strange chemistry that had locked Pinkhos Menakhem and Basheve in constant conflict and connection? No external imperative existed. Neither Alma nor Bashevis was averse to divorce and Bashevis professed his opposition, in principle, to the institution of marriage. They had no children between them—not that this would have stopped either of them from ending a union, given their past behavior. Something beyond honor, duty, and responsibility held Bashevis and Alma together. Most of those who knew them, however, remained mystified about what that element could be.

If Bashevis was moved to marry Alma because he believed Israel Joshua and was hoping that domestic stability would galvanize his writing, he soon found that he had made a big mistake. Initially, the relationship was anything but a palliative for the writer's block that continued to plague him. During 1937, the year the couple met, Bashevis published two short stories and two literary sketches; in 1938, he did not produce a single word in print. On the surface, matters improved in 1939, but that was because he was no longer writing fiction. Instead, he periodically reviewed the work of other writers for a Yiddish monthly, *Di tsukunft*, and he had a weekly curiosity column in the *Forverts*. Entitled "It's Worthwhile Knowing," the series was based on selections taken from English language newspapers. Bashevis often chose topics of psychological interest, such as "Crimes Committed by Women Due to Unhappy Family Life,"[17] "People Who Enjoy Hurting Others and People Who Get Pleasure From Being Hurt,"[18] and "What is Platonic

Love?".[19] The pieces were engaging, but they betrayed the anemia of his career.

Bashevis expressed his self-contempt and humiliation with a gesture both dramatic and profoundly revealing: he refused to dignify these articles with his beloved pseudonym. Instead of signing them *Bashevis*, he used the pen name Yitskhok Varshavsky—The Man From Warsaw. Other than cameo appearances in *Di tsukunft*, Bashevis was concealed until 1943. In 1942, he disappeared altogether, to be replaced by another invention, D. Segal, who also wrote no fiction. Varshavsky's essence shifted over time to include works of fiction, but the name Bashevis was reserved for the author's proudest works.[20]

Part of Bashevis's difficulty was the very fact of his marriage to Alma, or so it seemed to him. She was the very essence of what he believed he needed to overcome in order to thrive in America: "I lived in dire straits, physically and emotionally, torn asunder within myself....Here I was writing articles against assimilation and I was living with a woman produced by generations of assimilation....She told me all kinds of stories about her family, but I couldn't write about them because I knew neither the country nor the circumstances."[21]

Bashevis emerged out of hiding in 1943, demonstrating that his formidable intelligence and creative spirit had not been dormant during his period of stagnation. In addition to two noteworthy short stories, he published two sparkling articles that year that delineated and interpreted the state of Yiddish letters in Poland and in the United States. Each article is brilliant on its own; taken together, they provide a compact literary and cultural overview of the circumstances that Bashevis had been exploring and bemoaning since his arrival on American soil. The insights he had put forward in his early letters to Ravitch could not, however, fully anticipate the misery with which Bashevis now had to recognize the devastation to all that he called home.

"Concerning Yiddish Literature in Poland" was published in *Di tsukunft*.[22] Bashevis opens with an overview of literary events in Poland from the arrival of the Enlightenment as a mass movement at the beginning of World War I through the experimentations of the postwar period. Once again, as he had done a decade earlier in *Globus*, he makes clear his disdain for writers who tried to make political points through literature and who reviled those who chose to stand outside the radical circle. Soon, however, Bashevis gets to the heart of his discussion—that the politics were besides the point: "The truth was that Polish Yiddish literature could be neither proletarian nor capitalist.... It was simple to be worldly by negating the old manners, but quite a different thing to be worldly in a positive way."[23] The Polish-Yiddish writer did not have experience with secular life as it was lived by non-Jews. He had neither the inside knowledge nor the linguistic capability necessary for depicting a non-Jewish world. And the traditional Jewish world, rooted as it was in ancient religion, customs, and philosophy, was not what the writer wanted to explore. At the same time, the new secular Jews held little inspiration for him either—presuming he could have found the language to describe their activities: "The synthesis of Jew and Gentile, or of Jew and human being, could speak to his sense of logic, but not to that subconscious spring that is the source of creativity."[24]

The Yiddish writer in Poland was therefore left with two alternatives: he could criticize and tear down traditional Jewish life, as the earliest *Haskole* (Enlightenment) writers had done; or he could reach back to age-old Jewish values, elevating them above cultural concerns. In the end, the literature remained problematic: the orthodox Jew found it impious; the radical Jew found its idiom old-fashioned and irrelevant. As Bashevis summarized the situation: "Not only the Yiddish writer but his work, his *oeuvre*, was in a bind. A contradiction ran through this literature's entire existence. It was godly without a god, worldly without a world."[25]

Still, as long as Jewish life existed in Poland, a richly diverse language and a marvelous potential for characterization existed as well: "Form must *surround* literature in order for literature to have form. The spirit must be malleable for the artist to give it shape.... Every shtetl in Poland, every Jewish alleyway, had its own character.... In Warsaw you could distinguish the Jews who lived in certain streets—Grzybowska, Twarda, Sliska, Panska, Gnojna—from those who lived in others—Nalewa [Nalewki], Franciszkanska, Mila, Kupiecka. The potential heroes of Yiddish literature were wandering the city, simply begging to be described."[26] Here were the lives, and the language to describe them, that eluded the Yiddish writer who wanted to forge a secular, modern path. Pulsing with vigor, they were available as long as Polish Jewry could remain intact.

With apparent nonchalance, Bashevis describes some of the characters he knew in the *literatn-farayn*: Trunk, Ravitch, Tseytlin, a strange character named Hershele, who virtually lived at the Club—the people he had known while he was cutting his literary teeth. Significantly, he omitted his brother, a luxury or perhaps a discourtesy he did not allow himself in later years. Gradually, Bashevis's strategy becomes clear: he wants to illustrate the energy and exuberance of that former center of Yiddish literary endeavor. By recreating the liveliness of the Club and setting it within the larger context of Jewish cultural, political, and religious foment, Bashevis reveals his enormous loss, a loss he comprehended already in 1943, despite his incomplete knowledge of the heartbreaking statistics that would ultimately emerge. The reader understands, even before the final, wrenching, sentences of the article: "All we have done here is to illuminate a few aspects of Yiddish literature in Poland and the conditions under which it existed. For the Yiddish writer who comes from there, the very ground from which he derived literary sustenance has been destroyed along with Jewish Poland. His characters are dead. Their language has been silenced. All that he has to draw from are memories."[27]

In the *Tsukunft* article, Bashevis for the first time put forth the predicament that would consume him for the rest of his creative existence: how to remain true to himself, to his spiritual and intellectual sources, to his internal landscape, when his artistic foundation had been destroyed. How would he manage to keep his writing alive when the objects of his aesthetic attention were dead? Although he had no answers, and although he could not realize how profound his plight would be as it unfolded through subsequent years, Bashevis was able to articulate his position—and that of every Yiddish writer—when others were only beginning to reel from the shock.

However dramatic and anguished his essay, Bashevis was sure he had not revealed the full extent of the tragedy as he was experiencing it: "I bought the *Tsukunft* and, in a cafeteria, I read through my article, 'Concerning Yiddish literature in Poland.' How falsely articles portray life! How false is everything the pen writes! It would be better to tell the truth in a conversation, in unmediated speech. Literature is built on lies."[28]

Bashevis, in 1943, was completely trapped in a no-man's-land, caught between a dead past and an impossible future. He was cut off, not only from the spiritual sustenance of his origins, but also from potential nourishment in his new environment. A Yiddish writer in America, he was marginal—rendered tongueless and mute—as he pointed out in his painfully perceptive article, "Problems of Yiddish Prose in America."[29] The problem for the Eastern-European-Jewish writer transplanted onto American soil was that he could not use his native language to describe his new life.

Interbellum Poland had posed literary difficulties because traditional culture and speech had remained more fertile for the imagination than the modern social or political trends that were taking root there. In the United States, the situation was reversed; Yiddish, with its links to ancient religion, with its meanderings throughout European history, was inadequate to the melody and cadence of a brassy new milieu.

In a word, Yiddish in America was obsolete. The reason was twofold, having to do both with the language and with American culture. Bashevis explains that, in the course of its resettlement, Yiddish had lost essential elements of its being: "First, scores of provincialisms which were more or less tolerated in their place of origin have disappeared, victims of emigration. Secondly, emigration has also harmed many widespread Yiddish words and expressions which, here in America, have lost their native vitality."[30]

An impoverished Yiddish, infiltrated by Americanisms, was an impediment to creativity. But the culture itself made the use of Yiddish virtually impossible for the artist wishing to describe his new environment: "Young American Jews are automatically barred from being portrayed in Yiddish fiction. Their speech and thought cannot be conveyed through words that expressed the speech and thought of other people in another time....A belletrist cannot work in a language that is inherently untranslatable. It is equally abhorrent to let the characters babble on in broken, error-ridden speech. One cannot create a literature within quotation marks!"[31]

Although Yiddish literature had been a thriving enterprise in the United States since the turn of the century, Bashevis virtually ignored its achievements in his gloomy assessment. Two major literary groups, *Di yunge* (The Young Ones) and *In zikh* (Inside the Self) had been producing poetry and prose that was beloved and acclaimed on both sides of the Atlantic. From the rakish yet poignant poetry of Moyshe Leyb Halpern and the calmly thought-ful beauty of Mani Leyb's lyrics to the salty and earthy prose of Dovid Ignatov and Dovid Opatoshu, *Di yunge* had worked to bring a flavor of urbanity to Yiddish literature. Their *In zikh* successors, notably Yankev Glatshteyn and Arn Glants-Leyeles, were instrumental in their efforts to expand the range and sophistication of linguistic and thematic possibilities in Yiddish poetry. All were committed to the enterprise of a vibrant literature in their native language on the soil of their adopted land.

Bashevis considered the entire phenomenon with a casual and almost dismissive observation that Yiddish poetry had managed to flourish in America because a poet is beholden to none of the strictures that inhibit the prose writer. That is a fine solution for some-one with a lyrical spirit, Bashevis wryly concedes. But what is the author of fiction to do, sitting in a country where his native language is weakened and is, in any case, completely incapable of rendering contemporary scenes and characters? The only solution, Bashevis concluded, was to use Yiddish to describe the world in which it had developed: "The Diaspora—the Jewish communities and their leaders, rabbis, ritual slaughterers, trustees and scholars; the pious shopkeeper and the artisan, the fervent housewife, the yeshiva boy and the child bride—this is and shall remain the subject of Yiddish literature and the determinant of its content and form."[32]

Even the Yiddish press, ostensibly committed to current events, is unlike its English language counterpart: "The Yiddish press is, naturally, bound to the present, but an enormous number of its articles are concerned with the past, both distant and recent. It is not by coincidence that a Yiddish newspaper's allotted pages are not filled with *news*, as in English language papers, but with descriptions of old Russia, of rabbis, rebbes, intercessors, apostates, false messiahs, bitter decrees.... This shows how profoundly Yiddish journalists and readers are immersed in the old ways, in yesterday."[33]

Although Bashevis asserts that the writer who is drawn to Yiddish is, in the first place, used to adapting to alien environments, he cannot elude the inevitable conclusion that there is no real way to maintain Yiddish: "However, nothing here can alter the fact that this way of life is vanishing, if it has not already vanished without a trace."[34] As in his sad pronouncement on the history of Yiddish literature in Poland, Bashevis ends on an elegiac note: "Our mother tongue has grown old. The mother is already a grandmother and a great grandmother. She wandered with us from Germany to Poland, Russia, Rumania. Now she is in America, but in spirit she still lives in the old country—in her memories. She is beginning to forget her own language, mixing in many corrupted English words, making comical mistakes and confusing one language with the other. However, this is only when she tries to be modern, to keep pace with the times and show her worldliness. When she starts talking about the past (through the mouth of a true talent), pearls drop from her lips. She remembers what happened fifty years ago better and more clearly than what happened this morning."[35]

The pronouncement was unambiguous: Bashevis was the true talent who would turn his attention to the past of his parents and grandparents, away from a present and future that represented the absence of all that they had held dear. He was not a cosmopolitan who could eagerly adopt another culture and its language. He had found himself in a new land and married to a woman who knew nothing of Warsaw, Bilgoray, yeshiva life, dietary laws, or ritual purity. He would never return to Krochmalna Street, but he would keep that scene alive and teeming with activity. His characters would speak the endless dialect varieties of Polish cities, towns, and *shtetlekh*. Their conflicts would be the eternal Jewish conflicts around God, the community, and their private Jewish souls. Ironically, perhaps, his refusal to leave the memory of his Polish heritage allowed Bashevis to avoid all mention of the catastrophe that was occurring even as he constructed his polemics. Whether his silence was due solely to agony, or whether it was abetted by self-absorption, remains an open question.

In the decades that followed, Bashevis changed his tune somewhat, because it was impossible for him to remain forever in the past. He also discovered that he could write about Holocaust survivors and refugees. Although he never abandoned his core cast of Polish Jews, the reasons for his loyalty changed, becoming even more complex and sad than they had been in 1943. In that year, however, he spoke with the certainty of one who knows his situation could not get worse but who is prepared, despite all odds, to maintain his artistic authenticity.

Bashevis's written statements, as dire as they were, did not reach the heart of his lonely despair during the years of the Holocaust. Even years later, he was unable to fully address the absolute misery of that period, and he retreated into his lifelong habit of relying on himself for comfort. This time, however, he could not find his way out of the sadness through fiction: "During the War, I often comforted my friend, Arn Tseytlin, and assured him that his family would return to him, but I knew that my words had no weight. About what had happened to *my* loved ones, I never spoke to anyone, not even those closest to me. How could anyone help me? Why make someone else sad, even for a minute? Why increase the ocean of suffering? I was silent and remained silent."[36]

The pattern of artistic growth and accompanying emotional trauma was, unfortunately, to continue. Bashevis's two remarkably inventive essays, together with the new stories, marked the end of his writer's block. And the following year, the true force of his creative energy was cut loose from its fetters. In 1944, he experienced an artistic dream together with a personal nightmare: he got the upper hand in his struggle with the gigantic influence of his brother, but he did so literally over Israel Joshua's dead body.

Singer with his cousin Esther, the youngest daughter of Basheve's
brother, Yoysef. They are pictured in Zakopane, a resort town south of
Crakow, in the Carpathian Mountains. [From the Archives of
the YIVO Institute for Jewish Research]

Asher the Dairyman, whom Singer later described in his recollections of his Warsaw childhood, *In My Father's Court*. [From the Archives of the YIVO Institute for Jewish Research]

Singer's common-law wife, Ronye, and their son, Israel (the Israeli journalist Israel Zamir). [From the Archives of the YIVO Institute for Jewish Research]

A group of young Yiddish writers in Warsaw, 1930s. From left to right:
Kadye Molodovsky, Yoysef Kirman, Yoysef Opatoshu, Arn Tseytlin,
Meylekh Ravitch; center rear, Singer. [From the Archives of the
YIVO Institute for Jewish Research]

Singer at the Warsaw Yiddish Writers' Club
on Tlomacki Street. [From the Archives of the YIVO
Institute for Jewish Research]

Singer and Bella Dykaar, Coney Island, mid-1930s. Bella, whom
Singer met at Seagate, was the widow of the sculptor Morris Dykaar.
[From the Archives of the YIVO Institute for Jewish Research]

FACING PAGE
Above: Singer and his brother, Israel Joshua. The photo appeared in the
rotogravure section of the *Forverts* on May 1, 1935, with the caption "Two
Brothers and Both Writers." *Below:* Singer in a group at Mountaindale,
N.Y., where he first met Alma Haimann Wassermann, his future wife.
[From the Archives of the YIVO Institute for Jewish Research]

Portrait of Singer with Alma. [From the Archives of
the YIVO Institute for Jewish Research]

Singer, Dvora Menashe, New York Senator
Jacob Javits, Molly Picon, others. [From the Archives
of the YIVO Institute for Jewish Research]

Singer with Saul Bellow. [From the Archives of
the YIVO Institute for Jewish Research]

Singer receiving the Nobel Prize for Literature, Stockholm, 1978. [From the Archives of the YIVO Institute for Jewish Research]

FACING PAGE
Above: A scene from the Chelsea Theater Center production of *Yentl:* Tovah Feldshuh as Yentl and Lynn Ann Leveredge as Hadass. *Below:* Singer, surrounded by books and memorabilia, in his 86th Street study. [From the Archives of the YIVO Institute for Jewish Research]

Singer autographing copies of *Shosha*, Miami.
[© The Miami Herald/Battle Vaughan]

Singer and Alma sharing a meal. [© The Miami Herald/Joe Rimkus, Jr.]

Singer drawing himself at a writers' workshop at the
University of Miami. [© The Miami Herald]

Singer in old age. [© The Miami Herald]

6

ON November 17, 1945,[1] Bashevis laid the foundation for his literary memorial to the Jews of Warsaw and the *shtetlekh* of Poland. *Di familye mushkat* (*The Family Moskat*) erects a world that its author knew was gone forever. Yet, by stubbornly refusing to acknowledge Hitler's destruction, Bashevis immortalized that world, capturing it—with all its conflicts, inconsistencies, weaknesses, and nobility—perpetually on the verge of annihilation, but forever alive.

Bashevis's two previous novels, *Der sotn in goray* (*Satan in Goray*) and *Der zindiker meshiekh* (*The Sinful Messiah*) had been set in distant European history. Now, with *The Family Moskat*, Bashevis jumped into the twentieth century. Moreover, through the figure of Oyzer Heshl Banet, Singer introduced his emblematic protagonist. In one version or another, this lonely, brilliant scholar, with his philosophical musings, his penchant for multiple sexual relationships, his dislike of children, and his endless struggle with faith, accompanied Bashevis throughout his long and distinguished career.

The novel's first pages are packed with description, as if Bashevis had hoped to preserve his ruined home by recording every detail of its existence: "A porter wearing a hat with a brass badge carried an enormous basket of coal strapped to his shoulders with thick rope. A janitor in an oilcloth cap and blue apron was sweeping a square of pavement with a long broom. Youngsters, their little lovelocks flapping under octagonal caps, were pouring out of the doors of the Hebrew schools, their patched pants peeping out from between the skirts of their long coats."[2]

But the new novel was not only the remembrance of a culture and a physical environment. It also commemorated Bashevis's family, especially Israel Joshua, who had died suddenly of a heart attack the previous year. On the night of Israel Joshua's death, at the age of fifty, he had eaten dinner with Bashevis and Alma and had seemed in fine form; by the next morning, February 10, 1944, and without warning, he was gone.

For all his rebellion, Bashevis recognized his brother, author of such renowned works as *Yoshe Kalb*, *Steel and Iron*, and *The Brothers Ashkenazi*, as a "spiritual father" and dedicated *The Family Moskat* to him. Having pushed Israel Joshua away in his attempt to establish his own independence as a writer and as a man, Bashevis now had to face the fact that, through a trick of fate, he had vanquished his older sibling in the battle of life and literature. But the victory was empty and the victor was filled with guilt. He had been ungrateful and childishly willful. Now he had lost his only direct link to the past. His German-Jewish wife could not fill the gap. He still had Hinde Esther in England. But he had years before distanced himself from his epileptic and dramatic sister, trying to explain her to himself by creating the lonely, hysterical Rekhele in *Der sotn in goray*. Nothing could ameliorate the horrendous misfortune that had blighted Bashevis's life. He was spiritually homeless, terribly alone.

The need to erase or deny his dual loss of family and community led Bashevis to develop the literary technique that became a hallmark of his writing. Throughout the rest of his career, he merged autobiographical facts and fiction so seamlessly that it was often impossible to tease the two apart. While maddening to critics and would-be biographers, Bashevis's technique served an important psychological function. His flight into fiction had initially cushioned him from too-painful reality; now, the infusion of reality into his fiction provided relief from his forsaken solitude. The conflicts and abandonments of childhood had overwhelmed him, but there had always been hope for amelioration—and he could tune out while he was waiting.

Now, with everyone dead, he could turn only to fiction for the prospect of improved self-esteem and more stable relationships. Over time, Bashevis managed to "forget" that he had adored his sister and been terrified of her; he submerged his impotent competition with his brother; he recalled his father as a perfect Jew. In certain of his later works, he fictionalized autobiography, ostensibly to protect but possibly also to tease.

The Family Moskat, in contrast, is fiction filled with autobiographical information, almost as if Bashevis had included it without knowledge or volition. The similarity is not limited to the invention of Oyzer Heshl, who closely resembles his creator: a brilliant man from a rabbinic background who leaves the fold but cannot ignore the calling, who is depressed enough to spend whole days lying in bed. In addition, details of Bashevis's childhood and young adulthood—names and identifying features—spring to life once again: Oyzer Heshl's paternal grandmother, like Bashevis's paternal great-grandmother, Hinde, "had worn a ritual fringed garment, like a man, and had made the New Year's pilgrimages to the Chassidic court of the rabbi of Belz."[3] Hadassah, Oyzer Heshl's first love and second wife, lives close to Krochmalna Street during her first marriage;[4] Oyzer Heshl takes a job at the rabbinic seminary Takhkemoni, where Bashevis himself had for a time been a student;[5] Oyzer Heshl is related to the Bilgoray rabbi.[6] Even Tlomackie Street—albeit not the Writers' Club, but rather the Great Synagogue—plays a fateful role in the novel. It is there that Oyzer Heshl first meets Abram Shapiro, who, like the older men in Bashevis's own life, takes him under his voluminous wing and sweeps him into the tumultuous Moskat family.

Bashevis did not completely recreate himself and his situation in *The Family Moskat*, and the differences are telling. Oyzer Heshl has no brothers. His sister is the salt of the earth; simple and homebound, she raises her children as best she can within the constraints of poverty and dislocation. Oyzer Heshl's mother, Finkl, is equally uncomplicated and conventional. Her first husband, Oyzer Heshl's father, had abandoned her, returned to his mother, and finally divorced Finkl. Oyzer Heshl becomes the virtual head of the family, although his maternal grandfather proves to be a powerful and idealizable figure. Oyzer Heshl's father disappears, and is later reported to have died "half-insane."[7]

For all that the novel is a memorial to Warsaw, Oyzer Heshl's true home remains Tereshpol Minor, his birthplace and his grandfather's domain. Clearly modeled on Bilgoray, the village is poor in material resources but rich in spirit. When he has already left home, gone to Warsaw, and from there traveled to study in Switzerland, Oyzer Heshl returns to Tereshpol Minor. He finds himself alone with his thoughts at evening prayers, his grandfather near to him: "There was a heavy odor that seemed to [Oyzer Heshl] to be compounded of candle wax, dust, fast days, and eternity. He stood silent. Here in the dimness everything he had experienced in alien places seemed to be without meaning. Time had flown like an illusion. This was his true home, this was where he belonged. Here was where he would come for refuge when everything else failed."[8]

In its Yiddish original, *The Family Moskat* ends with a group of partisans fighting in the Polish woods; the final apocalyptic paragraph is reminiscent of Prophets. The English version lacks this uplifting concluding chapter. Instead, those who have not already died remain stranded in Warsaw, bleakly aware that they will perish. "Death is the Messiah. That's the real truth," read the last lines in translation. Yet, as hopeless as the situation may be for the Jews of Warsaw, Bashevis allows for a ray of optimism in Palestine and the United States. Oyzer Heshl's son, David, whom he has characteristically neglected, immigrates to Palestine, thereby eluding the fate of those who remain in Poland. Oyzer Heshl, who refuses to leave Warsaw, muses about the other safe place for Jews: "In America people were going to the theater, eating in restaurants, dancing, listening to music."[9] The conclusion of the novel, in both languages, underscores both Bashevis's distance from the physical suffering of World War II and the depth of his identification with the victims. While he was eating in restaurants and walking freely through the streets of New York, and while his estranged son was growing up in the relative safety of Palestine, Bashevis's fellow Polish Jews were facing extermination.

Nonetheless, for all that *The Family Moskat* was a commemoration of a lost place, a lost people, and a lost brother, it was also a reflection of Bashevis's personal exile from all that he had known and cherished. Oyzer Heshl's travels, first to Warsaw from Tereshpol Minor, and then from Warsaw to Switzerland, are a fictionalized representation of Bashevis's own expatriation. From Poland—

which encompassed both Warsaw and Bilgoray for him—to New York, where he put down ambivalent roots, he never forgot that he was a transplant onto alien and barren-feeling soil. In *The Family Moskat*, Oyzer Heshl struggles to define himself between Tereshpol Minor and Warsaw; for Bashevis, the split in loyalty and the locus of longing lay rather between Poland—including his two home bases—and the United States. Some of Oyzer Heshl's reactions are therefore clear translations back from Bashevis's own experiences in America, although the descriptions lack the "autobiographical" resonance that characterizes more direct parallels.

Bashevis's mixed response to New York, as his letters to Ravitch revealed, are reflected in Oyzer Heshl's opinion of Switzerland: "Switzerland is beautiful, but everything is so strange: the people, the scenery, the customs. I am sometimes even a stranger to myself...Warsaw seems so distant, like a bewitched city."[10] Moreover, Oyzer Heshl's bewilderment during his first moments in Warsaw resembles Bashevis's wonderment at the full-throttle pace of New York: "On the wide thoroughfare, paved with rectangular cobblestones, carriages bowled along, the horses seeming to charge straight at the knots of pedestrians. Red-painted tramcars went clanging by....He took a few steps and then stood still, leaning against a street lamp as though to protect himself against the hurrying throngs."[11]

Bashevis's conflict about living in the United States went hand-in-hand with bouts of nostalgia for Warsaw. Oyzer Heshl was Bashevis's mouthpiece for the philosophical conflicts that he could not resolve. The dislocation caused by his geographical moves only intensified the internal fragmentations that constantly threatened him. Always unhappy and seeking a solution to his existential conundrum, Oyzer Heshl epitomized intellectual sophistication and social naivete. Oyzer Heshl's second wife, Hadassah, in contrast, was the essence of social polish and intellectual sincerity. She read cosmopolitan literature, but at the same time, she retained an ingenuous adherence to the truths of her childhood. To the extent that every character in *The Family Moskat* represented something about Bashevis himself, it was Hadassah who personified his inability to face the destruction of old-world values. He chose Hadassah, the embodiment of traditional refinement and delicacy—despite her modern and rebellious behavior—to express his ache for home: "Warsaw, dear city of mine, how sad I am! Already before I have left you, I long for you. I look at your crooked roofs, your factory chimneys, your thickly clouded skies, and I realize how deeply rooted you are in my heart. I know it will be good to live in a strange country, but when my time comes to die I want to lie in the cemetery on the Gensha, near my beloved grandmother."[12]

Hadassah was perfect for Bashevis's articulations of yearning. More importantly, as a member of the Moskat clan, she underscored the extent to which Oyzer Heshl, like Bashevis himself, lacked skills that the wealthy and urbane seem to possess from birth. *The Family Moskat* was written against the backdrop of Bashevis's introduction to Alma's kin, whose Jewish background differed vastly from his own, and whose cultural preferences definitely did not include Eastern European Jewry. (Alma's only sister, Lisa, who also lived in New York, had fled from Germany to Italy before immigrating to the United States.)

The Moskat family was strictly Eastern European, yet the difference between their level of sophistication and that of Oyzer Heshl echoed perceived differences in culture between Eastern and Western Europe, even on American soil. The connection between fiction and reality was close. Certain scenes depicting Oyzer Heshl's insecurity around the Moskats, especially in the presence of Hadassah, resemble descriptions of Bashevis's own clumsy manners. Oyzer Heshl's first meal at the Moskat home, for example, is a study in the awe of a provincial at the easy savoir-faire of city people—especially affluent ones: "The knife and fork trembled in his hand and tapped against the plate. He did not know whether to take a bite out of the slice of bread in front of him or break off a piece. With his fork he took up a piece of sour pickle from a plate, but it seemed to disappear—and fell out of his sleeve a moment later."[13] Eleanor Foa Dienstag, Lisa's daughter, remembers: "I think that from my parents' perspective, he was very unsophisticated socially in all those ways. He was a kind of primitive person from a lower-class culture—crumbs falling down the front of his suit or things of that sort.... He practically tore the chicken bones...."[14]

Later, when Oyzer Heshl has become better acquainted with Hadassah, the true love of his life, and they are actually planning to elope to Switzerland together, he muses: "...it seemed to him that she was entirely too fragile ever to be his wife and that he was too uncouth ever to please her. Back of it all there must be a trick somewhere, an error that at the last moment would arise to negate everything."[15] Again, Eleanor Foa Dienstag comments: "I was raised with the notion that Yiddish and people who spoke Yiddish and those kinds of Jews were lower-class Jews. But nonetheless, my parents respected Isaac's intellectual talents and gifts."[16]

The deprecation of his language must have been particularly galling to Bashevis, who was mourning the loss of an entire Yiddish-speaking empire. He reflected on the problem through Oyzer Heshl, whose mother cannot communicate with her grandchildren. Oyzer Heshl bemoans the linguistic rift in his family with a fervor that clashes with his abstract and philosophic stance in life—not to mention his elaborate dislike of children and his denial of their significance: "David knew some Yiddish; Dacha understood only Polish. It was impossible for the grandmother to have any conversation with the child. She had asked: 'Do you love your papa?'—this in Yiddish—and when the child made no answer, had commented: 'A little *shikse.*'"[17]

The Moskats, despite their high-class tastes and opulent habits, were by no means perfect: Bashevis depicts them as effete and self-indulgent. Moreover, the family member who serves as the mouthpiece for the novel's most probing truths is a Moskat through marriage. Abram Shapiro, with his bulk, his penchant for mistresses, his gluttony, and his loneliness, is hardly a model of decorum or traditional religious piety. Yet, it is Abram who first understands that the problem of anti-Semitism is real and nasty; it is he who first brings Oyzer Heshl to the Moskats, thereby changing the lives of the entire family; he is responsible for many of the novel's saltier comments concerning the world that Bashevis was memorializing. Of all the Moskats, only Abram is capable of saying: "Once I knew the genealogy of all Warsaw. Now I've lost track. There's a proverb: 'Family prestige is in the cemetery.'"[18] Bashevis hints that the outsider, even if he is superficially flawed, nevertheless carries within him a source of wisdom and perspective that elude the more pedigreed.

To the extent that he knew of the disdain with which Alma's family regarded him, Bashevis retaliated through Abram. At the same time, Abram is dissolute and ridiculous, trying to seduce every woman in sight, and in the process deeply wounding not only his wife, but his loyal mistress as well. Abram's grotesque excesses represent an element of Bashevis's self-image that he continued to explore throughout his career. A peculiar detail suggests that Abram's ugly, immoderate hedonism and consequent self-loathing also applied to his creator, at least in fantasy: Bashevis was in the habit of signing his notes with the caricature of a pig.

But Abram's behavior, no matter how low, was matched in depravity by society as a whole. Righteous Jews were increasingly difficult to find. A central scene in *The Family Moskat* highlights Bashevis's use of grotesque imagery to indicate the role of modern ideas and institutions, including the press, in the collapse of social order. Abram has inveigled Oyzer Heshl and Hadassah into attending a masked ball, organized by the Jewish press,[19] where Oyzer Heshl meets Barbara, the woman who will quickly become his mistress. The masquerade, where costumed revelers immodestly and irreverently flout religious prohibitions, epitomizes the loss of profound Jewish values: "The overheated atmosphere was full of shrieks, giggling, and laughter, a confusion of odors and colors. A man in a rabbinical fur hat swayed with a woman whose mask had slipped down to her nose. On the stage, in front of the musicians, towered an enormous figure with a helmet on his head and a breastplate of mail."[20]

The ball heralds Oyzer Heshl's passage into another stage of his existence, with the communist sympathizer and convert from Judaism, Barbara Fischelsohn. Simultaneously, it vividly reveals the novel's central theme: the dissolution of Jewish Warsaw. Hadassah wanders through the cacophony and lawlessness of the ball, unable to rely on her Uncle Abram, who is in a daze, and unable to find Oyzer Heshl, who is beginning his new affair. She is confused: "A bewildering variety of masked figures went by: Russian generals with epaulets, Polish grandees in elegant caftans, Germans in spiked helmets, rabbis in fur hats, yeshivah students in velvet skullcaps; sidelocks dangling below their ears."[21] The scene is a turning point in the novel, signaling the virtual disruption of the marriage between Oyzer Heshl and Hadassah. Moreover, after the ball, Abram suffers the heart attack from which he will never recover and Hadassah's cousin Masha, who has married a non-Jew, makes a suicide attempt. It is the end of an era; Jewish Warsaw has broken down. Not the Nazis, but the Jews themselves, are responsible for their communal demise.

Had Bashevis written *The Family Moskat* before the Holocaust, his prediction of cultural ruin would have been prescient beyond challenge. The scene at the ball, and the subsequent disruption of enduring if troubled relationships and customs, might have seemed a prophetic warning about the end of Eastern European Jewry. Not only in the United States, but in Poland as well, the forces of assimilation and secularism had created profound changes that would forever alter the content and behaviors of Jewish life. However, Bashevis began this novel knowing the fate of Eastern European Jewry. Why focus on the internal loss of values and morality? Why end the novel with the acknowledged destruction of Jewish Warsaw willfully obscured?

Bashevis never showed any interest in war stories or battle scenes; yet his situation of *The Family Moskat* within definable time but outside the present was not due to aesthetic delicacy alone. His previous novels had helped him wrestle with his feelings about his conservative upbringing and the profound subject of his sister's mental state. This novel was the place where he might have forced himself to acknowledge that his world was gone forever. But, by avoiding the Holocaust, and by stressing the destruction of Eastern–European–Jewish values *before* the events of Hitler's devastation, Bashevis could hope to assuage some of his guilt at having survived, while all that was dearest to him had perished.

As a keen, if passive, observer of historical events, Bashevis was not ignorant of the discrepancy between his fate and that of his family and friends. Perhaps he did not mark the discordant coincidence that, during the weeks of the Warsaw Ghetto uprising in 1943, the musical *Oklahoma* celebrated its debut on Broadway, but he was certainly aware that he would most likely be dead if he had remained in Poland. His articles in the *Forverts* for March of that year reveal his understandable preoccupation: "Airplanes and What Has Been Discovered About Them During the War;"[22] "The Germans Have a 'System' for Everything, and the System Will Do Them In;"[23] "When Will the Power of Nazi Germany Burst?;"[24] "How the Invasion of Europe will Occur."[25] Bashevis also continued to mourn the loss of his brother, realizing with renewed intensity that, if not for Israel Joshua, he might never have come to the

United States. The novel provides ample suggestion that Bashevis was attempting to come to terms with his own survival while others, most specifically, beloved members of his own family, had died. Instead of confronting his guilt, however, he tried to run from it, leaving his characters in limbo and even insinuating that they were to blame for their fate.

In the concluding section of the novel, Leah Moskat and her second husband, Koppel, return to Warsaw from the United States for a Passover celebration. The holiday commemoration and gathering of Moskats also includes several relatives from Palestine. The only members of the extended family who do not attend this huge and final reunion are Leah's son, Meyerl, called Mendy in America, and Oyzer Heshl's son, David, who stays behind in Palestine. But the ceremony of salvation and deliverance takes a cruel twist. First, Koppel dies of a heart attack, possibly due to excessive excitement. Then the Germans invade Poland, virtually ensuring that none of the visitors will return to the freedom of their new homes. By the end of the novel, the ruin of Warsaw is imminent, and the destiny of its Jews is all too clear. For the city's inhabitants, the only alternative to the threat of death is escape. Oyzer Heshl makes the deliberate decision not to flee eastward with Barbara. In response to her plea, "I don't see the sense of remaining with the Nazis," he answers laconically: "The whole family's remaining. It's all the same to me. I want to die."[26]

Unlike Oyzer Heshl, whose choices are pitifully limited, Leah and her fellow sojourners have made a fatal but unnecessary choice by returning to Warsaw on the eve of war. Once they enjoyed carefree liberty; now they are stranded, existing at the mercy of their captors. Bashevis completed *The Family Moskat* with an implication, probably unconsciously arrived at, that those who were about to perish had elected to remain in Poland. They had played a part in their own demise. Moreover, Jewish Poland had been defunct before the Nazis ever set foot on Eastern European soil. Therefore, Bashevis could reason, he had abandoned nothing of value when he was clever enough to quit Poland. In his simple act of survival, he was innocent of any wrongdoing. He had merely followed his brother and found himself in the only viable spot, outside of Palestine, where a Jew could still contemplate a future—meager and desiccated though it might be.

Bashevis had declared himself a Zionist in his correspondence with Ravitch; and Oyzer Heshl, in answer to Abram's query about whether he is still a Zionist, allows that "'I don't believe we'll be left in peace unless we are strong.'"[27] Nonetheless, Bashevis did not don the mantle of political engagement, which had been the domain of his brother. Although he might unwillingly have become Israel Joshua's successor at the *Forverts* and in New York, he would not, and probably could not, succeed him as a writer on social issues. The most he could do in *The Family Moskat* was to adopt the form that Israel Joshua had employed with such mastery in *The Brothers Ashkenazi*: the large-scale, expansive historical novel.

The loss of Israel Joshua, which would have been immense at any time, hit Bashevis with particular force because of his social and historical circumstances. He did not fashion any character in *The Family Moskat* who directly resembled his older brother—in contrast, for example, to the figure of Aharon in his later novel, *Der sertifikat* (*The Certificate*; literally, *The Visa*), who is unmistakably an unflattering version of Israel Joshua. Instead, Bashevis created the novel's mighty patriarch, Meshulam Moskat. Meshulam's similarity to Israel Joshua rests in their comparable position: each one, when he dies, takes a world to the grave with him. For Bashevis, the death of his brother and the death of his culture, while not causally related, could never be separated psychologically. Through Meshulam, he attempted to convey all that was powerful and vibrant about traditional Eastern Europe. Ironically and tragically, the one person in Bashevis's immediate intimate environment capable of appreciating such a connection had been Israel Joshua himself. Now there was nobody.

In contrast to Oyzer Heshl, Meshulam is virile and generative. Oyzer Heshl contributes to the next generation, but, like Bashevis, he does so unwillingly and without involvement. In addition, Oyzer Heshl, like Bashevis and unlike Meshulam, is incapable of properly sustaining his family. Meshulam knows his place and controls his environment with an iron will. Oyzer Heshl, perpetually ill at ease with his surroundings, is happiest on the edge of chaos—at least then he feels alive: "A long-forgotten adventurousness seized him. It was good to be in a strange house with a strange woman, without money, in a complicated situation."[28] Bashevis reveals Meshulam's world as outmoded but he nonetheless contrasts it favorably with Oyzer Heshl's depleted modern domain.

The spiritual and emotional space inhabited by Meshulam and by Israel Joshua was forever lost. Bashevis may have envied, criticized, and ignored his brother; he may have begun to thrive artistically partly as a result of Israel Joshua's death. But nothing could compensate for the presence of his father figure and mentor: Bashevis was alone, forlorn, and bereft.

In *The Family Moskat*, Bashevis's primary domestic focus was his brother and the environment that had nurtured him. At the same time, however, he set up a theme that would reappear in many later works. In the novel, three women compete for Oyzer Heshl's love. The dynamic of one man fending off three women eventually became a hallmark of Bashevis's work. In later creations, one of the women is usually a type like Bashevis's sister, Hinde Esther: the hysterical, wild, panicky, and irrational woman who had emerged so vividly from the pages of *Der sotn in goray*. *The Family Moskat* contains no such character. Instead, two of the women, Adele and Barbara, reveal aspects of Bashevis's consort, Ronye, and his wife, Alma—they are assimilated, cool, and manipulative. The soft, other-worldly Hadassah seems drawn from outside personal experience altogether.

With *The Family Moskat*, Bashevis created an historical novel that reflected, not only his need to memorialize the culture of Jewish Poland, but also his desire to continue the literary tradition that Israel Joshua had mastered. Earlier in 1945, however, he had articulated his response to the Holocaust in a form all his own. Between January and April of that year, Bashevis published three short stories that come as close to perfection as anything he ever penned. Bashevis's need to deny the destruction of his world, even as he was forced to admit it, can be seen in these three companion stories which, while written during the same time period as *The Family Moskat*, nonetheless have a deeply different point of view. The novel memorialized Warsaw, with its big-city sophistication and modernity; the picture of provincial life provided by Tereshpol Minor, although important for Oyzer Heshl's story, functioned as background. In contrast, "Short Friday,"[29] "The Little Shoemakers,"[30] and "Gimpel the Fool"[31] all highlight the *shtetl* landscape and atmosphere that had fed Bashevis's imagination during his time in Bilgoray. (Significantly, none of these carefully crafted stories appeared in the *Forverts*. Perhaps Bashevis wanted to protect them from the eagle eyes and imperious decisions of the paper's editor, Abe Cahan; his caution was well-grounded. Cahan had a habit of insisting on capricious changes, as Bashevis later recalled: "He demanded every day of the week changes from me. There's a section in *The Family Moskat* that I wrote in an hour—six pages—to meet a deadline. Every time I look into the book I recognize it." Matters reached such a pitch between the two that Cahan once threatened to force Bashevis to conclude *The Family Moskat* within four weeks, whereupon Bashevis stopped writing altogether. The stand-off was resolved through mediation by others on the paper's staff.)[32]

"The Little Shoemakers" and "Gimpel the Fool" are both set in Frampol—north of Bilgoray—and both feature a character named Gimpel, but here the resemblance ends. "The Little Shoemakers" tells the story of a humble cobbler, whose family has been in the business since some time after the Chmielnicki pogroms. Bashevis leaves it to the educated reader to know that the towns he mentions are in Poland and that the Chmielnicki pogroms, which occurred in 1648, were the worst mass killings of Jews prior to Hitler's Holocaust. "Gimpel the Fool" relates the triumph of a modest baker who manages to maintain his dignity and his truth, despite the townspeople's primitive cruelty and his wife's whorelike and crude maneuvers.

The two works differ fundamentally in that "Gimpel the Fool" cannot be located in a specific historical period; it occurs at some point in the premodern era. "The Little Shoemakers" begins in the post-Chmielnicki era and ends after the Holocaust. Moreover, Gimpel remains in the old world, while Abba Shuster (the name means Father Shoemaker), the patriarch of the cobbler family, winds up in in the United States, joining his seven sons, all of whom had emigrated from Poland a generation earlier.

Abba finds himself alone in Europe, after his offspring—led by the eldest, Gimpel—have left Europe, and his wife has died in a cholera epidemic. He attempts to continue living as he and his forebears have always done, but history intrudes upon his simple existence: "One morning, while Abba was wandering among his thoughts, he heard a tremendous crash. The old man shook in his bones: the blast of the Messiah's trumpet! He dropped the boot he had been working on and ran out in ecstasy. But it was not Elijah the prophet proclaiming the Messiah. Nazi planes were bombing Frampol."[33] Abba escapes from Frampol and makes his way to Romania, where he is sheltered; from there, his sons are able to arrange passage for him out of Europe.

While the narrative approximates a classic American success story, Bashevis has not created a typical immigration saga. Abba's sons live in suburban New Jersey, where "Their seven homes, surrounded by gardens, stood on the shore of a lake. Every day they drove to the shoe factory, owned by Gimpel...." Moreover, the sons, although obviously Americanized since their long-ago voyage to the new land, retain respect for their father and his traditional European customs. They continue to maintain Jewish rituals and proudly observe the old ways. Although the language of the family is English, "The grand-children and great-grandchildren, who did not know a word of Yiddish, actually learned a few phrases. They had heard the legends of Frampol and the little shoemakers and the first Abba of the family line." Most amazingly, a kind of counter-assimilation has taken place in the New Jersey shtetl: "Even the Gentiles in the neighborhood were fairly well acquainted with this history."[34]

The story imitates Biblical style and includes Biblical allusions. When Abba arrives in America, for example, he feels like Jacob arriving in Egypt to find his long-lost son, Joseph: "He saw huge buildings and towers, but mistook them for the pyramids of Egypt.... He felt, he had lived through the same experience in a previous incarnation. His beard began to tremble; a hoarse sob rose from his chest. A forgotten passage from the Bible stuck in his gullet. Blindly he embraced one of his sons and sobbed out, 'Is this you? Alive?' He had meant to say: 'Now let me die, since I have seen thy face, because thou art yet alive.'"[35]

At the conclusion of "The little Shoemakers," Abba and his sons revive their age-old tradition of singing at work. Abba sits at a bench in the little shoemaker's hut that his sons have built for him; he uses the old equipment from Frampol, which he had one day discovered in a closet. Gone is the melancholy which had plagued him since his arrival in America. Looking around at his seven sons, Abba muses: "No, praise God, they had not become idolaters in

Egypt. They had not forgotten their heritage, nor had they lost themselves among the unworthy."[36]

Bashevis clearly intends his story to emphasize that Hitler—like Pharaoh—is powerless to destroy Jewish tradition and resilience. Jews may be enslaved and killed, their homes and communities ransacked, and their spirits temporarily bowed. But, in the end, they will prevail and continue to thrive and reproduce. By referring to the Bible, and by providing abundant references to the countless times in Jewish history when annihilation seemed imminent yet did not occur, he implies—without ever stating so explicitly—that this latest catastrophe will be overcome.

"The Little Shoemakers" ends on a benign and cheerful note, managing to deny the truth that Bashevis shortly afterwards began to admit in *The Family Moskat*. With the destruction of Jewish Poland and a thousand years of culture, there *would* be an eternal change in the fortunes of Bashevis and of all Jews.

In "The Little Shoemakers," Bashevis effectively suggested that Eastern European Jewry could be replanted on American soil. In "Gimpel the Fool," he went further, safeguarding Frampol by snatching it from history altogether. On the surface, the town is not worth salvaging. Populated with unsavory characters who savagely bait and tease the unfortunate Gimpel, it is a small-time Sodom. But Frampol also harbors Gimpel, an unassuming orphan who gently puts up with the pranks his neighbors play. Gimpel, who is not at all a fool, decides that if people want to make fun of him, they must have a reason. He endures their treatment, and his persistence pays off in strange ways. His marriage to Elka causes him torment, since she mistreats him and produces one bastard after another; but the union also provides Gimpel with a previously unknown sense of security. In the years he spends with Elka, he blossoms with wisdom and achieves worldly riches. As the prosperous proprietor of his own bakery, surrounded by children who are as dear to him as biological offspring, Gimpel has the last laugh.

"The Little Shoemakers" makes its optimistic point about Jewish survival with strategic Biblical and historical allusions. "Gimpel the Fool," lacking an historical framework, relies instead on aspects of Jewish folkways and superstition. The citizens of Frampol pay scrupulous allegiance to the externals of religious life, but they totally ignore its moral imperatives. They marry Gimpel to Elka in a cemetery during a dysentery epidemic, hoping that their good deed will encourage the dead to intercede and avert harm to the community. They encourage Gimpel to celebrate the births of Elka's illegitimate children by naming them after his deceased parents, in accordance with custom. They insist that Gimpel throw lavish receptions in honor of the new arrivals. When Gimpel expresses his suspicion that the first child born to him after the wedding cannot be his, the schoolmaster brushes off his concern, telling him that "the very same thing had happened to Adam and Eve. Two they went up to bed, and four they descended."[37] Everything functions in Frampol in obedience of age-old, unchanging rules of Eastern European daily life. Yet, when it comes to violating common decency, the laws of Judaism that cannot be mind- lessly observed, the townspeople lack all compunction. They behave without compassion, shamelessly disregarding Gimpel's feelings and his dignity.

Of all Bashevis's stories, "Gimpel the Fool" has probably received the most attention. The work, which inaugurated Bashevis's career in English, has been scrutinized from every possible vantage point: is Gimpel admirable, perhaps even a saint, or is he the symbol of the downtrodden Eastern European Jew, helpless to defend himself against aggression? Is the story about Gimpel or about Frampol? Does Gimpel grow or remain on the margins of his potential? The original title of the story in Yiddish is *Gimpel tam*. *Tam* means both "fool" and "full, complete." Did Bashevis intend to portray Gimpel as the consummate dupe or as the sage he seems to be at the end of the work? And, above all, what is the meaning of the formulation Gimpel reaches as he puzzles through the mystery of his existence: "... I resolved that I would always believe what I was told. What's the good of *not* believing? Today it's your wife you don't believe; tomorrow it's God himself you won't take stock in."[38]

The story concludes with the message that truth is a subjective matter and faith is superior to mistrust: "No doubt the world is entirely an imaginary world, but it is only one step removed from the true world.... When the time comes [for death] I will go joy- fully. Whatever may be there, it will be real, without complication, without ridicule, without deception. God be praised: there even Gimpel cannot be deceived."

Together with "The Little Shoemakers" and the later *Family Moskat*, "Gimpel the Fool" reveals Bashevis's complex reactions to the devastation that had already changed his life irrevocably. Of the three works, it contains both the strongest statement of denial and the strongest assertion of faith in continuity. "The Little Shoemakers" declares that survivors will sustain the old world so that it will never be lost, and *The Family Moskat* expresses Bashevis's nearly nihilistic vision. But "Gimpel the Fool" insists that external rules are less significant for the continuity of Eastern-European-Jewish existence than the thoughts, memories, and longings developed and lovingly preserved by generations of Diaspora Jews. Faith is in the mind.

Bashevis suggests as well that the way to disseminate these cherished cultural truths is through storytelling. Whereas Abba Shuster happily transmits his values directly to his sons, and whereas Oyzer Heshl prepares to die without imparting the fruits of his obsessive musing, Gimpel tells stories to strangers: "... the longer I lived the more I understood that there were really no lies. Whatever doesn't really happen is dreamed at night. It happens to one if it doesn't happen to another, tomorrow if not today, or a century hence if not next year.... Going from place to place, eating at strange tables, it often happens that I spin yarns—improbable things that could never have happened—about devils, magicians, windmills, and the like."[39]

The Holocaust was something improbable that actually did happen, and, at the end of it, the citizens of hundreds of Frampols had perished. Try as he might, Bashevis remained unable to deal with the enormity of his catastrophe. His plight was not unusual among American Yiddish writers. They were all in a miserable position. Although they had eluded the fate suffered by their less fortunate European counterparts, they all had huge losses to mourn: homes that no longer existed, families that had been annihilated, friends whose faces they would never again see. But unlike Holocaust survivors, whose trauma had been direct, American Yiddish writers were several steps removed from the locus of their grief. They needed to formulate their anguish without seeming to appropriate experience they had not endured—that would have been a travesty against the survivors.

Furthermore, and inconceivably, although they themselves were young, with their futures still ahead of them, they had lost their readers. A decade earlier, they had written for an audience that was substantial, sophisticated, and hungry for the Yiddish word. Now, that readership had been decimated; what remained was a sad and demoralized reminder of flourishing times.

As in the normal process of mourning, Yiddish writers in America could not immediately absorb the scope of their bleak future, and they could not at first fully articulate their agony. Bashevis's need to deny what he simultaneously knew to be true emerges with touching clarity in his story "Short Friday." Set in the tiny and timeless village of Lapschitz, "Short Friday" has the warmth of "The Little Shoemakers" and the mythic resonance of "Gimpel the Fool." The story concerns a simple tailor, Shmul-Leibele, and his devoted wife, Shoshe, who live only to serve God and to treat one another with respect and tenderness. Of the many tasks they lovingly perform, their favorite is the preparation for *shabes* (Sabbath). They cook, bake, clean, and strengthen themselves spiritually. In their zeal to welcome this holiest day of the week, they are happy to spend a sleepless Thursday night so that everything will be ready in time.

On one particular *shabes*, Shmul-Leibele and Shoshe enjoy their meal as usual and retire to bed. It is the longest *shabes* of the year, and they feel especially blessed and rewarded. But, after satisfying their mutual sexual yearning, they feel a peculiar heaviness. Shoshe worries that something is burning in the oven, which cannot be extinguished during the day of rest. Shmul-Leibele discourages his wife from opening the flue, complaining that their little house would get too cold. But Shoshe's intuition is correct: the couple succumbs to asphyxiation.

After they die, Shmul-Leibele and Shoshe "wake up" in their mutual grave. They know they are dead—they are paralyzed and shards cover their eyes—but they can think, feel, and communicate with one another. They are unhappy about their fate, but they treat the situation with customary faith and acceptance: "'Shmul-Leibele, they've buried us already. It's all over.' 'Yes, Shoshe, praised be the true Judge! We are in God's hands.'" They are grateful to be lying side by side, united in death as they had been in life.

The story concludes as Shmul-Leibele and Shoshe are about to attain their otherworldly reward: "Yes, the brief years of turmoil and temptation had come to an end. Shmul-Leibele and Shoshe had reached the true world. Man and wife grew silent. In the stillness they heard the flapping of wings, a quiet singing. An angel of God had come to guide Shmul-Leibele the tailor and his wife, Shoshe, into Paradise."[40]

Shmul-Leibele and Shoshe die *b'neshike*, "with a kiss," the traditional term for holy Jews who die on Sabbath, the holiest day of the week. Bashevis leaves the couple on the verge of heavenly peace. But in the meantime, they are sealed in a never-changing grave where they can share their love and devotion, their piety and goodness, without fearing the cruel perversities of the living. They are truly safe from history, their blessedness protected. Bashevis's message is both poignant and beautiful: to those who perceive only chronological reality, the simple Jews of Eastern Europe are dead forever. For those who understand another realm, however—the realm of loving memory and ageless sanctity—these very Jews live on in death, shedding their radiance upon eternity.

Bashevis creates and maintains a strikingly loving tone in "The Little Shoemakers," "Gimpel the Fool," and "Short Friday." While readers have argued over Gimpel's willingness to be deceived, sometimes labeling him a masochist, he is a remarkably benign character with generous and profound views of humanity. Abba, who steadfastly relies on the Biblical truths that seem carved in his heart, never compromises his values and morality. Shmul-Leibele and Shoshe epitomize Jewish intimacy with godliness. All of them glow with warmth, virtue, and compassion. Bashevis, intent on capturing the essence of Eastern European Jewry, portrayed its finest examples, although he did not ignore malice and stupidity. Shortly thereafter, in *The Family Moskat*, he created characters who fairly jump off the page with vibrancy, who exemplify the consummate bravery of ordinary life, with its careless lusts, desperate strivings, breadth, and narrowness. It was a unique moment of loss, and Bashevis responded spontaneously with all the love and respect he felt for his people. Only rarely in the years after 1945 would he allow himself to express such elegant yet impossible perfection.

7

---•◆•---

AFTER the cataclysmic events of 1944 and 1945, Bashevis's life in the late 1940s calmed down considerably, at least outwardly. Although he had expressed his anguish quietly, his enormous distress over the loss of his brother, his culture, and his literary future had been obvious at the conclusion of World War II. Now, just a few years later, he seemed more settled, able to enjoy the trappings of normalcy. He had returned to full literary activity and had finally achieved the status of staff writer at the *Forverts*. His salary remained paltry, but Alma supplemented the family income through her work as a saleslady, starting with a seventeen-dollar-a-week job at Arnold Constable, a New York department store.[1] While Bashevis stayed at home and wrote, Alma found herself "joggling back and forth on the subway."[2] The couple ate dinners out in simple restaurants; despite their modest circumstances, they traveled extensively, initiating long trips to Europe as soon as the War ended.

But external appearances were deceiving. A major change was underway in Bashevis's life: he had entered the world of English translation. This development was to have huge ramifications for Bashevis, leading finally to the award of the Nobel prize almost thirty years later. Along the way, Bashevis, that sharp-witted, conflicted, sometimes harsh literary genius, would gradually yield to

Isaac Bashevis Singer—and even Isaac Singer—the quaint, pigeon-feeding vegetarian, the serene and gentle embodiment of timeless Eastern-European-Jewish values.

Bashevis's first work to be translated into English was *The Family Moskat*. It appeared in 1950, published by Alfred Knopf. Knopf had been Israel Joshua's publisher in English, and he had agreed to take on Bashevis's book because of the family relationship. Already at the time of this first translation, Bashevis was worrying about what to call himself. A letter from the publishing house refers to the confusion: "Did we agree on the form in which your name as author is to appear? It could be 'Isaac Singer' or 'Bashevis (Isaac Singer,)' but I do not think it can be 'Isaac Singer Bashevis,' which is merely confusing."[3]

The privilege of appearing in translation with Israel Joshua's publishers turned out to be a mixed blessing. First, Knopf insisted on certain changes in the novel for purposes of translation, an artistic insult that Bashevis neither forgot nor forgave.[4] Then, once the book came out, Knopf informed Bashevis that sales were poor. But Alma, who was working at Macy's in Manhattan at the time, believed that Knopf's report was inaccurate, if not a downright lie. From her vantage point, perhaps colored by the immigrant fear that her husband was being cheated, she took issue with the publisher's gloomy account, observing that the books were actually "selling like hotcakes."[5]

In a 1965 interview in *Harper's*, Bashevis claimed that the book had sold 35,000 copies—in part because it had been a book club choice—but that he had realized only about $2,000 from the deal. "I haven't grown rich from my works translated into English," he commented wryly at the time. There were reasons for the meager reward. Knopf had deducted a translator's fee from Bashevis's royalties. Moreover, the translator had died before finishing the manuscript, costing Bashevis "additional time and money to complete the job."[6]

Bashevis's recollections on the matter complain of anti-European bias and hint at Jewish anti-Semitism: "...the mail kept bringing envelopes with reviews from all over America. I found my picture in many newspapers and magazines. But with all that, I had the feeling that my book was not receiving the proper recognition." As it happened, Knopf was also the publisher of John Hersey's *The*

Wall, which appeared just weeks after *The Family Moskat*. Both authors had written about Warsaw, and Knopf evidently favored Hersey's work. The slight was not lost on Bashevis: "True, I had written from experience, while Hersey had compiled a work based on reports. But the Jewish readers in America preferred to hear the story from an American rather than from a Jew. Knopf gave all its backing to Hersey."[7] Where Israel Joshua had once outshone Bashevis in Knopf's eyes, now it was supposedly John Hersey. Not surprisingly, Bashevis left Knopf as soon as he could, affiliating himself with Noonday Press and its editor, Cecil Hemley, who knew a good deal about Yiddish. When Noonday merged with Farrar Straus in 1960, Bashevis found the publisher with whom he would remain for the rest of his life.[8]

But the real break for Bashevis, his introduction to American readers who could appreciate him, was the 1952 appearance, in the prestigious *Partisan Review*, of "Gimpel the Fool," masterfully translated by Saul Bellow. Although not European-born, Bellow was ideally suited to render Bashevis into English for a cosmopolitan audience. He spoke fluent, richly idiomatic Yiddish and, like Bashevis, had grown up in a strictly orthodox home, complete with one grandfather who was a *khosid* and one grandfather who was a *misnaged* (an opponent of Hasidism); he understood the milieu that Bashevis had created. Nonetheless, he was at first reluctant to undertake the assignment. Approached by Eliezer Greenberg who, together with Irving Howe, was compiling an anthology of Yiddish literature in translation, Bellow initially declined. He was teaching at Princeton University and finishing his novel, *The Adventures of Augie March*. He simply didn't have the time, he told Greenberg. But Greenberg, undeterred, suggested that he could come to Bellow and read the Yiddish to him; Bellow could translate right onto the typewriter.

And so it was—which allowed Greenberg to exercise a bit of deception. He omitted the overt anti-Christian references contained in the Yiddish original.

Over forty years later, Saul Bellow recalled Bashevis with ambivalence and some heat, recounting, in Yiddish, the unsatisfying details of their relationship. Long after the success of "Gimpel," when the two met at a social gathering, Bellow asked Bashevis why he had never been invited to translate additional stories. Bashevis replied that if the works were greeted with acclaim, "they'll say it's you, not me." Clearly, Bellow was not one of those men with whom Bashevis felt comfortable. Many years later, on the occasion of his Nobel award, Bashevis would stoop to mock Bellow, a fellow laureate and the very man who, although eleven years younger than Bashevis, had nonetheless managed to "put him on the map" of English-language literary life.[9]

Bellow's rendition of "Gimpel" was followed in the *Partisan Review* by "From the Diary of One Not Born," "translated" by Nancy Gross,[10] who collaborated with Bashevis to produce the story in English, although she herself knew no Yiddish. Bashevis was unfriendly and ultimately vicious to Bellow, but he realized that the early translations into English of his stories, rather than his novel, had given him his American start.[11]

Even so, Bashevis began making it into the bigger magazines, including *Harper's*, only after Noonday merged with Farrar, Straus & Giroux. The unhappy experience with Alfred Knopf, who had helped Israel Joshua achieve a name among American readers, may have played a role in the subtle yet unmistakable shift from Bashevis to Isaac Bashevis Singer. Consciously or not, he had learned that Bashevis, the *enfant terrible*, would never capture the heart of an American audience. Those who had known him from the beginning might scoff, but Bashevis had correctly, if intuitively, perceived that for readers of English, an Eastern European Jew had to be old-fashioned, mild-mannered, even naive in order to be believable. Whether or not he knew what he was doing, Bashevis was never the innocent he claimed to be, according to Saul Bellow: "He was sophisticated. He was an opportunist. He was a careerist."[12]

The works by Bashevis that came out in English between 1950 and 1970—*The Magician of Lublin, The Slave, The Manor, The Estate, Short Friday, The Spinoza of Market Street, A Crown of Feathers*—were set almost entirely in Eastern Europe. His first volume of short stories, *Gimpel the Fool and Other Stories*, contained some of the works that the author had penned while still in Poland. Initially, the reliance on Eastern Europe was compatible with Bashevis's life as a recent immigrant. But, as the years passed, Warsaw and Bilgoray became less and less a part of his total experience. By the time he won the Nobel prize, in 1978, the man who now

called himself Isaac Singer had been in the United States for forty-
three years—well over half his lifetime.

The need to find a balance in his writing between Europe and the
United States, between memory and current events, between commemoration and critique, affected Bashevis as he approached both
his Yiddish and his English audiences. In each language, he was in
constant conflict and flux.

At the same time that the figure of Isaac Singer was in its embry-
onic stages, Bashevis was writing in the *Forverts* under at least three
names: Yitskhok Bashevis, Y. Varshavsky ("The man from Warsaw"), and D. Segal. As always, he reserved Bashevis, as he was
known to his Yiddish readers, for his highest literary efforts. Varshavsky and Segal were the names he used for "lesser" or more
popular items, such as his musings about the current state of Yiddish literature, including its politics and its morals.

Eventually, Bashevis began to write about Eastern European
Jews in America, a process that was to occupy him more and more
as the years progressed. In Yiddish, he published these works as
Varshavsky. In addition, the original Yiddish of *In My Father's
Court*, *Dem tatns bezdin-shtub*, appeared under Varshavsky's
name. Bashevis's dilemma was clear: he wanted both to branch out
in his American milieu and to perpetuate the events and the people
of his European past. But he did not fully respect the works he
wrote as Varshavsky. As far as the readership of the *Forverts* was
concerned, Bashevis wished to disassociate himself aesthetically,
both from the quasi-autobiographical flavor of his immigrant stories and from the memoiristic and elegiac voice that served to
memorialize his family. In English, however, Isaac Bashevis Singer
had no comparable restrictions. Moreover, these new efforts fit the
image he was effecting: they were homespun and personal, filled
with warmth and pathos.

Early in the 1960s, two novels made their way into English
translation.[13] *The Magician of Lublin*[14] concerns Yasha Mazur,
who, after a lifetime of expansive exploits and boundless lust,
retreats to self-imposed confinement, depriving himself of all external temptations. In *The Slave*,[15] Jacob, a deeply religious man who
has remained spiritually free despite physical enslavement, finds
himself passionately involved with a non-Jewish woman.

The two novels differ in their historical and geographical settings. *The Magician of Lublin* takes place in and around the city of Lublin; the era is premodern but nonspecific. *The Slave* begins in rural Poland and concludes in Palestine; like *Satan in Goray*, it occurs after the Chmielnicki massacres of 1648. Nonetheless, the works are similar in a deeper, functional way. Both present a man who finds himself in an alien environment where he knows he does not belong. Yasha willfully capitalizes on his extraordinary skill as a showman, losing his bearings in the process, whereas Jacob has no control over his situation: he is simply captured. But each man discovers what it means to be attracted to the non-Jewish world and each falls in love with a non-Jewish woman.

Yasha, the magician, juggles a nice Jewish wife, whom he takes for granted, a pitiable non-Jewish mistress and performance partner, whom he maligns, and a beautiful non-Jewish widow, whom he idealizes. Ultimately, he eschews all intimacy with women, but not before his mistress has committed suicide and his distant love has abandoned him. In contrast, Jacob, the slave, finds a true soulmate in Wanda, who converts to Judaism and becomes known as Sarah.

Despite the lures of the non-Jewish world, or at least, of non-Jewish women, both Jacob and Yasha are deeply and consummately religious Jews. Jacob's strife is sexual, not spiritual; even in captivity, he is intent on maintaining his faith, and he attempts to carve all of the Torah's 613 *mitsves* (commandments) on a rock in order not to violate these laws. Yasha's conflicts are more abstract, and his ultimate solution is more extreme. Yet he, too, retains his essential Jewishness, although he must isolate himself from all other stimuli to focus on it.

What was Bashevis seeking to communicate in these two novels? Like his characters, he was intrigued by his non-Jewish milieu and discovered that he was accepted there, at least superficially. Simultaneously, though, he was psychologically worlds away from his new environment and felt painfully out of place. The novels in English were greeted with interest and enthusiasm by the press, but the reviews often revealed a lack of comprehension. Critics pronounced variously on the vision of humanity portrayed in *The Magician of Lublin* and *The Slave*. They were especially intrigued by the "folkloristic" evocation of a backward Poland in which Jews were barely tolerated. Writing in *The New York Times*, for instance, Orville Prescott compared *The Slave* to *Pilgrim's Progress* by John Bunyan, and concluded by saying of the novel, "Mr. Singer's accounts of demons, werewolves, vampires, dibbuks and even of smoks are fine. His picture of the state of life in Poland 300 years ago is a revelation. Nevertheless, the necessities of his allegory, its folk-story simplicity, insure that 'The Slave' always seems a little unreal and very far away. The life in 'The Slave' is general to all humanity, not the kind of fictional life that readers can easily share vicariously."[16]

But Bashevis's problem was as much personal as cultural. In his home life, he was contending with the same issues that preoccupied him in his writing. He continued to be immersed in the endless arguments and conflicts of his life in Poland, and his Yiddish readership understood his position. Yet he was married to a woman from a completely assimilated, non-Yiddish-speaking home who could understand neither his language nor his religious grappling. For Bashevis, Judaism meant the orthodoxy he had known at home. He once remarked to a young student at Hebrew Union College, the Reform rabbinic seminary: "My father would consider all of you *goyim*. [non-Jews]"[17] For a man of Bashevis's background, Alma was scarcely Jewish at all.

Bashevis's sensitivity to his position among non-Jews as he revealed it in *The Magician of Lublin* was still evident years after the publication of the novel. In 1983, when asked about Magda's suicide, Bashevis explained that she had been forced to kill herself because she had made an anti-Semitic comment to Yasha, and she knew he would never forgive her. [18]

The English-language press did not manifest any understanding of Bashevis's struggles. The books of short stories he published in the fifties and sixties appealed because of references to the supernatural or mythical. Orville Prescott reported about *Short Friday* in *The New York Times* that "...even as artful a writer as Mr. Singer can't maintain a uniformly high standard in 16 stories. Several are flat and tiresome. One, 'Yentl the Yeshiva Boy,' about a girl with a man's mind or soul, comes perilously close to being silly. So one must conclude that Isaac Bashevis Singer is an uneven writer as well as a greatly gifted one; and that the peculiar quality of his work is probably too special for most tastes."[19]

These American critics had no way of recognizing that a story like "Yentl" was not about a silly girl from a backward community but rather a work that concerned the longing to study in an environment that forbade such pursuits by females. Perhaps "Yentl" was Bashevis's imaginative rendering of his great-grandmother Hinde's frustrated aspirations, the study of a misfit even within a so-called monolithic Jewish culture. Whatever Bashevis's inspiration, the story is yet another exploration of the clash between the individual and an environment that is both familiar and deeply uncomfortable. Bashevis had seen that conflict first-hand, in the gender confusion that had spanned generations in his family and that had especially affected his parents and his sister. But his English readers had no concept of the ways in which Yentl's trials reflected his own observations.

In 1954, Bashevis's final link to the tumultuous world of Krochmalna Street was severed. His sister, Hinde Esther Kreitman, died in London at age sixty-three. For Bashevis, the loss could hardly have been trivial, given Hindele's influence on his early development, and given the fact that she was the last surviving member of his nuclear family. Yet, if he felt grieved by her death, he did not publicize the point. He did dedicate *The Seance* to her, but the tribute was muted and marred by an unfortunate printer's error: "In memory of my beloved sister Minda Esther." Moreover, Bashevis refused to romanticize his sister in his memoirs; for him, she remained forever fascinating but at the same time dangerous.

Bashevis's ambivalence towards Hindele during the last years of her life was obvious from his behavior. On one hand, he had gone to England to visit her and to introduce Alma to her as soon as World War II was over. The trip was no easy jaunt, since it represented an immense financial drain for the penurious couple. In addition, Europe was in ruins and food was short. Bashevis's need to reconnect with his sister, whom he had not seen since the late 1920s, must have been powerful.[20] On the other hand, both before and after the visit, he avoided Hindele and refused to be of help, even when she beseeched him.

In one letter, from 1944, Hindele begs him three times to answer her.[21] In 1948, she is still asking him: "For God's sake, answer me soon!" Her request, in the same letter, that Bashevis arrange for her to come to America seems to have fallen on deaf ears, despite his sister's revelation that Avrom, her husband, had not worked for two years.[22]

Bashevis's neglect of his sister had not been limited to silence and the unwillingness to bring her to the United States. He was capable of complete coldness towards her, on one occasion flatly denying her request for much-needed funds. During that period, Hindele was troubled by noisy neighbors, who, according to her, deliberately banged on her ceiling in the middle of the night. The disturbance was especially grievous because of her frail health. Finally, she managed to procure another apartment, but she needed 200 pounds for "key-money." She wrote to Bashevis, entreating him to help her, but he refused, explaining that she would have to live with her situation.[23]

Perhaps the trip to London had, once and for all, discouraged Bashevis. He adored and respected his sister: "She did not write as well as I. J. Singer, but I do not know of a single woman in Yiddish literature who wrote better than she did." At the same time, she aroused anxiety and tremendous disappointment in him: "When I came to London, she was weirdly glad to see me. She loved me with a great love that often seemed to me exaggerated and frightening.... Even those who could not get along with her praised her good-heartedness and refinement. But who can live with a volcano? After a few days of listening to her complaints and blame, I became weary. She could literally drive a person crazy."[24]

Hindele was, and always would be, the model of female excitement and passion for Bashevis. He would subsequently, again and again, recreate his sister in fiction.[25] However, he knew he could be overwhelmed by such energy, and he needed to avoid her and anyone who too closely resembled her. On that visit, Bashevis discovered that, for marriage, he needed someone more like Alma: "the total opposite" of Hindele.[26]

Bashevis was now completely separated from all direct familial connection to his past. It is impossible to know how his public personality would have developed, had he not found himself in New York, orphaned and without siblings. During the 1950s and 1960s, Bashevis was not yet Isaac Singer, the simple, old-fashioned sprite, but he was on his way. And it was largely his English-language critics who set him on this path. Through a combination of ignorance and misguided indulgence, they communicated to Bashevis that the only way to successfully memorialize his beloved Eastern European Jews was to stick them—and himself—into a timeless *shtetl*, to cut himself from the same cloth he had created in "Short Friday." Orville Prescott concluded his review of *Short Friday* with the comment that "Those unfamiliar with the folklore of Polish Jews may find that the chief interest of some of these stories is anthropological, information about the customs and ideas of a backward and isolated community."[27] It is difficult to imagine what part of this mind-boggling *New York Times* essay would have been more hurtful and insulting to Bashevis: the reduction of his art to local color, or the notion that his lost world had been crude and uncivilized. Prescott's ignorance is matched only by his condescension, with its whiff of anti-Semitism.

A rare exception to the attitude of deprecation, unwitting or otherwise, was Richard Elman, who reviewed *In My Father's Court* in *The New York Times*: "Bashevis Singer excels in the sensuous depiction of the physical world, whereas his Warshowsky [Varshavsky] persona would seem to have a more didactic moral point of view and an almost total recall of long-vanished people and events." Elman was unusual in his comprehension that Bashevis and Varshavsky served separate functions in the author's creative apparatus. In addition, he suggested that readers avoid the tendency to regard Bashevis as an assimilated American Jew: "The appearance of 'In My Father's Court' should... serve as a necessary corrective for those Singer enthusiasts who have been all too eager... to confuse their easy alienations with his felt sense of loss, or to interpret his abiding skepticism (itself a part of his commitment to Jewishness) as the expression of the 'black' spirit in modern man."[28] Elman did not warn against the other, and growing, popular view of Bashevis's work—that it was simple, if not naive.

The Yiddish press, in contrast, acknowledged Bashevis's sophistication, but it viewed his accomplishments with suspicion and dislike. As a social critic, Bashevis in Yiddish was harsh and conservative, completely unlike Isaac Bashevis Singer, the apolitical, wryly unworldly creature he was becoming in English. His remarks in the *Forverts* seemed calculated to offend whatever Socialists still remained as readers: "It may sound like terrible *apikorses* [heresy], but conservative governments in America, England, France, have handled Jews no worse than liberal governments....The Jew's worst enemies were always those elements that the modern Jew convinced himself (really hypnotized himself) were his friends."[29]

In only one area, literature, were Bashevis's pronouncements similar in Yiddish and English. Although his statements in English lacked the bite of those in Yiddish, the philosophy was the same: "...analysis in art is as alien an element as, for example, emotion in mathematics or physics."[30]

Bashevis's detractors in the Yiddish press took whatever opportunities they could to make him look cynical and hypocritical. He was in particular disfavor at the communist *Morgn-frayhayt*, no doubt because everything he stood for deviated sharply from the newspaper's ideology. Whenever they could, the columnists of *In der yidisher prese* (*In the Yiddish Press*), which quoted items from other Yiddish newspapers, gleefully maligned Bashevis. They had plenty of ammunition: his own words. They caught him swaggering, for example, during a radio interview: "...one thing is a fact— that my contact with the non-Jewish world and with very young people is really a perfect one.... Varshavsky-Bashevis has nothing to complain about. In his work, there is no lack of vulgarity, eroticism, various kinds of demons, and he makes fine business from that."[31] Bashevis's remarks would likely have shocked his English readers, but he could be certain that they would never learn of his disdainful boasts. The interview aired on WEVD, named after socialist leader Eugene V. Debs, and known in Yiddish-accented English as "The Station That Speaks Your Lengvege."

In a particularly mean-spirited, and yet completely typical example of the insular passion that characterized Yiddish journalism in post–World War II America, the *Morgn-frayhayt* reprinted an article from the *Forverts* (December 26, 1963). Bashevis, speaking as Varshavsky, had railed against course literature, asserting that: "The whole world of entertainment is so immersed in dirt that the boundary between world and underworld has almost disappeared. The judges read this dirty literature and hear the same vulgar jokes as the thief." The response in the *Morgn-frayhayt* read: "A hearty congratulations, Mr. Yitskhok Varshavsky, for moralizing against Yitskhok Bashevis. Truly, congratulations."[32]

The author of this arch reaction did not care, and probably did not perceive, the painful inner dissension beneath Varshavsky-Bashevis's two-faced insincerity. Bashevis was both judge and thief, both moral critic and trickster. Finding a place in America meant relinquishing part of his essence. The more he became Isaac Bashevis Singer, the less he could continue to be Bashevis.

Bashevis's restless search for a mediated existence between old world and new, between Bashevis and Isaac, found concrete expression in his travels during the 1950s and 1960s. Bashevis once asked his friend Ophra Alyagon when she was visiting him in New York: "What is there to see in the world that you don't have here? Everything a person is capable of seeing is already inside of him."[33] Despite Bashevis's pronouncement, the Singers continued their pattern, established in the 1940s, of taking long foreign trips. Two of their favorite spots were Israel and Switzerland,[34] illustrating Bashevis's uneasy attempt to harmonize his attachment to tradition and his captivation with new circumstances.

Israel was an obvious choice. It was the Jewish homeland, and, in his youth, Bashevis had thought of himself as a Zionist; moreover, his son and grandchildren were there. Switzerland was less likely: an insulated country not known for its friendliness to Jews.

Bashevis had used Switzerland, in *The Family Moskat,* to illustrate Oyzer Heshl's experience of feeling lost and alien in a new environment. The fictional representation fit Bashevis's own first reaction to Switzerland. Even in calm, peaceful, prosperous, French-speaking Lausanne, he felt out of place: "I passed enormous churches, where candles burned and women knelt. I passed the Jewish synagogue, which was shut. Evidently, there was no *minyen* during the week." The scene, empty of Jews, may have aroused in Bashevis a futile longing for kosher food. In any case, he had entered a vegetarian restaurant, although he was still a meat-eater at the time. But the foray provided scant comfort: "A few young men were sitting there who looked like idealists....They ate dairy foods and dreamed of eternal peace....I understood better why the protagonist of *The Family Moskat*, Oyzer Heshl, couldn't stay there for long."[35]

In the context of Alma's experience, the attraction to Switzerland made sense. She had studied there as a young woman and, later, the country had provided refuge for her and her first husband, when they fled Germany in 1936. Switzerland was an ideal location for Jews who refused to go to Germany: one could find order, cleanliness, and even linguistic comfort without having to make the discomfiting and perhaps humiliating decision to enter the former realm of the Nazi regime.

Bashevis refused ever to set foot in Germany. Not so Alma. Once, when he was to receive an award in Dortmund, he delegated Alma to represent him. The proposed trip sparked a fight between the two, because Bashevis wanted her to deliver a speech that he had written; she thought she should deliver a speech of her own, about herself. On that occasion, Alma prevailed.

The consequences of the marital tiff were negligible, but the disagreement pointed to a fundamental and lasting contradiction in Bashevis's life. He could not be, simultaneously, the worldly-wise and sharp-witted gadfly that Yiddish journalists loved to hate, and the frail and childlike anthropological guide that American critics and readers read with damp-eyed nostalgia. He no longer had a home in Eastern Europe, and Western Europe was no substitute. Yet he would never become Americanized: He was a Yiddish writer adrift in a world where few people knew his heritage— although many imagined they did—and where those closest to him could not understand Yiddish.

Bashevis's attempt to integrate the two divergent claims on his life was not a success. Gradually, he effected a deep compromise. Most formidable were the concessions he made concerning his name. Bashevis needed to integrate his developing American life into his fiction. No longer a greenhorn, he would never cease to be a transplanted Polish Jew. The postwar years may have eased the sheer agony of the Holocaust, but Bashevis continued to be reminded of the catastrophe that had forever diminished his existence. As a way of expressing his changing but nonetheless complicated circumstances, he developed a narrative device in which a successful Yiddish writer living in New York was contacted by a series of zany Holocaust survivors. They confided to him their stories about Eastern Europe and the aftermath of World War II. Although many of these stories later appeared in English in the prestigious *New Yorker*, in Yiddish, the author refused to dignify them with the signature *Bashevis*, because he could not bring himself to acknowledge this foray into a new cultural environment.

Beyond his writing, however, Bashevis's effort to consolidate his European and American experiences also influenced nonliterary aspects of his lifestyle—his dwelling, his attire, even his diet. These behaviors served a dual purpose. They brought him closer to the milieu he had left behind in Poland, and they served to reassure him that he would not lose his Eastern-European-Jewish essence, despite a growing comfort in his new environment. All the members of Bashevis's immediate family were now dead. By setting up subtle boundaries between himself and his adoptive home, he could allow Isaac Singer to develop freely, without losing Yitskhok Bashevis. He did not have to fear that the son of Pinkhos Menakhem and Basheve, the brother of Israel Joshua, Hinde Esther, and Moyshe, would disappear from the world. The concrete gestures that kept alive his connection to the past also maintained Bashevis's link to those whom he had ambivalently loved, and whom he now endlessly mourned.

In 1965, the Singers moved into the Belnord Apartment House on a corner of Broadway and 86th Street. They had migrated to Manhattan from Brooklyn long before and had lived for twenty years at 103rd Street and Central Park West. Subsequently, they had spent some years on 72nd Street, off Columbus Avenue. They obviously enjoyed the ambiance on the Upper West Side, with its ethnic mix, its simple coffee shops, its down-to-earth atmosphere. Although there were no doubt other features that made the 86th Street location attractive, the building's construction was especially appealing to Bashevis because it contained a courtyard. His friend and translator, Dorothea Straus, recalls that: "Singer once told me that he chose it because it reminded him of his childhood home on Krochmalna Street in Warsaw."[36]

The courtyard provides a clue to the transformation that Bashevis was undergoing during the 1950s and 1960s. Although he was making decisive life changes, the shift was as much backwards as forwards. In subtle and probably unconscious ways, he was creating himself as a new-world version of his father. Beyond finding a place to live that could remind him of Krochmalna Street, Bashevis effected a particular and consistent style of dress and established his own dietary laws. Both maneuvers established him as a hybrid: no one would mistake him for his father, Pinkhos Menakhem, and countless Jews like him, but he nevertheless resembled his forebears. Bashevis was probably neither devious nor jaded enough to construct an entire external lifestyle for the purposes of publicity. More likely, he was cleaving to some version of the manners and boundaries with which he had been raised, even as he became increasingly unmoored from his years in Poland.

Richard Elman described Bashevis's customary apparel in the 1960s: "He wore the same severe costume every time I visited: a pair of dark suit trousers and a stark white cotton dress shirt, and plain black shoes...."[37] Bashevis's ubiquitous blue suit, while not literally reminiscent of Hasidic garb, nonetheless revealed him as different and other-worldly. At the ceremony for which that other-worldly quality was most lavishly recognized, the Nobel prize ceremony, Eric Pace would later write in *The New York Times*: "When he gave his Nobel prize lecture in Stockholm yesterday, he wore a plain blue suit, the same outfit in which he has been seen for years around New York."[38] Perhaps Bashevis's impulse to wear the same outfit in private as well as in public was a specific identification with his father, who had to be prepared at any time for people entering his home to seek counsel. This may also help explain why Singer insisted, for most of his years in New York, on having his telephone number listed and on spending time with all sorts of visitors. A rabbi does not hide himself from the public. As Singer remarked to Mark Golub, while referring to his comfort with the Yiddish language: "...in Yiddish, I feel like a man at home—you take off your jacket—although I don't take off my tie and jacket at home, but this is my own business."[39]

The most striking constraint that Bashevis created for himself in the United States was his strict vegetarianism. The resolve to avoid meat and fish matches the profile of a man erecting barriers between himself and his milieu.[40]

The conversion to vegetarianism came relatively late for Bashevis: he was almost sixty years old. It is therefore unlikely that the decision stemmed from lifelong feelings of compassion for animals, despite Bashevis's assertion, in *Love and Exile*, that he had been haunted since childhood by the scream of a mouse being tortured by a cat.[41] More likely, his determination not to eat flesh was connected to post-Holocaust feelings of revulsion against human cruelty, misuse of power, and disregard for life. At the same time, Bashevis's close regulation of what entered his body was a secular version of *kashrus*, the Jewish dietary laws.

Bashevis discussed his vegetarianism in several distinct ways, which together hint at the complex meanings of the stance for him.

First, he implied that he had been a vegetarian for much longer than was actually the case, although he never explicitly lied. The subterfuge is evident, for example, in his *Love and Exile*, where the admittedly autobiographical protagonist is already a vegetarian on the ocean voyage to America in 1935. Eventually, this implication made its way into the English-language press as a complete falsehood: "Singer has been a vegetarian since his early youth."[42]

In the years after the Nobel prize, when his fate as Isaac Singer, Eastern European *naif*, was forever sealed, Bashevis made light of his stance, quipping, for example, that: "I am a vegetarian for the sake of health—the health of the chicken!"[43]

Yet, there were, as well, serious statements in which Bashevis acknowledged how deeply the subject affected him and how earnestly he took the decision. In Yiddish, Bashevis was explicit about the spiritual longings contained in his vegetarianism: "My whole life I felt that it is an insult to eat living creatures... I thought to myself, how can I speak of God's mercy when I myself am cruel and eat the creatures which I should love."[44] Bashevis evidently enjoyed talking about his vegetarianism: "I always liked meat and I think it is perfectly healthy. But I feel animals are not made to be killed. I have my two birds, they are such lovely creatures—the thought of someone eating them makes me sick. I realize that in this world things are made so animals and people have to kill each other. It can't be helped. But it is not my duty to help in this destruction....No human being has what animals have. They should be our teachers and masters, not our food. They are humble, they have humility, they are sincere. They are not something to eat, they are God's beautiful creation."[45]

In a later interview, Bashevis related an account that could have been a short story, so powerfully does it evoke the moral yet deeply personal reasons he might have had for swearing off the consumption of living creatures: "I wasn't a vegetarian from childhood. It started some 10 years ago when a bird I was attached to fell into a narrow vase. He could have stayed afloat, I suppose, but I wasn't at home to help him get out. The effort and the despair must have killed him. I said to myself that now is the time or never."[46]

Bashevis had a particular connection to birds. Of all creatures, they were the only ones who played a part in his daily existence.

Mirra Ginsburg, one of Bashevis's early translators, tells a story that, in her opinion, explained his affection: one day a parakeet flew into Bashevis's apartment. He was so delighted with this unusual and fortuitous event that he determined not to eat meat again. The event also led to his owning a series of parakeets.[47]

As much as Bashevis clearly loved birds, he seemed also to have identified with them. When his original parakeet disappeared as mysteriously as it had shown up, Bashevis declared publicly that he had lost his faith in God. When a neighbor asked incredulously how he could utter such a statement, he turned on her, shaking a finger in her face: "God doesn't need you to defend Him," he retorted. Bashevis's reaction suggests his conviction that the fate of the bird was comparable to his own. Both he and the bird were equally important—and equally insignificant—in the cosmic scheme.

In 1968, Bashevis commented: "I feel that since I'm a vegetarian that not only man, but even the animals belong to my community. They suffer just as we do. They are made of blood and flesh. To me a pigeon is a part of my community."[48] In part, the public affection coincided with the development of Isaac Bashevis Singer; over the years, the sight of the little old man feeding pigeons on the Upper West Side became increasingly familiar to his admirers. At home, Singer allowed his parakeets to fly uncaged, until he decided that the freedom was dangerous for them: "I suffered so much when they suffered, when they got sick, got lost or fell down, that in a way I am happy I don't have them anymore."[49]

Bashevis's vegetarianism certainly goes deeper than the need to create a persona who would appeal to an audience longing for a benign Eastern European grandfather. The self-imposed prohibition against exerting power over any living creature was linked in his mind to the events of the Holocaust. The story "Pigeons," published in January, 1966, approximately four years after he had become a complete vegetarian, expresses in fiction his views about animal intelligence and human cruelty.[50]

The story takes place in pre–World War II Warsaw. The protagonist, an elderly Jewish professor named Vladislav Eibeschutz, finds his life increasingly constricted by age, the death of his wife, and growing anti-Semitism. As his connection to other people diminishes, his involvement with birds expands. The apartment he shares with Tekla, his frail but loyal Polish housekeeper, resembles a giant cage: parakeets, canaries, and parrots fly free. The professor, heedless of his own rest, regulates the amount of light in the apartment according to the needs of the birds; he does not want to disturb their rhythms of sleep and wakefulness. On the street, the professor's only companions are the pigeons he devotedly tends.

One day, while out feeding the pigeons, the professor is the victim of an anti-Semitic attack. Mortally wounded by a blow to the head, he expires during the following night. After his death, he is praised and honored as a great scholar by the very colleagues who had forgotten or ignored him during his waning years. But his truest friends are the pigeons. Forming an aerial honor guard, they escort the professor's coffin to the cemetery. Then, their task completed, they fly off. By the next day, someone has painted a swastika on the professor's door, and most of the pigeons, sensing that their existence is in danger, refuse to accept the food that Tekla brings them. Those that do come down are wary: "They pecked at the food hesitantly, glancing around as if afraid to be caught defying some avian ban. The smell of char and rot came up from the gutter, the acrid stench of imminent destruction."[51]

Who are these pigeons? According to the professor, pigeons resemble Jews: "Pigeons have no weapons in the fight for survival. They sustain themselves almost entirely on the scraps that people throw them. They fear noise, flee the smallest dog. They don't even chase away the sparrows that steal their food. The pigeon, like the Jew, thrives on peace, quietude, and good will."[52]

During the crucial years after the Holocaust, Bashevis came to believe that, by eating meat, he was condoning the killing of innocent living things. He would not emulate those who had murdered his people.

Insofar as Bashevis's vegetarianism also represented a shift backwards, towards the life he had known in Poland, he could look to a specific role model: Meylekh Ravitch, one of his few friends, and also an older sibling figure, had been a vegetarian since the 1920s. Bashevis was actively aware of Ravitch's vegetarianism. Sometimes he joked about it, teasing his friend as he did in a 1943 letter: "How is your *parnose* [livelihood]? And how is your health? Are you still eating grass?" Eventually, however, he came to reveal just how seriously he took the issue. In a letter dated November 4, 1962, concerning an upcoming visit to Montreal, Bashevis told Ravitch: "It seems that I will be in Montreal on January 18, 1963, at the Jewish Congress. I'll address them on the 18th and the 20th. If so, I could perhaps lecture at the library on the 19th. Do me a favor and tell the librarian that the *only* people I envy in the world are the vegetarians. I myself am almost a vegetarian, but when I am invited to someone's home I don't want to be tricky or pretentious or stuffy. Quite often my wife brings me a bit of chicken. When I am alone, I never eat meat and I mainly eat alone because she works."[53]

However long it took Bashevis to draw his important conclusions, he did not include Alma in the process of his transformation. She reported that Bashevis simply came to her one day and said, "I want to stop eating meat. Will you help me?"[54] Characteristically, and significantly, the move to vegetarianism created another barrier between husband and wife. Years later, in 1975, Alma described the situation with good humor and unrepentance: "My three favorite dishes are turkey, goulash, rare roast beef, but my husband's been a vegetarian for the past thirteen years, no meat or fish—he does eat eggs—so a big part in our life is played by mushrooms. I make sauteed mushrooms every day. He loves them."[55]

By the time Isaac Bashevis Singer won the Nobel prize, vegetarianism was as integral and unquestioned a part of his public personality as *kashrus* had been to his father. By attributing his decision to compassion, Bashevis avoided any discussion of spiritual and bodily purity. Yet, long before he stopped eating meat, the future vegetarian had hinted at his sense of inner pollution through the comical doodle that he used as a signature: it was a pig.

The earliest appearance of Bashevis's pig may have occurred only after he had left Poland. On a postcard to Ravitch in 1937, Bashevis writes simply: "*A sheynem dank. Ikh bin a—*"(Thank you very much. I am a—) followed by the drawing of a pig. There is nothing further in the correspondence.[56] Given the harsh Jewish prohibition against eating pork, Bashevis's self-description implies a sense of self as unclean, despite the attempt at joviality. Evidently, he no longer considered himself an unblemished Jew.

Later, in America, Bashevis tended to use the pig doodle when writing English. Alma reports that, during their courtship, he often signed his letters to her with a pig.[57] He also employed it in dedications to Elizabeth Shub, one of his earliest translators and herself a member of an illustrious Yiddish literary family: "He used to do something very cute when a book came out, some of the things I'd translate, he would always do a little drawing... which was very cute. He loved pigs. He loved pigs.... That was the trademark. Book after book." Why would he use such an autograph? Ms. Shub: "He's a pig."[58]

The pig, the quintessential symbol of Jewish uncleanliness, represented all that Isaac Bashevis Singer was becoming. An amusing anecdote he told years later nonetheless reveals his continued and painful awareness that he had disappointed his father: "My father... considered all secular books blasphemy—pornography. So my father used to tell people when they asked him, 'What are your sons doing?' he would say, 'They sell newspapers.' He considered this a very dignified way to make a living. But a writer?! So after a while he began to believe in it. Once when he came to Warsaw and he asked me, 'Are you selling enough newspapers to make a living?' I said, 'Not too many, but somehow I manage.'"[59]

Bashevis had already transgressed while still in Poland, not only with his career choice but also with his sexuality. He had engaged in relationships with several women and had fathered a child out of wedlock. In the United States, his position was even worse. In the eyes of his parents, could they have seen him, he was defiled. By abandoning orthodoxy, he had rejected their values; by moving to the United States and marrying a German-Jewish woman who understood no Yiddish, he had thrown away a sacred lifestyle that was now facing extinction. Above all, if the Yiddish language stood for all that was purely Eastern European Jewish, Isaac Bashevis Singer's increasing attention to an English-reading public proved his corruption. He—a pig—had survived while millions of chaste souls had perished. He was debased.

Bashevis attempted to cleanse himself by adopting a dietary regimen that was even stricter than that of his father. Even so, he felt blameworthy. In a comment to television personality Dick Cavett in 1977, Singer bemoaned the fact that, although he would not eat any living creature, he could not stop himself from swatting at flies and mosquitos when they annoyed him; this lapse made him a bad vegetarian.

Bashevis's vegetarianism served to separate him from his American milieu and to connect him symbolically with his past. Yet, his feeling that he was degraded and shameful persisted unassuaged. Bashevis's continued self-chastisement may have resulted from a confrontation that occurred several years before his final conversion to vegetarianism. In 1955, Bashevis was reunited with Israel Zamir, the son he had not seen for twenty years. The encounter demonstrated unequivocally that he had been responsible for grave cruelty to an innocent and vulnerable human being, who was, moreover, his own flesh and blood. During the years that followed the first meeting, Bashevis would be reminded again and again of his human failures. Not only his son, but his wife as well, were forced to accept his lapses. That they did so merely exacerbated Bashevis's knowledge that he was corrupt.

8

————•————

AS early as *The Family Moskat*, Bashevis had revealed his view
that monogamy and parental responsibility were not for everyone.
Oyzer Heshl, the novel's protagonist, found the traditional roles
too confining and too demanding. Bashevis himself was not a family man. His mistrust of domestic ties may have stemmed from the
tumultuous and neglectful environment provided by Pinkhos
Menakhem and Basheve, and may have been exacerbated by the
antics of Hinde Esther. Although Bashevis failed to correct his
hurtful behavior—he seemed to need the drama to fuel his creative
energy—he recognized his effect on others. He was a negligent
husband, an unfit father, and he knew it.

A hint of Bashevis's remorse during the long hiatus in relations
with his son, Israel Zamir, is evident in the tormenting fantasies
that he apparently suffered during the years of World War II.
Zamir reveals that "Later, my father told me of dreams that he had.
His wife and son were in a convoy on its way to Auschwitz. He
would awaken frantic and mumble a prayer."[1] Nonetheless, after
1935, Bashevis made no attempt to repair the schism until twenty
years later when Zamir, who had just completed his military service, asked to visit his father.[2]

In fairness to Bashevis, however, Zamir's mother, Ronye, had
worked to stimulate Bashevis's fear, although she was not to blame

for the specific concentration-camp content of his fantasies. In 1940, after Palestine had been bombed, Ronye had written, demanding money and falsely claiming that their son had been wounded. It was not until father and son met, however, that this information emerged. Zamir, who initially refused to believe the tale, was obliged to accept it when Bashevis ferreted out the letter and showed it to him.[3]

Bashevis and Ronye had a bitter disagreement just after the War. Ronye wanted Bashevis to grant her a divorce, even though there had never been a marriage, so that Zamir could be legitimized. Bashevis refused, but offered to adopt the boy, now fifteen years of age, as if he were not already his son. Ronye was outraged. She wrote: "How can you complain about the fact that I believed your assurances and oaths that your undying love is stronger than all marriage contracts, that your brother, too, who never legally married his wife, was a model family man....Who could know that it was all talk, so that you could more easily exploit the opportunity of finding a person who would take you, a poor, sick, lonely person whose own brother almost didn't want the likes of you in his home."

About the so-called adoption, Ronye was almost beside herself. Zamir would be forever psychologically affected, "...and then I will have to reveal the entire truth to him, and you realize how much hatred the child will carry towards you." She was unable to understand why Bashevis was now refusing to grant her a *get*, a Jewish divorce. After all, Israel Joshua had simply gone to a rabbi when his son Yossele was small and sworn that he had been married years before. How could anyone prove that there had never been a wedding in Warsaw, now that all documentation had been burned? As a final threat, Ronye insisted that, if Bashevis did not grant the *get*, she would refuse to let him visit his son. In any case, he had behaved egregiously, writing letters full of love, and promising to come to them in Palestine, when all the while he was married to someone else.[4]

Whatever was transpiring between Bashevis and Ronye during the years after their separation, he evidently kept the existence of his son in the background of his American life.[5] But his silence did not signify a lack of awareness. As ever, Bashevis eventually turned his fearful fantasies into fiction, in *Enemies, A Love Story*.

Herman Broder, the protagonist of *Enemies*, had survived the Holocaust by hiding in a hayloft; now living in New York, he is shocked when his first wife, Tamara, whom he had presumed dead, suddenly turns up. He is already married to Yadwiga, the Polish woman who had hidden him and saved his life. He is also deeply involved with Masha, his mistress. Tamara, who resembles Ronye in her political convictions, informs Herman that both their children have perished. Herman must face the pain of that realization, coupled with the knowledge that he, like Bashevis himself, had been a reluctant, uninvolved father, a selfish and profligate womanizer.

The story of Herman, who rues his very existence, and who fears that his indifferent behavior represents a sinful and unforgivable core, hints at Bashevis's disgust regarding his own actions. As always, however, he seemed to experience more fully through fiction than through direct contact. When Bashevis finally met Zamir, the son quickly learned that his longing for warmth and indications of remorse from his father would go ungratified. "The only people he seemed to really love were the heroes of his stories. He could talk about them for hours. If I wanted to know my father, I would have to enter his inner world."[6]

As was his habit and his need, Bashevis turned the eventual meeting with his son into a short story. Interestingly, Zamir also wrote down his impressions of the 1955 encounter. He had come to the United States specifically to meet his father, who had agreed to pay for the voyage. In "The Son," Bashevis describes waiting for his son at the dock in New York. Zamir is slow to emerge from the boat, causing his anxious father to entertain the fantasy that he has jumped overboard. Of the first sight of his son, Bashevis says, "He came out slowly, hesitantly, and with an expression that said he didn't expect anybody to be waiting for him. He looked like the snapshot, but older. There were youthful wrinkles in his face and his clothes were mussy. He showed the shabbiness and neglect of a homeless young man who had been years in strange places, who had gone through a lot and become old before his time. His hair was tangled and matted, and it seemed to me there were wisps of straw and hay in it—like the hair of those who sleep in haylofts."[7] In Bashevis's imaginative recollection, his son, much like Herman Broder, has managed to hold onto his life, perhaps by hiding and perhaps by running. But his survival has taken a physical and psychological toll.

"I approached him and asked unsurely, '*Atah* Gigi?' He laughed. 'Yes, I'm Gigi.' We kissed and his stubble rubbed my cheeks like a potato grater. He was strange to me, yet I knew at the same time I was as devoted to him as any other father to his son. We stood still with that feeling of belonging together that needs no words."[8]

Zamir, on the other hand, worried that his father was ill and was unable to come and fetch him. Of the same first few minutes, he says "'Gigi,' he called, my nickname from childhood. It had been so long since I had heard it. 'Yes,' I answered, like a soldier counted at inspection. We shook hands. He gave me a dutiful kiss. We stood there, silent and embarrassed. I had carried this meeting in my heart all my life. Now that it was actually taking place, I was choked and exhausted.[9] . . . We were strangers. A mountain of alienation loomed between us."[10]

The only common reaction that Bashevis and Zamir report, as they wait for one another, is the fantasy that the meeting will not take place. Bashevis fears that his son is dead or hiding, and Zamir worries that his father is too infirm to pick him up.

Another moment that both men describe in their accounts assumes a different quality in Bashevis's fiction than in Zamir's memoir. Bashevis writes: ". . . the powers which determine the world had destined that he should come to New York and see his father. It was as if I heard his thoughts behind his skull. I was sure he too, like myself, was pondering the eternal questions. As if to try out my telepathic powers, I said to him, 'There are no accidents. If you are meant to live, you have to remain alive. It is destined so.' Surprised, he turned his head to me. 'Hey, you are a mind reader!' And he smiled, amazed, curious, and skeptical, as if I had played a fatherly trick on him."[11]

As Zamir reports the incident, he was disdainful rather than admiring: "'Son, there are no chance happenings in the world. If you are alive it means you were supposed to stay alive.' I was so astonished, I shuddered. Had he actually read my thoughts? Was fatherly intuition so powerful that it could break down all barriers with just one blow? Afterwards, I decided that he had probably been thinking about himself, his life, the family that had come apart, the son and wife he had left behind in Poland. . . . He did not send them any money. He said he had none.... When he said that there were no chance happenings in the world, he only meant to say that since we had met again, a father and son who had never been close, it could only be the will of providence...."[12]

Years later, Zamir recalled that his father had written to him in the 1930s, expressing his love, but that he, living far away from his father, was incapable of feeling that love. In a sympathetic moment, however, Zamir suggested that, for Bashevis, writing was equivalent to doing. If he said or wrote something, he felt that he had accomplished it. During their first meeting, for example, Bashevis had exclaimed: "Well, we must buy you some galoshes." The purchase never took place, but Zamir felt certain that, in Bashevis's mind, the discussion itself was as good as having bought the galoshes.[13] In this instance, Bashevis may have been acting like a chip off the old block; after all, his father, Pinkhos Menakhem, had come to believe his own fiction that Bashevis made his living by selling newspapers.

Whatever love Bashevis might have felt for Zamir, he was cruel when it came to encouraging his son's literary aspirations. Years after the two men met, the father, sounding more like the old Bashevis than the kindly old man he usually presented to the press, announced in *The New York Times* that he had never expected his son to produce anything of literary value. He went on to expound his criticism: "'I told him he had some good phrases...but in the beginning he says that the boat made its way like a blind man and it shook like a drunkard. I say either you compare the ship to a blind man or to a drunkard. You cannot do the two things together....He writes there was 'an abyss' between him and this father. I say 'an abyss' is not exact. If you say 'abyss' it should be a real abyss. If you say 'drunkard' it should be a real drunkard....He says 'a mountain of strangeness.' In literature a mountain is a mountain....I say Hebrew suffers from clichés. In English the clichés are young, and in Hebrew they are sacred—but they are still clichés.'"[14]

Bashevis's uncharacteristic public harshness reveals that, at his core, he was a writer. Nothing was more important than the integrity of fiction. If he had to sacrifice his son's feelings to make a literary point, so be it.

Nonetheless, considering that these blunt comments concern

Zamir's memories of his first encounter with his father, the sniping seems especially malicious, if it is even possible to quantify the brutality of attacking one's son's creativity in a major newspaper. Although he had not yet won the Nobel prize, Bashevis used the opportunity of an attentive *New York Times* reporter to unleash his hurt and consequent anger at Zamir for portraying their first meeting in a critical light. Moreover, Bashevis had been exposed as embellishing the event in order to make himself look more fatherly and benign. If Zamir was wounded by this attack, he certainly did not confront his father, as a subsequent anecdote confirms. In 1980, he presented his father with a collection of stories that he had written. Bashevis said to him, "Why do you have to write your own books when you can translate mine?" Reflecting on this moment, Zamir mused, "Well, it didn't bother me." In answer to a comment that such insouciance was hard to imagine under the circumstances, Zamir admitted that he *had* felt insulted, but that he had not said anything to his father.[15]

Although Bashevis remained distant from his own son, he was able to turn his literary talents to writing tales for children. The new venture, which resulted in over two dozen stories, brought him both recognition and publicity. There is no question that the notion of the little man who resonated so well with children did much to further the development of Bashevis into Isaac Singer. The impetus for writing children's books came from Elizabeth Shub,[16] who had already done many translations with Bashevis:

"I was newly divorced and I had just gotten my first job in children's books. I never had anything to do with children's books at Harper, and it occurred to me because he was so good and such a good storyteller that he would have to be able to write for children. So I said one day when I saw him, 'Isaac, how about doing a book for children?' And he said, 'O.K., if you translate it.' So I said, 'Sure, okay, I'll be glad to.' I think I nagged him a bit and then one day—I'll never forget this—he came and brought me this Hanukkah story in really awful jingles. It was so bad that the worst amateur couldn't have written it. I think we met at the Famous Cafeteria on 72nd Street, and I thought, 'God, what am I going to do here? I've asked him to do a children's book.' And some adult writers cannot write for children. I didn't know that then. This was just the beginning for me. I said, 'Isaac, I really don't think this works.' He looked at me, really angry, 'What do you know?' 'Maybe I don't know, but I don't think....' He'll never talk to me again, I thought. So then we parted, and I really felt terrible because I knew that many adult writers think it's very easy to write for children. They talk down and they don't really bother. And that doesn't work. It shows.

"Well, the next day, he called me up. 'All right, I wrote something else. Meet me.' I was thrilled and also scared to death because if I had to turn down something else, it would have been the end. So he came. He brought a story called 'Zlateh the Goat'... I read it and said, 'This is wonderful.'"[17]

Unlike most of his stories for adults, "Zlateh" directly addresses the virtues of an animal and, through cryptic references, hints at a comparison between the goat and human victims of persecution. During one particularly difficult winter, Zlateh's owner, Reuven the furrier, decides to sell her to the local butcher. He designates his son, Aaron, to perform the task; Aaron, who loves the goat as if she were a member of the family, reacts with devastated compliance.

The two embark on their sad journey, although Zlateh is at first unaware of anything amiss. Suddenly, they find themselves in a freak storm that soon becomes a monumental blizzard. Eventually, Zlateh realizes that her life is in danger: "Those humans in whom she had so much confidence had dragged her into a trap."[18] Just as Aaron and Zlateh are about to succumb to cold and exhaustion, they come upon a huge haystack.

Aaron and Zlateh remain hidden in the haystack for three days; Zlateh eats the hay and feeds Aaron with her milk. They are warm, cozy, and safe. Oblivious to the natural rhythms of night and day, and becoming faster friends than they had imagined possible, they are ignorant of the desperate search for them that is underway outside the haystack. By the time the two emerge, Aaron has decided that he will never part with his beloved friend. His grateful family agrees, and Zlateh returns home a heroine.

The stories for children, which were recognized with two Newberry prizes, reflect Bashevis at his most honest. Although "Zlateh" was created specifically with children in mind, other stories evidently were not. "Menaseh's Dream," for instance, first appeared in the *Forverts* in 1967, signed Varshavsky. The decision to make it into a story for children may have been based on the unusual clarity of the story's message: Menaseh, an orphan who longs for nothing more deeply than to be reunited with his lost parents, one day discovers a magical palace, where he encounters his family. His grandfather leads him through the mysterious place. In the first room are all the clothes he has ever worn in his life. In the second room, Menaseh discovers all the toys he has ever possessed. The third room contains the bubbles he had blown years before; the fourth room holds all the voices he has ever heard. The fifth room is reserved for all the stories he has ever heard. The sixth room preserves all his dreams. In the seventh room, Menaseh encounters his future.

The story is a touching and completely open fantasy about the capacity of the human being to retain the past, especially in dreams, words, and stories. If the moral were not clear enough through the imagery of the story, Singer makes it explicit in the story's final paragraph: "Among the undergrowth and wild mushrooms, little people in red jackets, gold caps, and green boots emerged. They danced in a circle and sang a song which is heard only by those who know that everything lives and nothing in time is ever lost."[19]

After his heartsick yet poignant stories of 1945, Bashevis rarely revealed such unconcealed longing for the past. Varshavsky could be sentimental; so could Isaac Singer. Bashevis could not. With children, however, he was willing to make points that he shunned in his writing for adults. Varshavsky and Bashevis could be politically engaged; Isaac Singer forbade himself any explicit partisan stance. But in a children's story, he could divulge his point in disguise, remaining relatively certain that he would not be found out by his youthful audience. In "The Wicked City," for instance, he counseled against assimilation. It was only late in his career, in 1983—after the Nobel prize—that he allowed the translation of The Penitent, a similarly conservative novel, to be published into English, although it had appeared in Yiddish a decade earlier.

It was inevitable that, having now embarked upon a new aspect of his career, Singer would find himself called upon to comment on his feelings about children. And so he did. In 1969, for example, he noted about his young readers, "Their literature is still preoccupied with kings, princesses, devils, demons, imps, werewolves and other old-fashioned creatures."[20] He penned "Why I Write for Children," which was eventually part of his presentation at the Nobel prize banquet, and which comprised a list of ten reasons why he valued his youthful audience. Singer's tone was witty and affectionate: "Children read books, not reviews.... They don't read to free themselves of guilt.... They have no use for psychology.... They detest sociology.... When a book is boring, they yawn openly.... They don't expect their beloved writer to redeem humanity."[21]

Nor was the publicity confined to the written word. There were also visits and personal appearances, during which Singer portrayed himself, or allowed himself to be portrayed, as a grandfatherly gentleman. There is, for example, the article—complete with a photo of the author in his dark suit—describing a visit Singer had paid to a fourth-grade class at Woodmere elementary school: "...the visit was a departure for the distinguished guest.... he was entertained rather than being on stage himself.... the students... dramatized one of his own stories and read to him originals of their own in imitation of his style.... The day was rounded out by singing Yiddish songs and questions fielded by students and answered informally by the guest."[22]

What was Bashevis's more private attitude towards children? Alma is characteristically blunt yet forgiving on the subject: "Basically, he didn't like children; but he made exceptions when he knew the family and he saw the children occasionally. He could play with them and organize little games with them, that was all right. But he got tired quickly and it wasn't his forte to play with children. The writing for children became part of his work and as such he took it very seriously."[23] Israel Zamir, the long-suffering son, reported with some bitterness that his father never bothered to get to know two of his four grandchildren, yet he portrayed himself publicly as a family man. America likes it when a writer sounds like a family man, Zamir noted wryly.[24] Elizabeth Shub mused that: "Children didn't exist. Better still, I think they didn't count. They existed, of course. They didn't count.... I never met his son. He never spoke of his grandchildren. The cuteness, the charm, it didn't interest him."[25]

In a rarely candid interview in Hebrew with Ophra Alyagon, Bashevis himself admitted that "I love music but I can live very nicely without it. I love family life, but I am not sure that a person really and truly cannot live without the family, cannot do without a family. I don't believe that a person cannot live without children. I know it's terrible to say so, but this is the truth." Yet, Alyagon remembers a moment when Bashevis had treated a young adolescent with respect, taking care not to humiliate him: In 1968, she was in New York and wanted to interview him but lacked money for a photographer. Friends of hers had a thirteen-year-old son whose hobby was photography. In a moment of inspiration, she enlisted the boy, who dressed up like a man, donning a suit and painting on a little mustache. Bashevis treated him like a grown-up, called him *Adoni* (Sir), and never let on that he knew he was not talking to an adult.[26]

At the end of the 1960s and the beginning of the 1970s, Isaac Bashevis Singer was no longer Yitskhok Bashevis, the sharp-tongued Yiddish writer who needed to distinguish himself from his brother. He also no longer needed to distance himself from his father, who now appeared as a figure to be admired and longed for. Both men were gone and Israel Joshua was virtually unknown outside Yiddish circles except among well-read Jews. Singer had cultivated a manner among English-speaking audiences that was friendly, charming in the extreme, superficially intimate: "I'm in the phone book," he would tell those who wished to contact him—and he was. He fed pigeons, professed his vegetarianism, and wrote for children.

The fun-loving Singer could resonate with the fantasies of a child and play along with an appealing deception. But that same spirit and charm were responsible for causing misery as well. The chief victim of Bashevis's neglect was Alma. Like his character Yasha Mazur, Bashevis evidently thought little of being unfaithful to his wife; and, like his character Herman Broder, he eventually found himself entangled with three different women at the same time.[27] The knot eventually unraveled, leaving Alma victorious, but none of the women emerged unscathed.

Bashevis justified his behavior with the statement that he was a bachelor, "...a bachelor in my soul. Even if I married a whole harem of women, I'd still act like a bachelor."[28] Bashevis surrounded himself with women as translators, admirers, and sources of inspiration. Anecdotes, largely unverifiable, abound concerning conquests in hotel rooms, on college campuses, in trains. As always, the line between actual experience and the author's imagination was fuzzy: "Sometimes, he once told me, he completed in writing what he wanted to realize in reality."[29]

The two women who captured Bashevis's attention more than momentarily were as different from one another as each one was from Alma. Dobe Gerber, a Holocaust survivor and native Yiddish speaker, was passionate and wildly emotional, a type like Bashevis's sister, Hinde Esther. Aliza Shevrin, one of Bashevis's translators, recalls Dobe: "She drank and she smoked, and you could see he hated it. He hated it but it must have been alluring to him. She would just march around at a dinner party, sipping little bits of left-over liquor from everybody."[30] Dobe became the model for Masha in *Enemies, A Love Story*.[31] Dvora Menashe was American-born, learned Yiddish only after years of knowing Bashevis, and was fifty years his junior.

What Dobe and Dvora had in common with one another, and also with Alma, was their willingness to take care of Bashevis, to view him as a combination of lover and little boy. At different times, each acted as his secretary, and each traveled with him; for a period, although the affair with Dobe had cooled before Dvora became a central figure in Bashevis's life, he employed both.[32] The arrangement repeated Bashevis's long-standing position of involvement with more than one woman. It was a situation that had begun in his earliest childhood; as an adult, he perpetuated the lifelong mixture of high drama and eroticism, combined with distance and distraction, that characterized his relations with women.

Sometimes, the orchestration did not run smoothly. On one occasion, for example, Bashevis traveled to Israel with Dobe. According to Zamir, the trip was planned around an honorary doctorate that Bashevis was to receive from the Hebrew University in Jerusalem: "He traveled to Israel with Dove [sic], and they stayed together at the Park Hotel in Tel Aviv. I remember that the three of us were sitting and talking in his room when, unannounced, Alma suddenly appeared. My father blushed, and Dove turned pale. 'Alma, what are you doing here?' he asked, fearful and annoyed. 'I came for the ceremony,' she answered calmly."

Ophra Alyagon reports a different version of the same event. According to her, Bashevis had written to say that he was coming to Israel, together with Dobe and her mother, to find an old-age home for the mother. Bashevis and Dobe stayed at the Park Hotel, and the mother lodged with Dobe's daughter, who lived in Israel. One day, Ophra, Dobe, and Bashevis returned to the hotel after a day visiting potential homes. The hotel receptionist stopped Bashevis, saying: "I have to talk to you. Your wife from New York is in your room." Bashevis told Dobe to stay downstairs, and he went upstairs to find Alma, who greeted him with tears and loud reproach. She had seen Dobe's clothing. He said, "Why did you come?" Alma retorted, "I'm your wife. I have every right to come. You're betraying me. And I had a suspicion that you were." He said, "Look, do you know how long this has been going on? It's been 25 years, did you know?" "No," Alma replied. Seeing an opening, Bashevis asked: "Well, did it bother you?" She admitted that it hadn't. That settled, Bashevis seized control of the situation. "Now stop this," he ordered, and took his wife to the Dan Hotel, which was across the street from the Park. He later told Ophra that jealousy had aroused both women; he had been running back and forth between the two for days. The adventure concluded with all three—Dobe, Alma, and Bashevis—looking at old age homes together.[33]

The story in both versions has the irony and intensity of a Singer story. The reality of daily life between Alma and Bashevis was sometimes much more grim, however, descending from sexual politics to nastiness and condescension. Some of this animus appears to have stemmed from Bashevis's resentment over Alma's German-Jewish heritage. Sylvia Weber, the wife of *Forverts* editor Shimen Weber, recalls that Bashevis would say about Alma: "She is a typical German—mean, selfish, and she thinks only of herself." Weber also remembered that Bashevis would insult his wife in front of people, saying, "This is why I married a German Jew, I can spit in her face, and in the next minute she'll say it rained."[34]

The writer Richard Elman, who himself found Bashevis "closed off, harsh, ruthless, manipulative, [and] cold," remembers witnessing a cruel conversation: "Once...when I asked him about Dostoevski after he'd confessed to having translated *The Possessed* into Yiddish while still in Warsaw, Bashevis would not speak about that Russian writer except to say he no longer read 'such books' until Alma Singer interrupted from the next room. 'Tell them the truth, Isaacal,' she said, 'about how you used to love Dostoevski....' Bashevis seemed to grow quite annoyed with her. 'Alma,' he said, 'when you write a novel and they'll come to interview you, you'll tell them about Dostoevski and Jacob Wasserman [sic] both together, but they are here to interview me so please, Alma, don't say another word... not even about Sholem Asch....' Afterwards he was smiling, as if his seeming exasperation had been a game they played regularly, but she was silent the rest of the evening."[35]

The slight to Alma was both subtle and extremely spiteful. The reference to Jakob Wassermann may have been a nod to her breadth of reading, since Wassermann had been a much lionized writer among German Jews in the interbellum period, but it was surely, as well, a jab at Alma for having been married to Walter Wassermann. In this way, Bashevis was demeaning her entire existence prior to her connection with him. The reference to Sholem Ash, who was the main Yiddish author familiar to German-Jewish readers, is similarly cutting. The German-Jewish love of Ash, with his attempts to unite Judaism and Christianity and his focus on Jesus as a figure for his fiction, was a source of joking deprecation among Yiddish intellectuals, who mocked the inability of German Jews to appreciate the depth of Yiddish literature and culture. With these allusions, Bashevis indicated to Alma her failure to understand his world, not to mention his writing.

Despite her hurt, Alma carried on, perhaps bolstered by a tendency to be selfish and stingy—just as her husband had said. Her niece, Eleanor Foa Dienstag, recalls: "She was notorious in our family for being ungenerous." Alma also retained her earlier habits of reluctant domesticity, as Dienstag knew from experience: "Just as my mother was a wonderful cook and sort of good in all those things, Alma never cooked. Ever. And they went out to breakfast."[36] Nonetheless, Alma's devotion to her husband was tenacious. She may not have understood his background or the profundity of his pain, but she knew that she was married to a great artist, and she was willing to do what she could to support him: "He's a genuine writer who can't fix himself a meal or wash dishes or do the shopping. He's got no idea of business, even when it has to do with publishing his own books."[37] By the early 1970s, Alma no longer needed to provide the major income for the couple, but for the first twenty-five years of their marriage, she was the breadwinner, capping her career with a ten-year stint at the elegant Manhattan department store, Lord & Taylor. In a rare, appreciative moment, Bashevis obliquely acknowledged his debt, referring to his wife as: "'An old-fashioned, good Jewish woman from Germany. Three days a week, she sells dresses at Lord & Taylor. Why not? For years we needed it. Now it's a habit.'"[38]

Alma, like Dobe and Dvora, accepted the fact that, like it or not, she could not have Bashevis exclusively to herself. For all that he professed his homespun simplicity to a public eager to see him that way, and for all that he wanted to view himself as a creature of natural lusts and simple erotic energy, he remained a prisoner of his earliest complex and unfulfilling attachments. Singer was a consummate master of casual acquaintanceship, whether with students, reporters, adoring women, or strangers who recognized him as he walked the Upper West Side and sat at his favorite luncheonettes. These relationships, which provided a fantasy of pre-Holocaust perfection for his admiring fans, did not threaten to immerse Singer in the desperate straits of real attachment. It was quite different with a wife, a son, a grandchild: the constraints of *family* posed a danger to him of recreating the rejection, depression, and hysteria that he had needed to escape through his writing. The prospect of living closely with such terrible possibilities was more than he could tolerate without the threat of losing his integrity. Unfortunately, perhaps, the coming years would allow him increasing opportunity to retreat from intimacy, as he became more and more the unchallenged representative of a disappearing community. His old audience had decreasing chance to question his perspective, and his new one did not know how to.

9

---◆---

BY the early 1970s, Yitskhok Bashevis had lost the competition with Isaac Bashevis Singer. Yitskhok Bashevis, the sophisticated Yiddish writer whose imagination had once shuttled between Warsaw and Bilgoray, between his father's Hasidic spirit and his mother's rational understanding, between secular art and religious devotion, was all but eclipsed. In his place, Isaac Bashevis Singer, the English-language chronicler of immigrant life and container of a vanished realm, was stepping into the limelight with increasing confidence and energy.

In 1974, Singer won his second National Book Award for *A Crown of Feathers*.[1] His acceptance speech revealed the extent to which his center had shifted: "I am glad to get this award testifying to the fact that I am considered an American writer, even though I write in Yiddish. I have lived in the United States longer than I have lived in Poland and I have developed deep roots here. Many of my stories take place in New York and elsewhere in America. My heroes are, like myself, naturalized Americans who love this country not less than those who were born here....I keep on studying English and enjoying the resources of this language. Only in such a lavish and giving country as the United States is it possible for a writer who writes in a foreign language to get a national award. No man who lives here remains a stranger."[2]

But if Singer believed that his audience loved him for his growing American sensibility and his expanding knowledge of English, he was sadly mistaken. For all that he was trying to keep up with his changing circumstances, most of his public wanted him to stay just where he had come from; moreover, his readers clamored with unabated enthusiasm for *shtetl*, Jewish ritual, and Jewish demons. Any fantasies Singer may still have entertained about the transfer of his talents to a modern, urban, American milieu were forever dashed on October 5, 1978. On that day, he won the Nobel prize for literature.

Announcing its choice, the Swedish Academy cited Singer's "redeeming melancholy, sense of humor and...clear-sightedness free of illusion....[Singer's work describes] the world and life of Eastern European Jewry, such as it was lived in cities and villages, in poverty and persecution, and imbued with sincere piety and rites combined with blind faith and superstition. Its language was Yiddish—the language of the simple people."

Singer's fate was sealed. No one had the slightest interest in Bashevis, the immigrant genius, the former *enfant terrible* turned world-weary Jeremiah. The press and electronic media resonated with the idea that this prize commemorated the work of a homespun and humble soul who had faithfully represented the beautiful but tragic world of a moral and pious society that had been cruelly extinguished by the Nazi Holocaust.[3]

Typically, there was plenty of misinformation and stereotype as well. *The Washington Post* announced that: "...Singer writes about the nearly vanished world of Eastern European Hasidim, a world known to Americans through 'Fiddler on the Roof,'.... Elements of the supernatural legend and folklore appear throughout Singer's work, which is deeply rooted in the rich communal life of small villages but often explores how that life was transformed in the Warsaw ghetto and passage to the New World."[4]

The article went on to state that "Singer's world has been uprooted and threatened—first by the Nazis and Communists in Eastern Europe, then by demographic pressures in New York's Lower East side, where although some stores still bear signs in Yiddish, they are now outnumbered by signs in Spanish."[5] The photo accompanying the article showed the Nobel laureate wearing a yarmulke—definitely not a frequent occurrence. The *Los Angeles*

Times contained a laudatory editorial, stating that "The world of the Central European ghetto that is typically the setting for Singer's large body of novels and short stories is unfamiliar to most people." The front-page article called Singer the last great American writer in the tradition of Sholom Aleichem and Sholem Ash.[6] Whatever the *Los Angeles Times* meant by the "American tradition" of Sholom Aleichem and Sholem Ash, it is unlikely that this was what Bashevis had meant when he had told his National Book Award audience that he was glad to be regarded as an American writer.

If he had watched television, Singer might have felt slighted to learn that David Brinkley had mispronounced his name when announcing the story of the award on the NBC-TV news report.[7] Even more incredible than the fact that Singer's name could be mispronounced on national television at the moment of his greatest importance was the deep confusion about who he was. A few days after the announcement of the prize, a *Washington Post* article by Roger Rosenblatt appeared with the headline: "Isaac Stern: Like a Character of His Own."[8] The article was knowledgeable enough and concerned the similarity between Singer and the character of the young author in his story, "A Friend of Kafka." But the headline revealed all too clearly that, although he was better known to the American public than some of the Nobel laureates who had preceded him, Singer was still a dark horse: "The unexpected award even took Singer's New York publishers, Farrar, Straus and Giroux, by surprise. They had scheduled an auction of several hundred of Singer's books just several days before the prize was announced."[9]

Unfortunately, some of the misunderstanding was more fundamental than merely a question of pronunciation or misspelling. Peter S. Prescott, reporting in the Oct. 16, 1978 issue of *Newsweek*, understandably erred in stating that *The Family Moskat* was Singer's first full-length novel; but Prescott also assumed that Singer had enjoyed full control over the way his career transpired in the United States, attributing the slow beginnings of his fame in this country to Singer's devotion to Yiddish: "...fame has never meant much to Singer. If it had...he would not have waited until he was 46 to publish his first book in an English translation—the step that set him on his way to becoming a world-class writer...."

and now here he is, a Polish-American who has won the top prize without ever becoming (as so many American writers feel obliged to do) a prominent public figure as well."[10] And Ben Gallob in the *Chicago Sentinel*—which spelled Bashevis "Beshevis" in its head-line—comments with dazzling inaccuracy that "He wrote his first story during his first year of residence in the United States, 'Satan in Goray,' published in the Forward. Set in the 19th century, the book describes the ravages of the Cossacks and the mass murders of the Jews in Russia."[11]

The prize made Singer into a public figure, a position he had already assumed through his frequent public speaking engagements and lecture tours. Despite a diffident demeanor, Singer clearly enjoyed the limelight and actively wooed his audiences. As Lance Morrow reported in 1979: "For two months in the fall, and again for two months in the spring, Singer goes out lecturing to college audiences and other groups around the country."[12] In addition, while he generally refused to take political stands, he did make occasional exceptions. During one of these, he shared a taxi with the writer Alfred Kazin and the noted theologian, Abraham Joshua Heschel.

After Singer's death, Kazin recalled: "Of course, this is already a Singer story, like so many of my brief encounters with the man himself. Some years ago—I forget the exact date—some Leningrad Jews almost succeeded in hijacking a plane, were caught and sentenced to death. There was a big protest meeting in Washington. To my surprise I saw Singer. He had an almost total distrust of politics, political meetings and speeches. In the shuttle back to New York, he said almost ruefully, 'I don't usually do this.' I had heard him in the '60s expressing his amazement at the ignorance of 'nice Jewish boys behaving like revolutionaries who don't know how different America has been for the Jews.'... The writer and theologian Abraham Joshua Heschel, also returning from the Washington meeting, caught up with Singer as the plane landed. For reasons I found impossible to understand, they gave the impression of not having met before, or at least not for some time. In the taxi sitting with the two of them I was privileged to hear the most extraordinary reminiscences of Warsaw's old Jewish literary life, in a Yiddish more polished than I had heard before, except from Charney Vladeck, the Forward's old managing editor in his Socialist days, when he used to knock his proletarian audience dead with the elegance of his Yiddish. Some of the talk in the taxi was of course necrology—this writer dead, that one dead—the dead were just too many. But much of it was elegant shop talk about writers, magazines, old literary gatherings. I took it all as a gift, as I usually did with Singer. I insisted on leaving the taxi last, so that I could hear Heschel and Singer to the end. The driver finally had the last word. "Jesus, I thought I heard Jewish before in my life but Jesus, I never heard Jewish like that!"[13]

Whatever Singer might have been feeling concerning the misunderstanding of his current position, he fed the view of himself as just the man the Academy had described. Anecdotes abounded: when Alma came to tell him of the award, he recalled, "I didn't jump. I didn't dance. I couldn't believe it. But I said to her, 'In any case, let's eat breakfast. We have to eat. What do you think—you stop eating because of happiness?' Pressed to provide an informal understanding of his work, Singer replied: "Asking an author for an interpretation of his books is like asking a chicken what chemicals it used when it laid an egg." He went out of his way to appear as the quintessential grandfather: "Asked which of his works might have led to his winning the prize, Singer declined to say: 'If you have 10 children, you don't ask which one is the favorite. I have no favorites; my readers might have favorites, but I don't.'"[14] Just a week or so later, Singer quipped in a somewhat more modern vein to an audience at Bloomingdale's in Fresh Meadows, Queens, "I don't write messages. I just write stories...love stories, sex stories. No message."[15]

Clearly, Singer had no wish to challenge the Swedish Academy's assertion that he was the prototype of a quaint and naively logical people, whose aphoristic wisdom flowed from him naturally and with touching directness. As *The Southern Israelite* enthused: "And yet there is something particularly satisfying about Singer's selection and the way he received the news: 'Yesterday I was a Yiddish writer, today I'm a Nobel Laureate, tomorrow I'll be a Yiddish writer.' Singer is a Shayner Yid and a mensch."[16]

To his credit, Singer was modest about the award. Joking that "I didn't write for prizes—but since it came I take it like a man...," he also indicated that "Tolstoy was a candidate and some other writer got it...so the prize, while it's pleasant to get it, it doesn't prove really so much...." and even that "I'm grateful, but at the same time I am sorry that writers greater than I did not get it." Given his struggles with his brother, Singer may have been thinking of Israel Joshua as one of the literary heroes unacknowledged by the Swedish Academy. And he did mention his family, honoring his ancestry for the talent that had garnered him the prize: "Asked what led him to become a writer, Singer said his father had done some writing, as had his brother and sister, both now dead. 'I took a piece of paper and a pen and pencil and I tried to scribble....'"[17]

Perhaps Singer's need to defer to his family stemmed in part from the strange fact that he had received the ultimate reward for achievements that his parents, in particular his father, had disdained as sacrilegious. An article that appeared less than two weeks after the announcement of the prize indicates how much his parents and their reactions were on his mind at the time: "In his most recent book, *Shosha*, Singer writes of a rabbi's son who has affairs with three women at once, and who makes love to a friend's wife. Of this, he is sure, his parents would not have approved."[18]

Was he now a truly distinguished author or merely a *gantser knaker*, a self-important "big-shot" of whom his parents would never be proud? The question haunted the new Nobel laureate—and he was not confident of the answer. A cashier at Sheldon's, a neighborhood drugstore and luncheonette that Singer favored, remembers calling Singer to congratulate him on his great award. "I said, 'This is Bob from Sheldon's,' and Singer said, 'You can call me big shot. Everybody wants to call me Mr. but you can call me Big Shot.'"

Another account shows the same conflict. Singer is reported to have said, when reached on the big day: "'And now there are reporters here, and a photographer, and the phone is ringing, just like I was some kind of a big shot.' When a reporter suggested that in some circles Singer has been considered a big shot for some time, the writer answered, speaking with his marked Yiddish accent, 'Those are the most wonderful words to hear, because a real big shot is big whether he is recognized or not.'"[19] Singer had been talking about himself as a *gantser knaker*, which is used to mean "big shot" ironically and sometimes even pejoratively in Yiddish. The American reporter had, of course, not understood that Singer was probably poking fun at himself. At the same time, Singer was happy to be thought of as a real big shot, even if his parents would not have appreciated the assessment and even if he would never, in his own mind, rival his brother.

The *Washington Post*, perhaps seeking to inject some excitement into an award around which there was not much gossip, reported that: "Rumors in Stockholm before the announcement suggested a conflict within the academy between a faction favoring British novelist Graham Greene and another backing Turkish writer Yasar Kemal, which might have encouraged a compromise choice."[20]

If Singer had been preoccupied with the Nobel prize, he gave no hint of it; neither did he indicate any knowledge of the possible controversy around the award of the prize. "Some of my friends have said from time to time, 'I wish you the Nobel prize'.... But never did I know I was really being considered."[21] Other anecdotes cast doubt on this innocence. Mirra Ginsburg, one of Singer's earliest translators who is also a prominent translator of Russian literature, tells of being invited to a reception at the Swedish Consulate shortly before the award of the prize. At first, she did not understand why she had been included. Then she saw Singer and inquired after her friend and colleague, Elizabeth Shub. Explaining that Ms. Shub had not been invited, Singer added: "She's just a translator." Ginsburg retorted: "Well, who am I?" She understood that Singer may well have suspected that he was being "interviewed" for the Nobel prize, and that he was not inclined to be generous to his long-time collaborators.[22] In particular, Singer may have excluded Shub because, as the daughter of a renowned Yiddish literary critic, she was in a position to compare the potential laureate to other Yiddish writers. Alma Singer echoed the idea that the invitation to the Swedish Embassy for a cocktail party seemed to be a prelude to the award of the prize.[23]

In striking contrast to Singer's protestations of ignorance, his son, Israel Zamir, spoke with open jubilance about *his* Nobel fantasies for his father. An article in the *Jerusalem Post*, with the headline "How Singer's kibbutznik son heard the news," reports: "He was plating metals at the kibbutz's metal plating plant when he heard on the three o'clock news Thursday that his father...had won the Nobel prize for Literature. In an excited voice he told *The Jerusalem Post* that he couldn't believe it. 'In 1967 when S.Y. Agnon received the prize, I was sure that father didn't have a chance anymore, because they wouldn't give the prize to another Jewish writer. Last year when Saul Bellow received the prize then I knew that was it, he being both an American and Jewish writer."[24] Alma Singer suggests that her husband's supposed lack of interest may not have been completely genuine. She confirmed that, when Bellow won the Nobel prize in 1976, Singer was upset, believing that his chances for winning the prize had evaporated.[25]

Zamir, living in a small country that tended to view Yiddish as the symbol of Eastern–European–Jewish submissiveness and fear, spoke as a provincial wanting to appear astute and sophisticated about Nobel politics. His father, a more urbane and cosmopolitan person, nonetheless wanted to appear anything but worldly-wise and aware, regardless of how much he actually understood. At the same time, Singer's award may have fulfilled a dream of his son's to be recognized in the reflected glory of the "objective" acclaim his father was receiving. To be the abandoned son of an obscure Yiddish writer would surely not have granted Zamir a sense of mirrored glory. To be the son of the Nobel laureate for literature for 1978 was a different story.

Ironically, Singer's reward for upholding the vigor of Eastern European Jewry came just as he was starting to address the demise of that world. The publication of *Shosha* occurred in 1978, and *Enemies, A Love Story* was published in 1972. Both of these novels admit that Polish Jewry had been destroyed, except in memory. *Enemies* was the first of Singer's novels published in English that explicitly discussed the Holocaust, with its physical, psychological, and religious devastation. Moreover, in *Enemies*, Singer indirectly addresses the issue of his increasingly frequent appearances in translation.

Herman Broder, the protagonist of the novel, is hardly a successful author in English. Rather, he is a ghost writer for the vulgarly good-natured but hypocritical Rabbi Milton Lampert. The notion of being a ghost writer is immensely fitting, however. Herman is himself a sort of ghost, haunted by the children he has lost in the Holocaust and by the wife he believes has died as well. Writing for Rabbi Lampert, Herman brings to life creations that are not authentically his own but that serve an important purpose to an American audience longing for spiritual substance.

Did Singer actually believe that his own translated writings were phony? Probably not, but if the musings of Herman Broder have validity for the thoughts of their author, then there was something mendacious about creating in one voice for consumption in another. Herman says: "As long as I don't see the reader I deceive and he doesn't see me, I can stand it. Besides, what I write for the rabbi doesn't do any harm. On the contrary."[26] A more radical statement about the difficulty in trying to render meaning from his native tongue into a foreign language occurs as Herman talks Yiddish to Yadwiga, his Polish wife. Yadwiga is about to convert, but, even when she becomes Jewish, she will never know Yiddish and will never, therefore, know Herman's most profound reality.

Herman regularly goes to the Bronx in pursuit of Masha, his Yiddish-speaking mistress, telling Yadwiga that he is off selling books. One day, out of frustration with Yadwiga, he blurts out his infidelity—but in Yiddish, which she is incapable of comprehending: "'Tonight I'll be eating supper in Philadelphia.' 'Who will you eat with? Alone?' He started talking to Yadwiga in Yiddish. 'Alone. That's what you think! I'll be eating with the Queen of Sheba. I'm as much a book salesman as you're the Pope's wife! That faker of a rabbi I work for—still, if it weren't for him, we'd be starving. And that female in the Bronx is a sphinx altogether. What with the three of you, it's an absolute miracle I haven't gone out of my mind. Pif-pof!'" Yadwiga responds to this unrecognized diatribe with the simple words: "'Talk so I can understand you!'"[27]

This passage is filled with Herman's rage and despair: fury at the ones who support, even love him, yet at the same time suppress his freedom of expression; and terror that he will not be capable of emotionally sustaining the pressures of his deception. Most of all, Herman admits his need to tell the truth and articulates the idea that truth may emerge and yet not destroy if it is transmitted so that no one can understand it. But what good is a truth that is not understood, and what happens to an individual who knows the truth, and even utters it, realizing that he will get no confirming response? Gimpel had made peace with the loneliness of his perceptions. Herman cannot.

Like Herman, Singer had a wife to whom he could not reveal himself in the original, and his position was even more complicated than that of his protagonist. He was understood by the Yiddish writers who knew his language, but they could not appreciate his situation as cultural interpreter. The readers who loved his work in English were not able to resonate with his history and the culture that he was literally trying to raise from the dead. They might be able to see the symbolic importance of Tamara, Herman's first wife, who turns up alive after Herman has presumed himself a widower. Singer could not be sure, however, that they would realize the depth of his urge to create Tamara and the importance of her existence, even within the limits of fiction.

There is no indication that Singer despised his audiences as much as Herman was capable of hating his hangers-on. Nonetheless, perhaps his compulsive quipping and hedging were a means of ridiculing his admirers for their incapacity to take in just how serious and grim he could be.

In the Yiddish-speaking world, news of the Nobel award did not evoke misinformation and misconceptions. Instead, it caused elation in some quarters and consternation in others. Singer's fans rejoiced; his foes mumbled their dissatisfaction. The respected Yiddish writer, Chaim Grade, author of such admired novels as *The Agune* and the monumental *Yeshiva*, went so far as to call the event a "great tragedy for the Jewish people."[28] Still, everyone understood that the Yiddish language had achieved public dignity in the eyes of the non-Jewish public.

In a series of bold headlines, the *Forverts* quickly appropriated its long-time employee:

> *YITSKHOK BASHEVIS-ZINGER KRIGT DI NOBEL-PREMYE;*
> *DOS ERSHTE MOL, AZ A YIDISH-SHRAYBER KRIGT NOBEL PRAYZ;*
> *BASHEVIS IZ ZINT ZAYN ERSHTN TOG IN AMERIKE GEVEN A MITGLID FUN "FORVERTS;"*
> *DI SHVEDISHE KOMISYE LOYBT DERIKER ZAYN GROYS VERK "IN MAYN TATNS BEZDN SHTUB."*

> YITSKHOK BASHEVIS-SINGER RECEIVES NOBEL PRIZE;
> THE FIRST TIME THAT A YIDDISH WRITER GETS NOBEL PRIZE.

BASHEVIS HAS BEEN A MEMBER OF THE
"FORVERTS" SINCE HIS FIRST DAY IN AMER-
ICA;
THE SWEDISH COMMISSION PRAISES MAINLY
HIS GREAT WORK "IN MY FATHER'S
COURT."

Significantly, the article refers to the author as Bashevis, except when quoting the Swedish Academy; it begins with an explicit distinction between Isaac Bashevis Singer and Yitskhok Bashevis: "Yitskhok Bashevis, famous in other languages as Isaac Bashevis-Singer, has received the Nobel prize for literature for the year 1978." But the paper's agenda was clearly not related to literary matters. Next to the lead article reporting the announcement of the prize was an editorial comment by the editor of the *Forverts*, Shimen Weber, claiming that, when he reached the author in Miami Beach, Bashevis's first words were: "Without the *Forverts* it would not have been possible." It is curious that Singer seems not to have expressed his gratitude to the paper elsewhere. Was he being extravagantly polite or frankly disingenuous? Or was Weber taking editorial liberties? In any case, the *Forverts* went to town, underscoring the idea of the Nobel prize for Yiddish, while virtually ignoring the author's unique talents as a writer.

Some of this focus served to bolster the position of the paper, as well as to enhance Weber's importance. Singer played along, contributing to the notion that the Nobel prize was a general honor more than a specific one for himself. As Weber put it in his editorial: "The *mazltov* we gave Bashevis is also a *mazltov* for all of us—writers and readers of Yiddish."[29] Singer went even further: "I am not the only winner of the Prize. I share it with all of my readers, and with all lovers of the Yiddish language."[30]

Not everyone appreciated Singer's generosity. As usual, the communist-leaning *Morgn-frayhayt* could not resist a jab at the latest recognition of the man who represented all they could not abide: "Emphasizing the very important and the positive in the act of the Swedish Academy, we must also honestly say that in the Yiddish writers' world, I. Bashevis-Singer has been and will be evaluated not at all unanimously with praise because of the sexual element and the reactionary mysticism of his writing—which definitely made his work into 'best sellers' in English and other languages. There are greater Yiddish writers, just to mention two: Elye Shekhtman and Avrom Sutskever."[31] And, several weeks later, columnist Ber Grin accused the *Forverts* of systematically building up "a Singer cult over a period of years."[32]

It was not only the writers themselves who grumbled about the ill-judgement of the Academy. A scene that took place at the Jewish Public Library in Montreal was typical:

"The old men were not impressed.

'*S'iz a shanda!*—It's a disgrace,' one feisty octogenarian declared.

'*S'past nisht!*—It's entirely inappropriate!' said another.

'*Tfu, tfu, tfu!*' iterated a third.

"It wasn't the fact that a Nobel prize for Yiddish had been so long in coming which irked them; it was the fact that once it arrived, it had gone to Isaac Bashevis Singer.

'They should have given it better to Chaim Grade!'

'No, no, not Grade. To *Peretz*! Peretz was the greatest of the Yiddish writers. The prize should have gone to him.'

"The colloquy continued for some time longer, but finally they reached consensus (no small feat among this contentious group): they agreed that Y. L. Peretz, the classic Yiddish writer who died in 1915, should have been awarded the 1978 Nobel prize in Literature. When the head librarian, who had come over to try to restore some semblance of order, heard this judgment, she patiently explained that the Swedish Academy could only award the prize to a writer who was still alive. This intelligence elicited an immediate and unanimous response. '*Akhhh!*' cried the old men, '*Antisemitn!*'" ("anti-Semites!").[33]

While Singer was not immune to the insults of his detractors, he did not have much time to brood during the weeks between the award of the prize and the actual festivities in Stockholm. He was the man of the hour, featured in a two-part interview in the pages of the *New York Times Magazine*, and feted by the American Jewish Committee. Its magazine, *Present Tense*, honored him for his "outstanding achievements in the literary world." Richard Maas, president of the Committee, noted that Singer was "an outstanding interpreter of a bygone era of European Jewish culture who has made that glorious page in Jewish history come alive for the world audience."[34]

Singer remained charming and modest during all the hubbub, but he could not deny that he was overwhelmed by the attention. *The Washington Post* reported that Singer was "finding that all the notoriety and excitement generated by the prize he won earlier this month is upsetting his quiet life-style and affecting his health. 'My doctor told me yesterday no more lectures, at least until the Nobel ceremony in Sweden in December,' said Singer at a forum at Virginia Commonwealth University yesterday. 'I've been so busy since the prize announcement I haven't written a word. It seems like ten years,' he said."[35]

Singer was accompanied to Stockholm by Alma, Shimen Weber, his editor, Roger Straus, and Straus's wife, Dorothea. Each in a different way had been close to him over the preceding years. Less so was Singer's son, Israel Zamir, who was present as well. It remains unclear whether Singer was using this opportunity to further his ties with his son, whether he wanted to show the Academy and the world that he was, indeed, a kindly family man, or whether he knew he would receive good coverage in Israel if his son, a reporter for the daily *Al Hamishmar*, were on the scene. Alma's sister and brother-in-law, with whom the Singers were in frequent contact in New York, were excluded from the party. Their daughter recalls: "My parents were very hurt...when Isaac got the Nobel prize; they were not invited, but other people were."[36]

Weber later devoted an entire issue of the *Forverts* to the Nobel festivities, but his actual presence on the scene was irrelevant. As a *New York Times* reporter mockingly pointed out: "Simon Weber, the managing editor, flew to Stockholm with Mr. Singer. If Yiddish was never before heard in the Swedish Academy, it is no less rare for The Forward to send a correspondent, let alone the managing editor, all the way to Europe just for a story. Still, because of the costs of cabling stories across the ocean, Mr. Weber wrote his article in New York and left it behind to be set in type. He included the news that Mr. Singer received a great ovation. Did anyone doubt that he deserved an ovation? Would anyone be brash enough to pose as a false prophet and say Mr. Singer would not get a great ovation?"[37]

And, of course, Singer did delight. But, while his quips and ironic comments around the ceremony were characteristically clever, the acceptance speech itself was serious, even grave. It made no excuses for Yiddish or the first writer to have won the Nobel prize in that language. Singer mesmerized the audience by uttering one sentence of his speech in Yiddish. It was an explicit expression of love and respect for his native tongue: "The high honor bestowed upon me by the Swedish Academy is also a recognition of the Yiddish language—a language of exile, without a land, without frontiers, not supported by any government...." *The New York Times* commemorated the occasion by publishing the quotation in Yiddish characters (with type set by the *Forverts*) and with a transcription supposedly supplied by Singer himself. It is hard to imagine, though, that Singer would have confused *melukhe* 'government' with the nonexistent *meluchoch*, as it finally appeared.[38]

The Swedish Academy was aware of the social conflicts that the young Bashevis had faced while maturing in the maelstrom of early twentieth-century Jewish life in Warsaw. Yet, in his introduction, the secretary of the Academy, Lars Gyllensten, revealed that the decision to recognize Singer was not based on Bashevis's aesthetic struggles: "Singer has perhaps given of his best as a consummate story teller and stylist in the short stories and in the numerous and fantastic novellas.... The passions and crazes are personified in these strange tales as demons, spectres and ghosts, all kinds of infernal or supernatural powers from the rich storehouse of Jewish popular belief or his own imagination.... The middle ages seem to spring to life again in Singer's works...."[39]

Reflecting on the festivities, Israel Zamir speculated wryly that his father's work had appealed to the Academy because "Bashevis talks about demons and they have their tradition of trolls." He further commented that, in his opinion, his father had not cared if the members of the Academy understood his work or not.[40]

In his speech, Singer simplified his original community to some extent, using the familiar, if incorrect, term "ghetto" to apply to his milieu in Warsaw: "The ghetto was not only a place of refuge for a persecuted minority but a great experiment in peace, in self-discipline and in humanism.... I was brought up among those people."[41] At the same time, he did not indulge in nostalgia. The compromise may have been a means of softening the gap between his own perceptions and those of his hosts. Gyllensten had provided a description of Warsaw that Singer's family would not have recognized as home: "His father was a Rabbi of the Hasid school of

piety, a spiritual mentor for a motley collection of people who
sought his help. Their language was Yiddish—the language of the
simple people and of the mothers.... It is Singer's language. And it
is a storehouse which has gathered fairytales and anecdotes, wisdom, superstitions and memories for hundreds of years...."

Nonetheless, Singer did not focus his speech on timeless spiritu-
ality and artless provincialism. Rather, he sought to situate himself
within an international elite of sophisticated modern writers and
thinkers: "I am not ashamed to admit that I belong to those who
fantasize that literature is capable of bringing new horizons and
new perspectives—philosophical, religious, esthetical and even
social. In the history of old Jewish literature there was never any
basic difference between the poet and the prophet. Our ancient
poetry often became law and a way of life. Some of my cronies in
the cafeteria near the Jewish Daily Forward in New York call me a
pessimist and a decadent, but there is always a background of faith
behind resignation. I found comfort in such pessimists and deca-
dents as Baudelaire, Verlaine, Edgar Allan Poe and Strindberg."

Even while seeming to respond to Gyllensten's comments,
Singer underscored his worldliness: "My interest in psychic
research made me find solace in such mystics as your Swedenborg
and in our own Rabbi Nachman Bratzlaver.... I often play with the
idea that when all social theories collapse and wars and revolutions
leave humanity in utter gloom, the poet—whom Plato banned
from his Republic—may rise up to save us all."

Citing writers with whom his audience would be familiar, Singer
sought to make sure that he would not be regarded as merely
parochial, even though he spent much of the remainder of his talk
paying homage to his family and to Yiddish—the language and
the culture it represented for him. After all the years, he remained
in conflict. Was he the sole survivor and inadequate representative
of a family that had embodied the ideals of Jewish orthodoxy?
Was he a secular but spiritual soul who had closely observed his
family's arguments and strife and managed to depict those ordeals
in their fullest controversy? Or was he simply a brilliant wastrel,
who had grabbed the benefits of intellectual privilege, ridden the
coattails of his fine and generous brother, and dishonestly claimed
his brother's mantle after Israel Joshua's sudden death? Perhaps
even worse to contemplate: had he attained recognition because he

had survived the Holocaust, while other, potentially greater, writers had perished? By tipping his hat to the literary and cosmopolitan Bashevis, he could maintain continuity with the self he had
known in that distant and now annihilated environment. But he
could not fail to recognize that the award was clearly for Singer and
not for Bashevis.

As if needing to resuscitate Bashevis, and even Yitskhok, Singer
took care to pay homage: to his parents, to his friend Tseytlin, and
above all, to his brother. Suggesting that his parents might well
have been perplexed by his fame as a secular artist, he went on to
explain that his home had nonetheless been the incubator for the
imagination that captivated his audience: "As a child I had heard
from my brother and master, I. J. Singer, who later wrote 'The
Brothers Ashkenazi,' all the arguments that the rationalists from
Spinoza to Max Nordau brought out against religion. I have heard
from my father and mother all the answers that faith in God could
offer those who doubt and search for the truth. In our home and in
many other homes the eternal questions were more actual than the
latest news in the Yiddish newspaper. In spite of all the disenchant-
ments and all my skepticism I believe that the nations of the world
can learn much from those Jews.... To me the Yiddish language
and the conduct of those who spoke it are all identical."

With these words, Singer elucidated his paradox: having gleaned
his sophisticated secular view at the edge of his conflict over orthodoxy and faith, he was now in the position of upholding the views
of his parents, even as he had to pay his respects to the brother who
had set the arguments in relief when he was still a child. Having
survived to preserve it all, he could not abandon his own views—he
was too much an artist for that—but he had to try and incorporate
all the quarrels into his writing, sequentially if not all at once. But
his audiences could not read him as the epitome of paradox; they
had to simplify in accordance with their own perspectives, which,
in general, could not encompass all the disharmony.

Characteristically, *The New York Times* omitted the comments
concerning Poe and Plato; even Israel Joshua was missing from the
report. Instead, the paper concentrated on Singer's remarks about
the Yiddish language and those who had spoken it. The impression
was one of unworldliness that reinforced the stereotype and failed
to reflect Singer's literary cosmopolitanism: "In his lecture he said

he thought there were lessons for the world in the Jews of the ghetto whom he has portrayed. They were people, he said, who were admirable in their way of thinking and their way of bringing up children and in their ability to find happiness where others saw only misery. 'The Yiddish mentality is not haughty,' he continued. 'It does not demand and command, but it muddles through, sneaks by, smuggles itself amidst the powers of destruction, knowing somewhere that God's plan for creation is still at the very beginning.'"[42]

The New York Times article made sure to include the quips and jokes that were always a delight to Singer's readers and that served to underscore the view of him as winsome and naive. Describing the audience of about 400, John Vinocur wrote: "Sitting on uncomfortable blue upholstered benches, they vigorously applauded, and they laughed hard when Mr. Singer joked after the speech that he was going to buy a new Yiddish typewriter with his $165,000 prize money.... The problem with his old typewriter, he said, was that after 40 years it had turned into a critic and refused to function when it did not like what he was writing."

Perhaps inadvertently, the *Times* article exposes Singer's cruel streak, revealing that the Nobel laureate had never resolved his feelings of competition towards sibling figures. Saul Bellow, whose earlier award of the prize had evidently rankled with Singer, had nonetheless helped launch his English-language career. Bellow was about ten years younger than Singer; but Bellow was a prominent American-Jewish writer at a time when Singer was unknown in the United States. His youth precluded his assuming the role of older brother and mentor, and he was all the more enraging for having reached the Nobel pinnacle first. Singer, who might have used his moment of glory to thank an old supporter, instead took the opportunity to put down his colleague. Vinocur writes: "In an interview before the lecture, in telling a visitor that he wanted to make his address simple, fast and understandable, he said he knew that many Nobel laureates before him took a heavy cosmic approach that he wanted to avoid. Referring to Saul Bellow, the 1976 laureate, the 1978 laureate said: 'I heard Bellow talked for 45 minutes and no one understood.'"[43]

Singer's subsequent actions showed that he was unrepentant about his behavior in Stockholm. Bellow wrote a letter of reproach, which Singer did not answer personally; instead, he delegated his secretary to compose a response. When Singer came to Chicago for a round of congratulations after he returned from Stockholm, Bellow attended the festivities, much to Singer's surprise. But Bellow had the last word, in Yiddish, telling the guest of honor that he had only come so that Singer would not have the satisfaction of saying that he had avoided him. Nonetheless, almost twenty years after the fact, Bellow still bristles at the memory of the insult: "I was deeply irritated."[44]

Clearly, the 1978 laureate might have talked with as much gravity and cosmic innuendo as he pleased; the public continued to recognize only what was poignant and seemingly humble in his remarks. Everyone wanted to view him as a kindly old grandfather. Even his post-presentation dinner was the subject of journalistic comment. Once again, Singer stood out as the unusual and somehow saintly Jew: "After the presentations, the Nobel laureates and Swedish royalty led 1200 guests through the cold, dark streets to the glittering Town Hall for the traditional banquet and ball. Banquet guests dined on lobster, duck, champagne and ice cream. But Singer, who's a vegetarian, had a special menu prepared just for him. He was served Israeli avocado, artichoke bottoms and a vegetable main dish."[45] Saul Bellow, reflecting on the VIP treatment, comments pointedly: "He may have been on a green diet, but he hadn't stopped drinking blood."[46] The fact that a number of the other Nobel honorees were Jews, who might have been uncomfortable consuming lobster, did not seem to concern anyone.

The greatest irony for Singer may have been the treatment he received in the *Forverts*, where he had flourished as Bashevis and wrangled publicly with the different aspects of his literary identity. No less than the American press, the *Forverts* sought to portray the man they now considered to be their possession in the warmest, most palatable light possible. The paper published a special Chanukah issue, dedicated to Singer, which appeared on December 24, 1978. That issue contained, among other things, Shimen Weber's "diary" of the Stockholm adventure. The tone of this document is as revealing and informative as the content.

"Perl fun der yidisher poezye" ("Pearls from Yiddish Poetry") was a regular column in the *Forverts*. In the special issue, the column contained an introduction concerning Bashevis's Nobel lec-

ture. In an evident move to create a similarity between Bashevis and other lovers of Yiddish, the selections themselves were all devoted to the subject of the Yiddish language. On the same page as the *Perl*, the *Forverts* reprinted the photo of Bashevis and his brother that had originally appeared in the rotogravure section of the paper in 1935, when Bashevis had first arrived in the States.[47] Years after that inauspicious moment, Singer recalled that, at the moment of his greatest triumph, "'I felt my brother standing there with me on the stage in Stockholm, sharing the prize and celebrating the victory of Yiddish....'"[48] Nonetheless, it was a different matter for the *Forverts* to remind the Yiddish-speaking world that the Man of the Hour was still Israel Joshua's younger brother. English readers were encouraged to view Singer as an innocuous old man, bravely shouldering an entire culture; Yiddish readers were presented with a link in the chain of literary and social tradition.

Weber's diary exposes the paper's stance with even greater clarity than the *Perl*, and it simultaneously sets up a strong division between Singer and Bashevis. Whoever Singer may be, the tone of the diary suggests, we are proud of him; but the real laureate is our own Bashevis. However, the *Forverts*'s description of Bashevis as a modest, simple, and familiar soul—intriguingly similar to the Singer so beloved by his English-reading public—has a false and disconcerting ring to anyone familiar with Bashevis the cynic and sophisticate. The paper was trying to conform to the English-speaking view of the Nobel laureate, but with a twist: the new Bashevis was more homespun and kindly than the original one, but he was personalized for people who knew their way around Judaism and Eastern-European-Jewish customs and mannerisms.

Perhaps inadvertently, Weber reveals the new vision, as well as his realization of a split, in the magically tinged introduction to his diary: "...when I tell my friends and colleagues at the *Forverts* what happened in Stockholm, I have the feeling that I am telling them a fairy tale, in which my imagination has transformed Cinderella into a Yiddish writer, my old friend Yitskhok Bashevis-Singer, whom we call simply Bashevis."[49]

The general allusion is clear: Bashevis, who has labored patiently and without proper recognition under the yoke of a dying language, one that has been defeated and annihilated by the decimation of its speakers by a cruel and murderous force, is suddenly elevated, magically transported to a real palace, in order to be rewarded for his efforts. But then the connection becomes less clear. Who is the fairy godmother? Perhaps the *Forverts*, or maybe Shimen Weber himself. Will the happy ending be the unification of Bashevis and Singer, Cinderella promoted to royalty and living in the palace of her adopted land? Most important—at least from the point of view of Weber—will Yiddish now live happily ever after in a fairy-tale position of prominence? Can the Court on Krochmalna Street in Warsaw be transported to the Court in Stockholm?

While not neglecting to give adequate attention to the pomp and circumstance of the occasion, Weber was writing for readers who longed to feel personally connected to current events within their increasingly isolated community. Therefore, he emphasized the homey side of the festivities, often referring to Singer as Bashevis-Singer when describing the ceremonial events and reserving Bashevis for the interactions with Jews. While the world at large read Bashevis's Nobel lecture, readers of the *Forverts* learned that, in the middle of the official greetings at the airport, a *kokhlefl*—literally a cooking spoon, someone who stirs things up—jumped at Bashevis and started kissing him, although Bashevis had never seen this man before. Weber reported that Bashevis had gone to synagogue on the Sabbath, together with the other Jewish Nobel prize winners, and that he had received the first "aliya," because of his position as a *kohen*, a member of the priestly class, and that there had been a number of Jews in that audience at his lecture who had never attended a ceremony at the Academy before, but who now felt themselves "as if at their own party."

Perhaps the most obvious example of Weber's attempt to write a modern Yiddish fairy tale is his account of the time Bashevis and Alma spent alone drinking coffee with the King and Queen of Sweden, after the banquet at the palace: "After the meal, the King and Queen summoned *Singer* and his wife separately to drink coffee and to chat. They spent 20 minutes alone. When *Bashevis* finished his coffee standing up and didn't know what to do with the cup, the Queen took it from him and carried it over to a little table. He told the queen about his nervousness at meeting a royal couple face to face—'Your Majesty knows I was not raised in a royal palace.' She assured him that she, too, was nervous before she met him, because she was unused to the company of a great writer such as Bashevis."[50]

Even the *Forverts* advertisements were susceptible to depicting Singer as a homespun hero. The Chanukah edition carried a message from EL AL: "EL AL Israel Airlines salutes the humble genius of Isaac Bashevis Singer." Under the photo appears a familiar-sounding quote: Singer says, "I will still live at the same address. I will still have the same telephone number. Do you think that winning a prize can change a man's character?"[51]

Singer himself emphasized that life would go on as usual for him: "No writer stops writing because he gets a prize," he said, "...what else is there to do, a man of my age?"[52] Very likely, he believed his own words, not realizing that the Nobel award might have an unexpected effect on him.

Years later, Saul Bellow indicated that he was capable of understanding Singer's position, despite his dismay at how he had been treated: "The Stockholm Prize elicited kinky reactions from everyone. Before the year was out I was ready to trade my gold medal for a beautiful house in the Canary Islands. But Singer in his own intricate fashion was really very conventional. He saw the Nobel prize as the crown of glory."[53]

Almost exactly one year after the 1978 announcement, *The New York Times* published an article entitled "Has the Nobel prize changed Singer's Life?" The article, which appeared in the Living section of the paper, featured the customary benign and spritely Singer, described with "blue, Rip Van Winkle eyes." Perhaps this designation was an unconscious association to periwinkle blue, but the effect suggests a man who has slept through history. The reporter notes that Singer had put dark glasses over these eyes, commenting: "Too bright out." Perhaps the Nobel laureate, who had not lost his sense of humor, was playing his own small joke, knowing that his American interviewer would not recognize the Yiddish literary affectation of wearing sunglasses when performing. In the interview, Singer discussed his worry over whether or not he had mailed a certain letter: "'I have such crises every day....I need suspense, not only in my novels, but in life itself. If there is not positive suspense, then there is negative suspense.'"

Moreover, Singer evidently needed to create anxiety and suspense in Alma. No doubt intending to illustrate Singer's genial side, the *Times* article reproduced an interaction between husband and wife. What appears instead is a cruelly teasing Singer and an obviously distressed Alma: "Two hours had passed by the time Mrs. Singer gently mentioned to her husband, whose energy showed no signs of flagging, that they ought to be thinking about dinner. The next day they were scheduled to leave for an eight-day stay in Florida.... 'I hear it's been very hot down there,' Mrs. Singer said. 'Maybe we shouldn't go,' her husband replied. 'Let's forget the whole thing.' A wry smile suggested he was gently teasing her, but she looked at him aghast. 'I'm all packed,' she said. 'So unpack,' he replied. 'But we've told everyone we're going,' she said. 'Didn't I have enough heat already this summer?' he said, obviously enjoying the byplay. 'We've made the reservations,' Mrs. Singer said. 'Then cancel them,' he said. 'But we can't cancel them. We have the Super Saver fare.' Isaac Bashevis Singer smiled benignly at his wife. 'So then,' he concluded, 'we will go.'"[54]

Sadly, Singer had been correct. The Nobel prize had not changed him. He maintained his self-presentation as the impish but mild old man, appealing to the audience who loved him but could never really understand all his intellect and complexity. He persisted in twitting Alma, who could not hope to match his wit or counter his mean flirtation. Unfortunately, business as usual for Singer continued to mean that he suffered from feelings of deep internal emptiness, which could only be held at bay by writing fiction and by creating fiction within his life. The world's highest literary acclaim had done nothing to alleviate the core of his malaise.

10

SINGER insisted that he would continue writing after the award of the Nobel prize: "...what else is there to do, a man of my age?"[1] During the thirteen years between 1978 and Singer's death in 1991, however, only two novels appeared in English. One of these, *The Penitent*, had been serialized in the *Forverts* ten years before it was introduced in translation. The other, *The King of the Fields*, seems to have made little critical impression, possibly because of its strangely distant setting and characters. In addition to the novels, Singer published some memoirs in translation, as well as several volumes of stories. Until 1987, he continued writing stories as well as longer works for the *Forverts*.

The slowdown, subtle as it was, may have been due partly to the advancement of years; after all, Singer had been seventy-four at the time of the award. But, even as he stepped back as a writer of novels and short stories, his public presence as an American celebrity increased during the same period. The expanded prominence occurred because Singer's works were now being "translated" from English prose to other media, often with the author's active participation. To the extent that he was consciously pursuing personal and cultural immortality, Singer's interest in having versions of his work produced in theater, film, and television makes sense. He had been nimbly diversifying his audience for years, a fact noted by

Christopher Lehmann-Haupt at the time of the Nobel award: "As for his appeal: one need only note that any writer who can command a following in such disparate publications as the *Jewish Daily Forward,* the *New Yorker, Commentary* and *Playboy* can scarcely be accused of cultural parochialism."[2] In his role as the sole survivor of Jewish Eastern Europe who could capture mainstream attention, Singer understood that he could use the broader forum to reach even more people than had been possible through the channels he had so far exploited.

At the same time, the world's most famous Yiddish author faced a dilemma. If he did not branch out, he would continue to attract only a limited and specialized following. But if he embraced a wider market, he risked the possibility that his culture would appear in approximate, diluted, or even stereotypical portrayals. Moreover, with greater fame would come intensified responsibility, since his audience trusted—not always correctly—that anything with his name attached to it was authentic. When *Teibele and Her Demon* arrived on Broadway in 1979, a *New York Post* reporter made the case that Singer had been instrumental in inspiring an entire revival of Jewish theater in New York: "Isaac Bashevis Singer, by being a practicing Jewish writer with high visibility... and therefore bringing attention to Jewish literature, must be credited as partly responsible for the current renaissance of Jewish-related theater in New York. Plays—some in English, some Yiddish—abound, and the plays are meant to have universal appeal, even if the majority of the audience is Jewish."[3] Singer nowhere indicated, however, that he was worried about having undue popular influence.

There are other, more personal reasons why Singer may have been interested in the changeover from the written word to other forms of communication. According to his son, Singer was after the money. Israel Zamir pointed to his father's materialism: Singer believed that writing for the theater would be lucrative, and that involving himself with movies could be even more profitable.

The specter of Israel Joshua remained as well. Despite his fame, Singer probably never trusted that he had overtaken Israel Joshua. In 1964, for example, twenty years after the elder Singer's death, he had dedicated his volume of stories, *Short Friday,* to his brother, again calling him "my teacher and master in literature" and adding

"I am still learning from him and his work."[4] Moreover, although Singer may have felt vindicated as a novelist by winning the Nobel prize, he had to remember that his older brother had, despite his tragically short life, managed to succeed brilliantly with the theater version of his novel, *Yoshe kalb*. Singer referred to his brother's work on the occasion of his own Broadway debut with *Yentl*: "The first really good play Singer remembers seeing was 'Yoshe Kalb,' an adaptation of his brother's novel which he saw in Paris on his way to America in 1935. In the opinion of the younger brother as well as the public and critics of the time, it was a masterwork of Yiddish theater. (It starred the great Yiddish actor, Maurice Schwartz, who, according to Singer, was 'a spectacle in himself.') I. J. Singer's other famous novel, 'The Brothers Ashkenazi,' was also adapted into an internationally successful Yiddish play."[5] Despite the overt praise, the competitive Singer may also have gained secret glee from the knowledge that his father, who harbored a religious aversion to the theater, would certainly have disapproved of Israel Joshua's *Yoshe kalb*. Years later, the Nobel laureate felt compelled to comment: "I remember my father saying in one of his sermons, 'The wicked sit day and night in the theater, eat pork and sin with loose women.'"[6]

The transfer of Singer's writing into other media had begun before the Nobel award, in a couple of cases much earlier: "Gimpel the Fool" had been adapted into a one-act play and performed at the Mermaid Theater in New York in 1963,[7] ten years after the appearance of the story in *The Partisan Review*. After that, another ten years passed before the Yale Repertory Theater staged a production of "The Mirror." The play was based on one of Singer's earliest short stories, a witty yet somber work about a young woman who is vain and stupid enough to be seduced by an imp.[8] The production, although it received a creditable review in *The New York Times*, was obviously not a hit and did not travel beyond New Haven. The *Times* article does not comment on the task of turning the story, which contained humor and romance as well as a somber meditation on temptation, into a successful play.

A documentary/fantasy production that aired on Public Television in 1972 brought greater acclaim for Singer than "The Mirror," and probably a larger audience as well. Produced by Bruce Davidson, with the help of a grant from the American Film Institute, *Singer's Nightmare and Mrs. Pupko's Beard* won a prize at the 1972

American Film Festival. This production combined the dramatization of a Singer short story, "The Beard," with what might be called
a dramatization of the author's life.[9] Singer appears full-blown as
the kindly grandfather who will some years later stand before the
King of Sweden. He is a gentle, otherworldly soul, writing longhand on pads of paper that somehow manage to look like parch-
ment. He peers with good-natured bewilderment at the adoring
young students who literally sit at his feet. Singer dreams his story,
as if he were a tribal mystic or soothsayer, rather than a sophisticated artist who cared deeply about the function and purpose of literature. Ironically, while the tale of Singer the writer may have
been fictionalized, the story of the bearded lady had its origin in
fact, according to Israel Zamir: "I remember...one day when we
were in a cafeteria on Broadway. Sitting at one of the tables in the
corner was a woman in her sixties with a long white beard, smok-
ing a cigar. Neither my father nor I could take our eyes off her. 'I
sense that she's got a fascinating story,' he whispered to me. A
friend of my father's entered the restaurant, and my father asked
him to introduce him to her. He moved to her table and ended up
talking with her for hours.... Not long after that encounter, his
story 'The Beard' came out."[10]

It was not until 1973, however, that Singer gained access to mainstream theater. Three years earlier, the Chelsea Theater Center's
Robert Kalfin had proposed a stage version of "Yentl the Yeshiva
Boy," and Singer "didn't want to discourage a man 'with good
will.'" Kalfin enlisted his friend Leah Napolin to help Singer turn
the story into a play. The product of their collaboration was first
performed at the Brooklyn Academy of Music, directed by Kalfin.[11]
A considerably trimmed version of *Yentl* opened on Broadway at
the Eugene O'Neill Theater on October 23, 1975.[12] Tova Feldshuh
mesmerized audiences in the title role. "Some time before, Singer
had abandoned his own screen treatment of *Yentl*, a film in which
Barbra Streisand was to star." Streisand went on to produce her version of *Yentl* without Singer's input.

Yentl's story piqued attention and attracted notice; audiences
were unused to a Jewish story in which a girl's hunger for learning
is so immense that it forces her to abandon her traditional female
role, pretend to be a man, marry a woman, and ultimately quit her
home, leaving behind the man and fellow student who has captured

her heart. In addition, such underlying issues as sexual preference, gender identity, and feminism aroused more controversy than if the story had simply concerned a rebellious female longing for knowledge. Some years later, for example, the *Jerusalem Post International* reviewed the Hebrew version of *Yentl* and titled the article "A Lesbian Fable."[13]

The departure from traditional orthodoxy caused a commotion when the play had its run in Brooklyn—especially during scenes that contained apparent nudity. On one occasion, for instance, "a class of yeshiva boys held up the play for fifteen minutes, shrieking and tittering." On another, "when a male character undressed...a husband in the audience took off his hat and put it over his wife's eyes. Later, when a female character appeared in the nude, the wife did the same for her husband."[14] Evidently, the anxiety was a reaction to dramatic sleight of hand: Tovah Feldshuh revealed that "...between you and me...I do not bare my chest. It's the movements of my wonderful leading man...that make you think so."[15]

Singer, however, steadfastly refused to enter into any kind of discussion about gender-related motives in writing the story. In an interview on the occasion of the O'Neill opening, Elenore Lester reported that: "In spite of Yentl's rebellion against orthodox sex customs, Singer doesn't see her as a women's liberationist. That would be mere sociology—a subject that doesn't interest him. 'Yentl doesn't want worldly things,' he says. 'She only wants to study Torah. And she wasn't fighting for other women—only for herself.'"[16] Singer may have written the story without consideration of modern feminism, but it is unlikely that he had forgotten his great-grandmother Temerl, with her startling habit of wearing the ritual fringes of a man and her unprecedented acceptance by the Belzer rebbe; nor had he been unaware of his mother Basheve's proclivity for study and her conflicts over the requirements and limitations imposed upon her as a female.

Feldshuh received rave reviews for her performance; ironically, she was compared with Barbra Streisand, who would only later take on the movie role of Yentl: "...people are saying 'No young girl except Barbra Streisand in recent years has originated a role and become a star a few nights later.'"[17] Feldshuh's performance was described as "so shiningly brilliant the young actress is immediately established in America's first rank." The play, in contrast, was criticized: "After the opening emotional rush, the script... bogs down in detail, wandering away from its dramatic arc. Scenes that were cut are now briefly described in narratives to the audience.... The dialogue is often awkward and some scenes are clumsy and aborted. Ultimately, the play looks stripped down and skimpy, much as the sets begin to on the big, Broadway stage."[18]

The play's shortcomings were not caused by lack of enthusiasm on the part of the actors and the director. Rather, they were a combination of the general problem of rendering a short story into a full-length play, and the specific difficulty of making the story believable. As Mendl Kohansky put the predicament when discussing the Hebrew version: "Even granted the sexual ignorance of a Jewish girl in a 19th-century *shtetl*, it boggles the mind that Haddasah [called Hadass in the English play] can live happily with Yentl for five months without discovering her husband's true sex. A literary magician like Bashevis Singer can make the reader believe anything, but the stage makes its own demands."[19]

Yentl's creators had to determine how many details of orthodox Jewish life to include, especially since part of the play's potential was its capacity to provide a colorful sense of Eastern European *shtetl* existence. The original version was changed for Broadway to be "less of a folk tale and more a psychological story of three individuals united in a strange love relationship."[20] It is difficult to imagine *Yentl* as a folk tale. In Singer's original, Yentl reveals herself to her beloved Avigdor and then realizes that she must either endure seeing him with another woman or relinquish her dreams of learning. Unable to tolerate the impossible repercussion of her self-disclosure, Yentl disappears. In the O'Neill production, "Three lives have been blasted and the community is in turmoil with speculation running to Satanic intervention. This element is cut to a cute chicken-plucking scene among three gossips and we are left with an upbeat ending that strangles the tale."[21]

Who had allowed such a radical and cheapened retelling of Singer's story? It may have been the author himself, who already had a notion of what the American theater-goer liked. Singer's first Yiddish theater experiences in Warsaw had involved imports from the United States, and he had understood the dramatic strategies of those unrefined productions: "'Our *Landsleit* [countrymen] will not be bored.... If a play bores them they start to talk to each other. So one way or another, by some stage trick—whether jokes or music or a wedding or a *kaddish* [prayer of mourning], you must entertain them.'"22 He had even written about the American Yiddish theater: "...the public must be given 'dynamite' to keep it quiet. Second Avenue experience shows that the most successful dramatic 'dynamite' is a scene where the *kaddish* and the wedding canopy were actually more than theatrical effects. They were the very essence of the Yiddish drama, the musical and even the comedy."23

Whatever Singer's reasons for condemning most Yiddish theater as vulgar entertainment, he used the same formulas—or acquiesced to them—when it came to adapting "Yentl, the Yeshiva Boy" for the American stage. And perhaps he was right, if the ecstatic response of Martin Gottfried in the *New York Post* is any example: "The lump in the throat, the thrill, the choked sob, the emotional rush—it is a phenomenon almost exclusive to the theater and when it happens, well, it's like sex. At the moment there is no other moment.... [Yentl's father] has died. Yentl goes to the synagogue where the Kaddish—the prayer for the dead—is to be said for him. She sits in the section to which women are relegated. The prayer begins and suddenly her voice rises over the others. The men gape at her, astounded by the audacity of a woman's praying.... The rabbi waves the objectors off. Her voice soars. Who would not be thrilled?"24

The cast worked hard to absorb the flavor of Singer's milieu. Feldshuh, although Jewish, and acquainted with Hebrew, had to study the way prayers would have been said in a Polish *shtetl*. In addition, she "invaded a Yeshiva dressed as a boy to observe the students' behavior."25 But the instruction went far beyond this: the cast had its own religious coach, an unusual orthodox rabbi whom the director had encountered one day on the Staten Island ferry. "It was not unusual, during rehearsal, to hear the stage manager announce, 'Tomorrow at one o'clock all the actors in the synagogue scene should see the rabbi.'... Rabbi Leonard Kaplan enjoyed advising the cast on ritual and its meaning. He showed them how to sway and bend while they pray, explained what it means to study the Talmud, and in general helped the cast understand the outlook of a religious Jew." Rabbi Kaplan "was not upset by his association with a play which contains nudity as well as a woman dressed as a man.... 'It is an abomination,'" he admitted, "'But so what?'"26

By the time the next adaptation of Singer's work arrived on Broadway, he had won the Nobel prize. *Teibele and Her Demon* had already enjoyed a run at the Guthrie Theater in Minneapolis (where, at least at the time that *Yentl* appeared on Broadway, David Feldshuh, Tovah's brother, was associate director),[27] in 1978, before the award of the prize. The play, written in collaboration with Eve Friedman, opened at the Brooks Atkinson Theater on December 16, 1979. The story[28] concerns an *agune*, an abandoned wife. According to Jewish law, such a woman cannot remarry unless she receives confirmation of her husband's death. Teibele continues her work as the proprietor of a dry goods store, assuaging her loneliness with evening chats in the company of her female friends.

One night, Teibele recounts a story she had read in a book bought from a peddler, about a demon who had lived with a woman and acted as her husband. The local teacher's helper, Alchonon, a man whose greatest ambition was to be a wedding jester, overhears Teibele's story and hatches his own plan. He comes to her and pretends to be the demon Hurmizah. In short, Teibele falls in love with Hurmizah, and the two have a rich and exciting affair—that is, until Alchonon dies during an epidemic. Teibele is seized with the strange desire to accompany his body to the grave, although she has no conscious awareness that he is her own Hurmizah.

Singer's story celebrates two simple people: Teibele reads the stereotypical romantic chapbooks designed for ignorant Jewish women, and Alchonon is a lowly teacher's helper, or *belfer*. Their status is humble, but together they temporarily escape the constraints of their society, through illicit sexuality and playful imagination. The story concludes with Singer's lucid and profound commentary on Teibele's solitary and lonely fate. Having lost both her husband and her demon, "Nothing was left to her of the past except a secret that could never be told and would be believed by no one. There are secrets that the heart cannot reveal to the lips. They are carried to the grave.... The dead will awaken one day, but their secrets will abide with the Almighty and His Judgment until the end of all generations."[29]

On Broadway, the story of Teibele was different, although Singer's basic premise remained. There, Alchonon begins to desire marriage with Teibele. To this end, he invents the information that Teibele's husband is dead, thereby freeing her from the *agune*'s prohibition and making her into an eligible widow. At the same time, as Hurmizah, he tells Teibele that he can no longer be her lover and recommends Alchonon as a replacement. Teibele, although at first opposed to the idea of marrying the shiftless Alchonon, soon complies. In the end, as Teibele is dying, the rabbi directs Alchonon to reinvent Hurmizah.

The play fails entirely to convey Singer's original point, that Eros can be a liberating antidote to the foolishness and senseless constraints of traditional Jewish law. Where *The Mirror* had been a social commentary that needed an imp and the supernatural to make its point, *Teibele and Her Demon* exploits a pseudo-demonic setting to emphasize the psychological needs of fragile human beings. Teibele was much too conventional to contemplate an extramarital affair, but helpless possession by a demon was acceptable. Once she had surrendered, she could find the liaison enjoyable and fulfilling. The superficial similarities of seduction, betrayal, and the supernatural, only serve to underscore the differences between the two stories.

The critics, who praised the cast, this time singling out F. Murray Abraham in his role as Alchonon, had harsh words for the play itself. They complained that the story was too thin for a full-length play and, as they had been with *Yentl*, they were troubled by the unbelievable plot: "we're confused, and we do feel cheated."[30] The play's flaws may have resulted in part from Singer's collaboration, once again with an American woman. For separate reasons, each of them may have failed to realize just how much was being lost in the translation. It was not only a question of changing fiction to dialogue, but also one of shifting a straight description of *shtetl* life into a rendition of that life. It is impossible to know, for instance, who decided that there should be a group sex scene in the play—a detail that completely violates Singer's original portrayal of the community. Was this Singer's idea of what a jaded American audience would require in order to keep it interested?

Not all critics of *Teibele and Her Demon* were oblivious to the corruption of the cultural treasure in the crossover to theater. The most specifically damning comments recognize that the *shtetl* is neither a prison of reactionary thinking from which one must flee, nor a bastion of virtue requiring endless nostalgic devotion: "Worst of all, the play works to strip the story of its dignity. A certain condescension toward the *shtetl*, from which Mr. Singer's work has always been notably free, has crept in. *Teibele* has regressed, half-heartedly and ungracefully, to an essentially earlier period of *shtetl* consciousness. *Teibele* has a lot of tentative, uneasy comedy at the wrong moments. At a bad time in her life, for instance, when at Hormizah's [sic] orders she is about to marry the repulsive Alchonon, Teibele finds 'A prayer to recite when the spirit is heavy'—and raises her eyes and adds 'Oy!' Although Stephen Kanee, the director, presumably directed or allowed Miss Esterman to play this moment for comedy, the authors must take responsibility for that cheap comic 'Oy!' Although Mr. Singer is given credit as coauthor, the play feels as though it had been adapted by some show-biz type not entirely in sympathy with his work."[31]

Eve Friedman, Singer's collaborator, was hardly a show-biz type: "I'm an English teacher for my living and a playwright, too." Friedman published these words in the Theater section of *The New York Times* on December 16, 1979, on the same day that *Teibele and Her Demon* opened on Broadway.[32] The essay, a history of the partnership between the two, purports to be a warm recollection of a growing friendship between a genius and his young but talented writing partner. In reality, Friedman's association with Singer ended in disappointment and rancor.

Singer and Friedman had first encountered one another six years previously at a P.E.N. cocktail party, where they had discovered their mutual dislike of alcohol. Although Singer was swept away by the intrusions that occur to people, particularly famous ones, at cocktail parties, Friedman recalls: "Suddenly I heard him call out, 'Eve! Please phone me. We'll talk some more. We'll have lunch. I'm in the book.'"

What followed was a lunch, a long afternoon of conversation, and the invitation to work together. Friedman relates that she gave the author an opportunity to change his mind; instead, the two initiated a cooperation that evidently lasted several years. Friedman sums up her comments with an appreciation of Singer as a creative genius who cannot be described as "like" anything. Such persons, she concludes "just are." At the same time, however, she hints at a different side of the genius when she demurs that, although she and

Singer "pray for success," the real pay-off for her was the chance to know him: "...my red-letter day was that first Saturday, our brave beginning—two authors who barely knew each other embarking on a creative journey. Once, on one of our walks I remarked to Isaac that his secret might be that he was a child at heart. 'No,' he quickly corrected, 'a man of 30. A 30-year-old man who has forgotten nothing.'"

The implication that Singer was responding to Friedman in at least a mock-seductive way is clear. And things were not always as sunny as Friedman suggests. Although the play had been scheduled to go to Broadway in the Fall of 1978, the producers (Joseph Kipness, Jule Styne, and Marvin A. Krauss) decided to take the play to Washington for an additional try-out. Friedman took legal action to prevent the venture. "'She enjoined us,' said Charlotte Dicker, the associate producer. 'She didn't want to go to Washington. She thought we had already gone out of town. The case was settled out of court, and now everything has been forgiven and forgotten.'"[33]

However others depicted him, Singer continued to appear as the bemused, otherworldly soul that the American public now expected and insisted upon. While the poster for *Teibele* showed "a barechested stud carrying off a passive maiden," Singer was described as "perhaps uncomfortable with the sexiness of the ads," even though he allowed that "Many of my readers, especially women,...might say, 'I wish I had a demon like this.'" Moreover, he professed to be largely uninterested in the actual production of the play: "He admits to not going to the theater very often. 'I'm not even one of those authors who visits his plays every night.'" Singer announced that the play was about "'a bohemian man who desires a woman he knows he has no chance with, because she's religious. So he tells her she has to make love to him or else he'll throw her to the black market.'"[34]

Just a few weeks before the opening of *Teibele and Her Demon*, Singer had made another debut. The new venture was a film version of *The Magician of Lublin*. This production, too, was advertised with a suggestive poster: a man in a tuxedo, covered by a cape that resembles the wings of an eagle, stands, wings unfurled, while at his feet cowers a naked woman. The blurb reads: "A spellbinding story of sex, charm, and supernatural forces."

Lars Gyllensten, the permanent secretary of the Swedish Academy, had commented specifically on *The Magician of Lublin*, contrasting it with *The Slave*: "Even boredom can become a restless passion, as with the main character in the tragi-comic picaresque novel *The Magician of Lublin* (1961), a kind of Jewish Don Juan and rogue, who ends up as an ascetic or saint. In a sense a counterpart to this book is *The Slave* (1962), really a legend of a lifelong, faithful love which becomes a compulsion.... The saint and rogue are near of kin."[35] Gyllensten's sophisticated and delicate discussion of the novel hints at some of the conflict that Bashevis, on his path to becoming Singer, had articulated in the 1960s. The book, although set in Europe, implicitly addresses the author's ambivalence to life in America, with its dangerous attractions and heartbreaking deficiencies; the film does none of that.

Like *Teibele and Her Demon*, the movie version of *The Magician of Lublin* had been in the making for a long time. Already in a 1965 article, Singer had mentioned selling the motion picture rights.[36] And Irving S. White, who eventually acquired the rights and wrote the original screenplay, tells a story of tragedy and delay. The first producer, Walter Reade, was killed in a skiing accident, and the original leading man, Laurence Harvey, died of cancer. In the end, the film was directed by Menahem Golan and produced by him and Yoram Globus. White also gave up part of the writing credit to Golan, and later stated that he was finally embarrassed to be cited at all, given the eventual mess of the screenplay.[37]

Despite its rocky beginnings, the timing of the film seemed unexpectedly felicitous: "After five years of great difficulties, Israeli filmmakers Menahem Golan and Yoram Globus finally managed to put together a production of 'The Magician of Lublin.'...On the final day of filming...the news flashed around the world: Singer had been awarded the 1978 Nobel prize for Literature.'"[38]

If the filmmakers dreamed of riding the Nobel crest to a blockbuster of their own, they must have been sadly disappointed. Perhaps because it was not an American film, the movie did not capture as much notice in New York as had *Teibele*. The reviews of the Broadway play do not even mention the movie, although the play's opening occurred about five weeks after the film's. The attention *The Magician of Lublin* did get was rather negative. Janet Maslin in the *New York Times* was dismissive: "To viewers unfamiliar with Mr. Singer's novel, the film may simply look like the story of an amorous, unprincipled man whose bizarre fate is not mysterious, just ill-explained.... 'The Magician of Lublin' sounds stilted much of the time, and Mr. Golan's attempts to strike a note of earthy charm are, for the most part, in vain."[39] J. Hoberman in the *Village Voice* pulled no punches: "Lavish and dismal, Menahem Golan's adaptation of Isaac Bashevis Singer's Magician of Lublin treads heavily on its source.... Squandering some convincing location work, Golan reduces Singer to a Harold Robbins entertainment of florid compositions and bombastic copulations."[40] Ironically, the film had been made in Berlin. "Producers Golan and Globus wanted to film 'The Magician of Lublin' in Poland. They argued that the movie was 'art, not politics,' but the Polish government declined to do business with an Israeli firm. 'So we went to Berlin instead,' said Globus. 'We rebuilt Lublin in the French sector, where many of the streets are paved in stone and look just like old Poland. All we had to do was take down the television antennas and fill the streets with droshkies and old cars.'"[41]

Golan's treatment of Singer's novel fails to preserve the conflict between worlds that was at the core of the original work. Unlike the novel, the film does not leave Yasha firmly ensconced in his cell, securely protected from outside enticements, yet forever vulnerable to temptations from within. Singer's struggle, both in *The Magician of Lublin* and in *The Slave*, had pivoted on the search for a place somewhere between the traditional world of Jewish Eastern Europe and the modern, essentially Christian, world of assimilation. In addition, Singer had been negotiating the sensitive issues of immigration and translation. Where did he fit? Was he a slave to his American audiences? Or was he a magician, an ordinary con man who beguiled his readers, employing tricks that they could not see through? The subtleties of Singer's torments were not for Golan to figure out, much less depict, but he proved unwilling or unable to contemplate spiritual and psychological themes. As Maslin put it: "Although Yasha, the magician, is frequently identified as a Jew in the course of the story, he is surely not a religious man. In fact, he seems to take particular pleasure in avoiding his Jewish origins— and his Jewish wife—by wooing Christian women. This is yet another sign of the vanity and arrogance that will eventually bring about a magical change in Yasha, a change which Mr. Golan is in no way equipped to render."[42]

Golan's personality may have prevented him from viewing Yasha's drama as an attempt to navigate his Jewish soul in the Diaspora. Perhaps for "veteran hack" Golan, as for so many of Singer's Yiddish readers, the big news was Yasha's sexuality. The movie's extremely secular approach did have one positive, if inadvertent, outcome: it spared its audience the nostalgia that might have plagued it under other circumstances. As J. Hoberman put it, granting a wry, back-handed compliment: "Coarse as it is, though, the film doesn't trade on the A-Yid-bin-Ich-un-a-Yid-vil-Ich-blaybn [I am a Jew and that's what I want to remain] sentimentality that's the bane of Jewish popular art. As my mother can tell you, a Fiddler it's not."[43]

Singer was silent concerning *The Magician of Lublin*. Not so when it came to Barbra Streisand's famous *Yentl*, which premiered on November 18, 1983. There had been a history of disagreement between Singer and Streisand. Singer mentioned the controversy more than once prior to the release of the film, calling Streisand's acquisition of rights to the film "a bargain," and talking about abandoning his own screen treatment of the story, in which she was to star. Singer's son put it more bluntly, explaining that Singer had indeed written a script of *Yentl*, and that Barbra Streisand hadn't liked it;[44] since she had bought the rights, however, Singer could not sell the option, a trick he had played on Irving White years before, over *The Magician of Lublin*.

It is possible that Streisand remained immune to the charm that Singer could usually wield with consummate skill and dramatic success. Roger Simon, who wrote the screenplay for *Enemies, A Love Story*, relates an anecdote about trying to do a rewrite for Streisand of *Prince of Tides*, in which she was to play a psychiatrist: "I went over to meet her and she loaded me down with about six versions of the script by various people plus all her transcriptions with various psychoanalysts about what it meant to be a psychiatrist.... A day and a half later, it's about 11:00 at night. I'm sitting up there reading, I don't remember what, and the phone rings—at 11:00 at night. This is someone I'd met once, right?... 'Do you think that in the third draft, we should use that scene...?' The greatest student in the history of Evelyn Wood could not have read whatever she was talking about. I said, 'Well, I haven't really read it yet.' Then she said to me, 'Your agent has asked me for too much money.' At 11:00. Not only did I not know what my agent was asking because I hadn't communicated with him on the subject. No negotiation had taken place of any sort. I just responded, 'Oh really, I didn't know.... I'll see if I can read this as quickly as I can....' One day later I received a case of expensive French wine with a thank you from the executives of Columbia for my time. And that was the end of that."[45]

Given both her temperament and her position, it is unlikely that Streisand would have allowed Singer to treat her as he had his collaborator Eve Friedman, for instance. In addition to devoting an immense amount of time to writing *Teibele* with him, Friedman had been willing to accept a "'contract'... dashed off by hand on a half sheet of foolscap. The terms were simple: share everything equally—work, money, author's credit."[46] These contracts were a regular and seemingly impromptu part of Singer's dealings—journalists Ophra Alyagon and Avrom Shulman both had them.[47]

The issue was more complicated, however, because, although the story had been invented by Singer, Streisand wanted to do *Yentl* for personal as well as aesthetic reasons. As Steve Hill, who played Yentl's father in the movie, put it: "The picture is dedicated to her father....She never knew him; he passed away when she was about 14 months old. I think she's fascinated with her identity."[48] Streisand turned *Yentl* into a virtual one-woman show, writing the screenplay (together with Jack Rosenthal), directing, producing, and starring in the film. Singer, clearly upset, recalled an earlier warning to Streisand: "I told her the human being doesn't have all the qualifications. She cannot be the actress, the producer...but she chose this way. So, if she succeeds, I will consider it a miracle."[49]

Singer had been cut out of the action, a position he obviously resented, in addition to whatever financial gripes he might have had. As Alma Singer later put it in her clear and succinct manner: "She didn't follow at all what my husband had written. She made something entirely different out of it. In the end this going to America and....It has absolutely nothing to do with what was intended."[50]

In a move that was uncharacteristically active and more like the old combative Bashevis than the new, mild Isaac Singer, the author "interviewed" himself, venting his anger in *The New York Times*. Although he inveighed in general against Streisand's rethinking of

Yentl's character and motives, he was particularly angry about two things: Yentl's journey to America, with which the film concludes, and Yentl's singing. About the immigration, he said: "Was going to America Miss Streisand's idea of a happy ending for Yentl? What would Yentl have done in America? Worked in a sweatshop 12 hours a day where there is no time for learning? Would she try to marry a salesman in New York, move to the Bronx or to Brooklyn and rent an apartment with an ice box and a dumbwaiter?"

Singer's anger seems to have been largely due to Streisand's reinterpretation of the original story's intent, which he continued to insist concerned solely a passion for learning: "Those who adapt novels or stories for the stage or for the screen must be masters of their profession and also have the decency to do the adaptation in the spirit of the writer." In the fluid way he had with imagination, Singer went on to picture Madame Bovary on the Riviera, Anna Karenina marrying an American millionaire, or Raskolnikov as a Wall Street banker. Clearly enjoying his own hyperbole, Singer simultaneously identified himself with some of his favorite authors, bemoaning the plight of the scorned genius.

A particular thorn in Singer's side was Streisand's decision to have Yentl sing. This objection, while he spoke about it in general terms, likely stemmed from his religious upbringing. He himself stated it as a departure from his own way of viewing things: "I did not find anything in her singing which reminded me of the songs in the studyhouses and Hasidic *shtibls*, which were a part of my youth and environment. As a matter of fact, I never imagined Yentl singing songs. The passion for learning and the passion for singing are not much related in my mind. There is almost no singing in my works."[51] Singer's comments did not reveal that, in his traditional world, and Yentl's, the legitimacy of hearing a woman's voice in song was the ongoing subject of heated debate.

The notion that a woman's voice is a sexual incitement, and therefore prohibited, dates back to the Talmud. Later, more stringent interpretations, argued that: "a woman's singing voice, under all circumstances, is to be considered a form of nudity, to be exposed exclusively to one's husband." Despite more liberal recent reinterpretations of the understanding among many Jews, the prohibition remains very much alive in certain established Orthodox circles: "The identification of a woman's voice as a likely source of sexual stimulation has led many modern Halakhic authorities [authorities on Jewish law] to ban, albeit with substantial dissent by other authorities, activities such as choirs of men and women together, women singing *Zemirot* in the presence of men other than their husbands, listening to records of women singing, and even women singing lullabies to their children in the hearing of men."[52]

Although Singer had abandoned orthodox Jewish practice, he had retained his familiar sensibilities. Even if he was not offended under ordinary circumstances by the sound of a woman singing, the notion of his Yentl raising her voice in song—especially in a House of Study—was a different matter. In the story as Singer had created it, the only anomaly to the strictures of conventional yeshiva life was Yentl's deception; once that was revealed, she was forced to leave, since she would not dream of openly defying either Law or custom. Even as she had broken rules in the pursuit of her studies, she remained a modest Jewish woman.

For Singer, Streisand's ignorant flouting of such a strong prohibition was nothing short of depravity. This was a place where the discrepancy between his past as Yitskhok or Bashevis and the present spin he was trying to put on himself as Isaac Singer clashed noisily. How could he hope to clear up a misunderstanding of his culture that saw artistic coherence in an historically impossible formulation? If he had read *Time Magazine*, he would have been hard-pressed to know where to begin his critique: "Composer Michel Legrand and Lyricists Marilyn and Alan Bergman have constructed the score as Yentl's running Talmudic commentary on the genesis of her womanly desires. (That's why Patinkin doesn't sing.) The songs begin in a liturgical mode.... As Yentl enters the real world of passion and deceit, the melodies become more secular.... [W]hen Yentl's thoughts turn from intellectual to sexual love, the songs are swimming strongly in the American pop mainstream. It is the most romantic, coherent and sophisticated original movie score since Gigi a quarter-century ago."[53]

While Singer was voluble about Barbra Streisand, the target of his invective remained regally removed. Instead, her fans took up the fight on her behalf. *The New York Times* published a full page of letters in response to Singer's "interview" with himself, and many of the readers were outraged that he could so malign *Yentl*. Some writers were more inventive than Streisand herself in under-

standing the story. Carol Matthau wrote to chastise Singer's refusal
to credit Streisand for bucking the Industry, at the same time
putting forth some ideas of her own: "I think the real ending of
'Yentl' is the holocaust. But the other possible ending is that she
came to America, as did Mr. Singer. Isn't it beautiful to opt for
life?" Another reader took Singer directly to task for his objection
to the singing: "...where in the work of I. B. Singer is there the
feeling for life that would be song in us?"[54]

Nor was the reaction to the movie limited to those interested in
protecting Streisand's reputation. The film made a splash because of
her fame, and its influence exceeded that of any other media venture
of which Singer was a part. Ironically, Singer had Streisand to thank
for her role in the preservation of his destroyed culture. But the
preservation had emerged as flawed and insulting to him, even as the
film reached an audience that was larger, and more diverse, than he
could have managed on his own. Perhaps the weirdest story of
influence occurred in a quarter that Singer could never have antici-
pated: "Workers at a Lubavich center in Southern California were
dumbfounded by the recent appearance of a six-year-old accompanied by his distraught, non-religious mother. It seems that after
viewing 'Yentl' with his family, the boy decided to become religious, study Torah and wear *tsitzes* and *paius* like Barbra Streisand.
Apparently taking his cue from the stubborn persistence of Yentl,
he kept up his campaign for religiosity until his desperate parents
relented and agreed to the child's plans. Unsure of how to proceed,
they brought the child to the Chasidic outreach center."[55]

Unfortunately, the more control Singer was able to exert in the
transfer of his written word to other media, and the more he, or his
adapters, clung to his tone and sensibility, the more circumscribed
the influence of the result—and the better its quality. Arguably,
Yentl provided the widest audience Singer was ever to have,
although it is questionable how many people link that story with
him, rather than with Streisand. Few viewers remember *The Cafeteria*, a television gem that aired just months before *Yentl* hit the
screen. A small production, based on a short story of the same
name that concerned a Holocaust survivor whom the narrator used
to see in a cafeteria in Manhattan, the tale has a supernatural twist.
Reviewers were enthusiastic, praising the director, Amram Nowak,
for his faithfulness to the original.

An exotic rendition of Singer into something else is David Schiff's opera, *Gimpel the Fool,* composed between 1975 and 1979, and performed in New York and Boston. Schiff also composed a divertimento from the opera for Chamber Music Northwest, replacing voices with instruments. The match was actually an especially fitting one. Schiff writes: "The idiom of *Gimpel* owes much to the sound of the klezmer band—the music of itinerant Jewish musicians in Eastern Europe....Instead of trying to imitate authentic klezmer music (which scarcely exists anymore) I sought to reconstruct the sound of this music from the traces it left in the works of Mahler, Stravinsky and Kurt Weill....To me, the interesting thing is to write a klezmer piece not using klezmer instruments...."[56] Schiff describes *Gimpel* as a translation of sorts, from his own, non-klezmer background, through the evidence of klezmer music in the works of classical composers (only one of whom was born Jewish), back to the original milieu in which the music had been authentic and integrated.

The final remake of a Singer work that was to occur during his lifetime was *Enemies, A Love Story,* written by Roger Simon and directed by Paul Mazursky. At the time the project began, Singer was already infirm, but he knew what he wanted, according to Mazursky, who visited him in Florida: "I decided it would be healthy if I could go down to meet him before I made the picture....So I arranged with his wife Alma to go down and meet him in Miami. He was spending most of his time there. In a big building on the water. Collins Avenue, I think. And she said, 'I'll meet you in the lobby.' And I flew to Miami and I rented a car and I drove to the place. There was Alma, and she said, 'I recognize you from your movies. Where do you want to meet Isaac? You want to meet him out by the pool or upstairs?—they have a room where you could sit and talk.' I said, 'Whatever's easiest for you is okay for me.' She said, 'Well, he's down by the pool now.' I said, 'Well, let's go down to the pool.' And we go out by the pool and it was a hot day. It looked like Hockney in Florida. And there seated at the pool like in a wheelchair is Isaac Singer with a little straw hat and a kind of—those wrong clothes that old Yiddish people wear. They're just the wrong jackets, the wrong pants. Winter clothes that he must have bought in the Lower East Side or up on 119th Street and Riverside Drive....And Alma said, 'Isaac, this is Paul

Mazursky. He's the boy who's going to make a movie out of *Enemies*.' I thought 'boy,' that's great. And he looked up at me and he took my hand. And he had a hard grip. And he said, 'I deedn't like what Barbra Streisand did with *Yentl*.' So I said, 'Mr. Singer, I promise you—no songs.' 'You're a good boy.'"[57]

This film, of which Singer was only dimly aware, turned out to be a great critical success. The production had combined an excellent screenplay, sensitive directing, and acting that effectively reproduced the mixture of sadness and vivacity that had enlivened the novel. The collaboration came about almost by accident. Roger Simon explains: "I knew Paul as a friend and I kept trying to get him to do one of my Moses Wine detective novels. One of them was just coming out and I was trying to convince him and he said, 'Well, you know, there's a book I'd like to do. Why don't you come to the office.' And he said, 'You ever read this book, *Enemies*?' I said 'Yeah.' He said, 'Well, it's real depressing. I don't think we should do it.' I said, 'Well it's great. It's really a masterpiece.' 'Well, read it again and call me back and tell me what you think.' So I took it home and I read it again. While I was reading it, I kept thinking, 'Gee this is great, this would make a masterpiece for a movie, except he's not going to want to do it and how am I going to convince him to do it?'...So, I walked into his office a couple of days later, or whatever it was, and he immediately said, 'Well, when do you want to start?'"

Unlike *The Magician of Lublin*, the film version of *Enemies* delves into psychological history. Although he did not know Singer, Roger Simon understood Herman Broder: "I think that when a man feels a loss in childhood of the mother for whatever reason...what you want to do is to bring a lot of women around you for fear that they're going to leave you....I think Herman loves all the women. There's just never enough because he's so needy."

Despite the later critical acclaim the film enjoyed,[58] Simon explained that "Every major studio in Hollywood turned it down....People would say that you might win the Academy Award but it's not going to make any money....I think what is really interesting is the resistance to making it considering that afterwards...it was the best reviewed movie of the year anywhere. And they knew that. You see, the thing is that when they read it, they all knew that but they were still resistant to making it [because it was too Jewish] and it was dark on top of that."[59]

Mazursky had a similar story to tell. Both men are American-born Jews and have no direct relationship to the world that Singer represented in his novel. However, Mazursky was careful to teach his actors about the Holocaust. Although the film has no death camp scenes, Mazursky obtained documentary footage, which the cast watched. Then he began to expose them to the situation of the survivors who, like Herman, had landed in New York after the War. "I then took them to the real locations, whatever I could still find, because most of this movie was shot in Montreal. I rehearsed in New York. I had two weeks of shooting in New York and then the rest in Montreal where I built all the apartments. I took them to Jewish delicatessens. Every day of rehearsal we would eat in another place. And the irony of ironies—it would be so—I knew it was going to happen, I hoped it would happen—the waiters who served us were Holocaust victims. And it didn't take but a snap of the finger to get a kind of—'Oh, yeah, Auschwitz. Oh, I was there, of course. What can I get you? Do you want borscht? Do you want potatoes? Auschwitz? Oh yeah.' That was great for the cast to see. The guys with the numbers."

By the time *Enemies* appeared, Singer was in his dotage. Mazursky recalls receiving a note, clearly written by Alma. It read, in part: "We were delighted with the great success your film *Enemies, A Love Story* had so far. We are wondering whether Isaac would be entitled to some additional royalties. As you know, Isaac is not able to continue working. It would be wonderful to get a little more money. Did you ever have time to look over the novels that Roger Straus sent you on our behalf? It would be wonderful to have another film made by you.... Fondly, Alma Singer and Isaac."[60]

Fortunately and unfortunately, the translations of Singer's work into other media have continued since his death: fortunately, because the public is treated to a version of his world, despite his demise; unfortunately, because the stereotypical and misinformed statements that inevitably accompany these renditions have also been perpetuated. The review in *The New York Times* of a 1994 production of *Shlemiel the First* (based on a children's work) epitomizes the situation. The play had originally been performed in 1974 at the Yale Repertory Theater, under the direction of Robert

Brustein, and the 1994 version, a musical, used his stage adaptation as well. While *The New York Times* review contains no errors, it delights in the formulaic and offensive idea of the busybody Jewish woman, a cliché Singer was careful to avoid: "Among the production's amiably clownish performances, Ms. Sokol's Yenta Pesha exudes a riveting comic ferocity. Scolding, gossiping and kvetching and wielding a giant floppy pickle like a lion tamer's whip, this queen of blintzes emerges as the story's ultimate know-it-all."[61]

It may be that Singer felt less obligated in his children's work to eschew stereotype, and he had advised Brustein at the time of the 1974 production that: "'My work should be done fast, like Shakespeare—not slow, like Chekhov.'" But it is unlikely that he would have enjoyed seeing his sophisticated world reduced to burlesque, even though the liveliness and originality of the production might have encouraged him. He certainly would not have known what to make of the pronouncement in *The New Yorker* that the musical was about "the imaginary town of Chelm, a village of fools invented by Isaac Bashevis Singer for his children's stories."[62] If he could have fully understood the ignorance that lay behind that statement, and if he was not merely aiming to be remembered as a literary genius, he might have concluded that he had failed in his effort to immortalize his beloved, complex Jewish Poland.

11

IN 1982, nineteen-year-old Meirav Zamir, one of Israel Zamir's four children, went to visit her grandfather in Florida. Singer was to live thirteen years after the award of the Nobel prize and much of that time—in the end, all of it—was spent at his home on Collins Avenue in Surfside, just north of Miami Beach. Alma and Isaac had instructed Meirav to take a cab from the airport. Greeting her in the lobby of their apartment house, the two immediately insisted on taking their astonished and weary visitor for a walk. Ms. Zamir recalls having to ask if she could leave her suitcase with the doorman. Meirav soon learned the reason for the foray, as the trio arrived at a nearby street, merely one short block long, but impressively named "Isaac Singer Boulevard." Her grandfather wanted to show her the street, demanding that she take photos of him next to the sign, all the while deprecating the "Boulevard." There were no more people to name the streets of Surfside after, he claimed, and the honor did not signify any display of respect for him. The walk itself was uncomfortable: the thing that struck Meirav about her grandfather was the rapidity of his pace—and Alma's complaint that Isaac was walking too fast.

Later, after they had come home and had had something to eat, during which time Alma was visibly anxious, worrying that Isaac was not being sufficiently cordial to his granddaughter, Alma took the teenager shopping in the super-upscale mall in Bal Harbour, a brief walk away from Collins Avenue and a world away from the sleepy, old-fashioned little shops on Harding Avenue, which abuts Isaac Singer Boulevard. Announcing "Come Meirav-ele, we need to buy something for you," Alma blithely waved away Meirav's protestations that she didn't need anything. Alma was firm: "I want your parents to know we bought you something." Wandering through the expensive shops, Alma cajoled, "Why don't you buy this for your mother, for your father, for your grandmother?" Meirav, who was traveling in modest style, kept asserting that she could not afford the likes of Neiman Marcus fashions. Alma, seeming not to comprehend, asserted, "Well, at least buy something for your grandmother." Meirav, sensing something wrong, but not knowing what, ended up buying a shirt, something she could ill afford, for her grandmother, Ronye—Isaac's common-law wife. Alma bought nothing.

As it turned out, part of the impetus for the shopping expedition was to leave Isaac alone: "He needs to rest," Alma explained. For dinner, they went to Sheldon's, the prosaic drugstore at the corner of Harding and Isaac Singer Boulevard. Alma wanted Meirav to have a hamburger, but Isaac, having just hours before lectured his granddaughter on the virtues of a vegetarian existence, contended that she should avoid meat. The meal was also accompanied by Alma's comments, stinging even years later, that the young woman was too heavy and should lose weight. The stressful first day ended abruptly when the three returned to the Singer apartment. Suddenly, Isaac said, "Well, it's time to go to bed—" and turned off the lights.

The next morning, Isaac awakened his granddaughter with the words: "We're going to go for a walk." However, the constitutional was not along the oceanfront, which lay directly outside the apartment building. The two did not even venture outdoors. Rather, Singer proceeded to march—or, more accurately, run—back and forth forty times along the corridor just outside his apartment. The atmosphere was filled with tension. By the second day, Meirav had taken to being by herself, encountering Isaac and Alma for a few moments before lights out. Sometimes, Alma took her along to be with friends, but she disliked those outings, because Alma's companions were—understandably enough—older women, and they were always talking about fashion and appearance.

When she got a chance to talk with her grandfather, in those rare moments when he appeared to be available to her, Meirav was amazed by his knowledge and understanding. They discussed the kibbutz, for example, and Singer's ideas were clear, advanced, and modern. At the same time, Singer could be hurtful in quite a different way from Alma. Meirav recalls that one day, as they were sitting and eating, Singer remarked: "You know, you look like your grandmother and not like me." The granddaughter countered that she did look like him, and also like his mother, Basheve. Singer adamantly denied the connection: "No, that isn't so." Meirav felt chastised by her grandfather for daring to imagine that she could look like his beloved mother. The comment was a dismissal of the young woman's reason for making the visit, a cold rejection of the bond that she was attempting to establish with her grandfather. With his brusque reaction, Bashevis also revealed that his need to maintain a unique attachment to his mother had not diminished simply because the Nobel laureate was now almost eighty years old. All in all, it was a "difficult and unpleasant" visit for Meirav. When they were not ignoring their granddaughter, Isaac and Alma argued about where to take her and what to do. She was happy to escape the oppressive atmosphere.[1]

Singer was now certifiably renowned. He was wealthy: his adjusted gross income from 1983 totalled over $575,000.[2] But he was no closer to vanquishing his internal misery than he had been twenty, thirty, or fifty years earlier. He could boast to his friend Ophra: "Do you know that they made of me a professor— in my old age? It does something for my ego. I'm not only a professor. I am a distinguished professor in the University of Miami. I get a very nice salary.... " At the same time, the man who had asserted that the Nobel prize would not change him was forced to make a significant alteration in his lifestyle: he had to get an unlisted phone number. The new situation was unpleasant; he felt more isolated and he worried that people might think he was being snobbish, a trait he disliked and one that did not fit him. As he explained: "I had to lose the telephone and to go into hiding.... There are so many crazy people in America that look for celebrities.... I nearly died from so many telephone calls, not from those I wanted, not from those I used to get before.... Who needs me has to try very hard to get my telephone number, and I'm sorry and I apologize.... "[3]

The accolades that had started pouring in after the 1978 award continued during the 1980s. In 1984, Singer became the sixteenth member of the Jewish-American Hall of Fame. The recognition, sponsored annually by the Magnes Museum in Berkeley, California, placed the author among such notables as Golda Meir and Jonas Salk. As part of the celebration, timed to coincide with Singer's eightieth birthday, the Museum issued a medal in gold, silver, pewter, and bronze: "The Singer medal is an exceptionally large piece, two inches in diameter and weighing two and one-half ounces. It has an unusual trapezoidal shape and was designed by Robert Russin, the artist who also prepared the medals honoring Albert Einstein and George Gershwin. The obverse features a front-facing portrait of Mr. Singer and his distinctive signature. The reverse carries a quote selected by the author and calligraphed in both English and Yiddish by Los Angeles artist Susan Fisher: 'Free Will is Life's Essence.'"[4]

Singer was also the recipient of the Handel Medallion, New York City's highest award, in June of 1986. The ceremony was a showcase of New York Jewish dignity, intelligence and art, all of it observed by the left-wing journalist, Morris Schappes: "Cultural Affairs commissioner Bess Myerson explained how fitting it was that the city's highest award go to an immigrant.... Barbara W. Tuchman defined Singer as 'the quintessential storyteller' whose tales, 'drawn from a foreign culture, are native American because they are natives of the world.'" The actor Eli Wallach read an excerpt from Singer's *Lost in America*; Mayor Edward I. Koch explained that the medallion itself was uniquely inscribed in both English and Yiddish, and Giora Feidman played klezmer music.[5]

Even at the very end of his life, Singer continued to receive honors. In 1990, he was elected to the American Academy of Arts, the only writer who did not write in English to be so inducted. He had become an American writer, a status that has lived on even after his death: in announcing the Nobel prize for literature award to Toni Morrison in 1993, for instance, *The New York Times* stated that "Other Americans who have won the prize in the last two decades are Joseph Brodsky [another immigrant], Isaac Bashevis Singer and Saul Bellow."[6]

Yet, with whom could Singer converse and spend valuable time? With whom could he desist from being the genial storyteller, while not having to suffer the accusation that he had sold out? He had outlived his few male friends: Weber, Ravitch, Tseytlin were all gone. These were men with whom he could speak Yiddish and recall his Polish home; they did not deprecate him for the choices he had made. While his American fans adored him, they would never understand him, and he found that controlling his impatience was becoming increasingly difficult.

An anecdote from the Miami years exemplifies Singer's loneliness. Lester Goran, who was instrumental in procuring Singer's Miami University appointment, but who came to rue their relationship, reports: "At a gathering at the Faculty Club at the University, what had been the usual lighthearted banter by Singer was interrupted when a man in the audience asked, 'How does it feel to be seventy-seven years young?' Singer was in a quick rage. 'Don't ask such questions! No one is years young. A man is years old. And it is not a joke. It is nothing to joke about. It is a terrible thing to be old, not a joke.' He stood alone in a room of perhaps two hundred people, immersed in the desolation that came from feeling perennially misunderstood. For all the millions of words he had written, he had not communicated his isolation."[7]

Eventually, Singer broke with both Dobe, his longtime mistress, and Dvora, his secretary during the late 1970s and 1980s. Dobe had gone to live in Israel; like Masha in *Enemies, A Love Story*, she had been unable to separate from her mother. The payments that Singer had made to her in the late 1970s were evidently insufficient to quell the pain that Dobe felt over her dismissal from his life. Dorothea Straus recalls that Singer had offered to pay her and had then reneged, an action that caused Dobe to threaten a lawsuit: "It would have ruined his career." In 1984, Singer's lawyer wrote to him: "It has been over a year since we have heard from Doba Gerber or her lawyer. It looks as if her legal efforts are over, since she appears to have fired her lawyer."

The rupture with Dvora was dramatic as well. A devoted student as well as a loyal caretaker, Dvora had undertaken to learn Yiddish; in 1982, she wrote to Singer in a voice filled with longing: "It is impossible for me to describe the terrible isolation and disharmony that I am living through.... The truth is I want to live with you alone—work on stories—study—translate—and grow. I want to grow in every way and you can help me.... But still—with all my destitution, I never forget, not for a single minute, how good and merciful God has been to us."[8] Dorothea Straus, who observed Singer and Dvora together, remembers: "...this was a rite, an erotic rite....They would order tapioca pudding and eat out of the same bowl. Now, this is some new kinky sex that I had never seen or heard of before. But it was very intense on both sides."[9] In the end, however, Singer became mistrustful of Dvora, suspecting her of trying to cheat him financially. As he had been capable of doing in the past, with other important people in his life—including his sister Ronye, and his common-law wife, Singer shut Dvora out of his life and cut her out of his will.

Now, of the significant women in his life, only Alma remained. Singer continued to be cruel to her in public. Just after winning the Nobel prize, for instance, he had brushed aside her attempt to celebrate their long years of connection and her role in supporting and nurturing his genius: "...his wife took the phone off the hook and came to sit beside him, nibble at the honey cake and recall the days of their courtship in 1937 when he told her his dream of being a renowned writer. 'I never said those things,' Singer grumped, hiding behind the first edition of the afternoon paper with headlines announcing his prize and thereby spoiling this section of film for the omnipresent television cameras. 'Yes, you did. You said it when we would go walking along Central Park West near 84th Street,' she said with a wistful smile. 'Don't believe anything I might have said on Central Park West. I have already forgotten. You must have dreamt those things,' said Singer, a man well-acquainted with dreams."[10]

For her part, Alma continued to hold her own, even though she seemed to madden Singer with her chatty illogic. Lester Goran was part of a typical exchange. He had been late for a breakfast meeting with the two because it had been raining, an excuse that Alma refused to accept. Since his car had a roof, why should the weather make any difference? Why would anyone fear skidding in a car? A car's rubber tires must make skidding impossible. How could other drivers make someone late? She had never heard of such a thing. Singer listened to the discussion in distress. "You two will drive me crazy....I'm going to run from this place." Finally, Alma made her concluding argument: "'Look out the window,' she said. 'Those people are running in the rain. Rain makes people hurry. How can

you be late because it's raining? I never heard such a thing.'"
Exhausted, Goran acquiesced. "'See Isaac,' she said. 'I was right.'"[11]

Yet, when the time came to take care of her ailing husband, Alma
was exemplary. Moreover, she showed unexpected psychological
understanding of his reactions. By the late 1980s, Singer was beginning to fail, an apparent victim of Alzheimer's disease. He lost his
ability for sustained focus, and he could not always recognize people. Alma describes a man who was at once pathetic and sweet:
"You know we had an apartment on the twelfth floor which was
tiny. It was just a living room and a bedroom and a kitchen. And
then when Isaac got unwell and I had nurses in and out, and he
wanted, just before he got sick, he wanted bookcases. He said he
must have a bookcase. So we put a recliner for the nurse and a
bookcase in the room, and it became crowded-looking. You know,
it wasn't nice anymore."

A larger apartment in the same building became available, but
Isaac didn't want to move. "But one day I said to myself, I'll take it
upon myself—he will like it. And we just took him. We went down
here the way it was and we put him in the afternoon in his bed over
there. He had a nice bedroom, beautiful bedroom, and I didn't
mention anything and he never complained. He was always afraid
of not having a bed because in his father's house there was a short-
age of sleeping quarters and someone always had to sleep on the
table because there were not enough beds. So he had the fear that
he wouldn't be able to sleep and I arranged it so that he had his
bed, and he took it as if nothing ever happened. I felt he would say
where do you take me and why did you change—nothing. He was
just happy....He got everything until the very end. It wasn't
easy."[12]

Even though he was unable to recognize even family members,
and although his memory was gone, Singer somehow managed
to cling to the most basic aspect of his identity: his essence as a
writer. Dorothea Straus remembers: "He was completely senile.
Not senile. He was just not there. Once in a while he would come
back and he would say things like, 'I certainly am the greatest
Yiddish writer living.' He would be out of it completely, like a
child, and then he would come back. And suddenly he was his old
self. But it always had to do with his writing."[13] And Zamir, who
visited for the last time about a year before his father's death, recalls

that Singer suddenly said to him: "'We're so poor. The publishers robbed us of everything.'"[14]

The reference to poverty indicated that little Yitskhok's deepest realities were still present within him. The sensitive boy who would become a famous writer survived until the end, after all the worldly sophistication, all the sexual curiosity, and all the knowledge had slipped away. Despite Alma's fervent efforts to keep him at home, eventually, Singer had to be hospitalized; he spent his last days in the Douglas Gardens Rest Home. Alma had struggled to care for her husband at home, and she witnessed his demise with helpless misery: "His eyes would open wide and he looked like a little boy, pleading for help; and I couldn't do a thing to save him. That look will always haunt me."[15]

At the time of Singer's death, Zamir had begged Alma to have him buried in Israel. Alma, who had no special love for the Jewish state, refused. Instead, Singer would be buried in New Jersey, where the Jewish cemeteries closest to the New York metropolitan area are located. Zamir was bitter and concerned about his father's immortality: "In Israel, Singer's grave would have become a pilgrimage site for Yiddishists, intellectuals, tourists of all kinds.... There would never be anyone to pay homage to my father in New Jersey."[16]

Epilogue

SURFSIDE, 1991. In a cheerful apartment, an old man lies list-
lessly on a couch. His eyes, once brilliant blue and filled with life,
are dull, drained of expression. He seems unable to notice the gentle Florida ocean outside his window; he recognizes no one. On his
lap is a sheet of paper; his fingers cradle a pencil. The old man's
hand moves ceaselessly in a gesture of writing. But what takes
shape is merely a scribble.[1]

Isaac Bashevis Singer, son of Pinkhos Menakhem and Basheve,
died on July 24, 1991. Alma Singer died on January 11, 1996.

NOTES

Prologue

1. Isaac Bashevis Singer (as Yitskhok Bashevis), Originally published in *Goldene keyt* 83 (1974): 74–88. Translated into English as *"Hanka,"* in *Passions,* (New York: Farrar, Straus & Giroux, 1975). Republished by Fawcett Crest, 1976, 20.
2. Isaac Bashevis Singer (as Yitskhok Bashevis), Originally published as *A gast af eyn nakht* in the *Forverts* (Nov. 17, 18, 24): 3; (Nov. 25): 3–8; (Dec. 1): 3. Translated into English as "A Night in Brazil," in *Old Love,* (New York: Farrar, Straus & Giroux, 1979). Republished by Fawcett Crest, 1980, 17.
3. Isaac Bashevis Singer (as Yitskhok Bashevis), Originally published as *Eyn emese libe* in *Goldene keyt* 81 (1973): 93–105. Translated into English as "One True Love," in *Passions,* (New York: Farrar, Straus & Giroux, 1975). Republished by Fawcett Crest, 1976, 129.

Chapter 1

1. Isaac Bashevis Singer, *In My Father's Court,* (New York: Farrar, Straus & Giroux, 1966), 155. Hereafter cited as *Court.*
2. Esther Kreitman, *Deborah,* (London: Virago, 1983), 153. Hereafter cited as Kreitman.
3. *Court,* 171.
4. Kreitman, 153.
5. Isaac Bashevis Singer (as Yitskhok Bashevis Zinger), *"Di mishpokhe,"* (Serialized in the *Forverts,* Feb. 2, 1982–Feb. 4, 1983), (May 12, 1982): 8. Hereafter cited as *Mishpokhe.*
6. *Court,* 175.
7. *Court,* 67.
8. *Court,* 175.
9. *Court,* 155.
10. Fern Marja Eckman, "Daily Closeup: Interrupted Melody," *New York Post,* July 6, 1972.
11. *Mishpokhe* (April 14, 1982): 8.
12. *Court,* 44.
13. I. J. Singer, *Of a World That Is No More,* (New York: Vanguard Press, 1970),

217

207. Hereafter cited as *World*. For a book-length, literary–critical study of Israel Joshua Singer, see Anita Norich, *The Homeless Imagination in the Fiction of Israel Joshua Singer*, (Bloomington: Indiana University Press, 1991).

14. Maurice Carr, "Uncle Yitzhak: A Memoir of I. B. Singer," *Commentary* 94: 6 (December, 1992): 25–32. Hereafter cited as Carr.

15. Kreitman, 236.

16. *World*, 33.

17. *Court*, 152, 189.

18. *Court*, 97.

19. *Court*, 99.

20. *Court*, 100.

21. *World*, 29–30.

22. *World*, 153.

23. *Mishpokhe* (April 9, 1982): 8.

24. *Court*, 47.

25. *Court*, 44.

26. *Court*, 141.

27. *Mishpokhe* (Feb. 17, 1982): 8; *World,* 82.

28. *Mishpokhe* (March 12, 1982): 8. In another version of the candle anecdote, Bashevis asserts that his grandfather was orphaned, raised by his aunt and uncle, and that the incident occurred with his aunt, not his mother. *"Der zeyde"* ("My Grandfather") first appeared in the *Forverts* on Oct. 1, 1955. Cited in Isaac Bashevis Singer, *Mayn tatns bezdin shtub [hemsheykhim-zamlung]*, Selection and Introduction by Chone Shmeruk (Jerusalem: The Magnes Press, The Hebrew University, 1996).

29. *Mishpokhe* (March 19, 1982): 8.

30. *Mishpokhe* (March 12, 1982): 8.

31. *World*, 82.

32. *World*, 82; *Mishpokhe* (March 12, 1982): 8.

33. *Mishpokhe* (March 12, 1982): 8.

34. *Mishpokhe* (March 19, 1982): 8.

35. *Court*, 47.

36. *World*, 82.

37. *Court*, 217.

38. *World*, 83.

39. *Mishpokhe* (April 2, 1982): 8.

40. *Mishpokhe* (April 8, 1982): 8.

41. *World*, 141.

42. Kreitman, 31.

43. I. J. Singer was born on November 5, 1893.

44. *World*, 69–70.

45. *World*, 241.

46. *Mishpokhe* (March 31, 1982): 8.

47. *Mishpokhe* (April 1, 1982): 8.

48. Carr, 27.

49. *World*, 29.

50. Kreitman, 10.

Chapter 2

* Brian Glanville, "Isaac Bashevis Singer: A Yiddish Original," *London Jewish Chronicle*, Sept. 21, 1962.
1. *Court*, 207.
2. *World*, 18.
3. *World*, 54.
4. *World*, 26.
5. *World*, 154.
6. *World*, 131.
7. *World*, 156.
8. *World*, 75.
9. *World*, 193–194.
10. *World*, 149.
11. *World*, 150.
12. *World*, 214.
13. *World*, 215.
14. *World*, 241.
15. Carr, 27, 28.
16. *Court*, 151.
17. *World*, 140.
18. *World*, 141.
19. *World*, 243.
20. Kreitman, 6.
21. Kreitman, 6.
22. Kreitman, 7.
23. Kreitman, 243.
24. Kreitman, 337.
25. *Court*, 151.
26. *Court*, 152.
27. Carr, 30.
28. The British writer, Clive Sinclair, discussed Esther's conflicts and behavior in a paper and subsequent discussion at the First International Isaac Bashevis Singer Conference, March 1993.
29. Carr, 30.
30. I am grateful to Dr. Robert Collins, Chair of Neurology, UCLA Medical School, for providing his opinion concerning Hinde Esther's epilepsy. I also thank Dr. John H. Menkes, Professor Emeritus of Neurology and Pediatrics, UCLA, who suggested to me that partial complex status epilepticus is extremely rare and does not usually result in behavior change. In his view, many of Hinde Esther's attacks were likely psychogenic.
31. *Mishpokhe* (Feb. 18, 1982): 8.
32. *Court*, 152, 155.
33. Kreitman, 235–236.
34. *Court*, 152.
35. Kreitman, vi.
36. *Court*, 160.

37. *Mishpokhe* (March 4, 1982): 8.
38. *Court,* 13.
39. *Court,* 15.
40. *Court,* 16.
41. *Court,* 56.
42. *Mishpokhe* (Feb. 25, 1982): 8.
43. *Court,* 27–28.
44. *Court,* 49.
45. *Court,* 110.
46. *Mishpokhe* (March 5, 1982): 8.
47. *Court,* 76.
48. *Court,* 77.
49. *Court,* 78.
50. *Court,* 79.
51. *Court,* 160.
52. *Court,* 211.
53. *Court,* 220–221.
54. *Court,* 203–204.
55. *Court,* 104.
56. *Court,* 211–212.
57. *Court,* 222–223.
58. *Court,* 224.

Chapter 3

1. Isaac Bashevis Singer, *Love and Exile,* (New York: Penguin Books, 1986), 37.
   This volume consists of three earlier published volumes: *A Little Boy in Search
   of God, A Young Man in Search of Love,* and *Lost In America.* These were originally serialized in the *Forverts* as *Gloybn un tsveyfl (Faith and Doubt)* between
   Nov. 14, 1974, and Jan. 3, 1975; between April 29, 1976, and Aug. 12, 1976; and
   between Feb. 3 and Dec. 7, 1978. Hereafter cited as *Love and Exile.*
2. Isaac Bashevis Singer, *"Figurn un epizodn fun literatn farayn"* (*Figures and
   Episodes from the Writers' Club*), *Forverts* (June 28, 1979): 3. Hereafter cited as
   Farayn. Farayn appeared in the *Forverts* from June 28, 1979–Jan. 10, 1980.
3. Carr, 29.
4. *Love and Exile,* 42.
5. Eric Pace, "An Unchanged Storyteller," *The New York Times,* December 9,
   1978; Paul Kresh, *Isaac Bashevis Singer: The Magician of West 86th Street,*
   (New York: Dial Press, 1979), 78.
6. *Farayn* (July 6, 1979): 3.
7. *Farayn* (July 5, 1979): 3.
8. *Farayn* (June 29, 1979): 3.
9. Z. Segalowicz, *Tlomatske 13* (Tlomackie 13) (Buenos Aires: Central Union of
   Polish Jews in Argentina, 1946), 9. Hereafter cited as Segalowicz.
10. *Farayn* (July 5, 1979): 3.
11. *Farayn* (June 28, 1979): 3.
12. *Farayn* (July 20, 1979): 3.

13. *Farayn* (June 28, 1979): 3.
14. *Farayn* (July 5, 1979): 3.
15. Segalowicz, 15.
16. *Farayn* (July 5, 1979): 3.
17. *Farayn* (July 6, 1979): 3.
18. *Farayn* (Aug. 24, 1979): 3.
19. H. D. Nomberg, *Oysgeklibene shriftn* (*Selected Works*), ed. Shmuel Rozhansky (Buenos Aires: Confederacion Pro-Cultura Judia, 1958), 12–13.
20. *Farayn* (July 6, 1979): 3.
21. *Farayn* (July 12, 1979): 3.
22. *Love and Exile*, 56.
23. This is according to a later statement by Bashevis. The name Yehoshue is pronounced Yehoshiye in certain dialects; hence the shortened form Shiye and the diminutive Shiyele.
24. *Farayn* (Dec. 21, 1979): 3.
25. Segalowicz, 97.
26. *Farayn* (July 13, 1979): 3.
27. *Farayn* (Sept. 14, 1979): 3.
28. *Farayn* (Dec. 6, 1979): 3.
29. *Farayn* (July 19, 1979): 3.
30. *Farayn* (June 29, 1979): 3.
31. *Farayn* (July 19, 1979): 3.
32. *Love and Exile*, 131.
33. *Farayn* (July 20, 1979): 3.
34. "*Af der elter*," which was signed, "Tse," [corresponding to two Yiddish letters] appeared in No. 60 of *Literarishe bleter* (Warsaw). The story begins on Krochmalna Street in Warsaw and ends in the *shtetl* Yuzefov, not far from Bilgoray. The protagonist, Reb Moyshe-Ber, outlives all of his family and, in advanced age, sires a son whom he names Yitskhok. The plot of "*Af der elter*" echoes the theme of birth and new beginnings that its author was experiencing at the time he penned the story.
35. *Farayn* (Sept. 28, 1979): 3.
36. *Farayn* (July 26, 1979): 3.
37. *Farayn* (Oct. 5, 1979): 3.
38. *Farayn* (July 26, 1979): 3.
39. *Farayn* (Sept. 20, 1979): 3.
40. Carr, 27.
41. Israel Zamir, *Journey to My Father: Isaac Bashevis Singer*, (New York: Arcade Publishing, 1994), 63, 74. Originally published in Hebrew as *Avi, Yitskhak Bashevis-Zinger*, (Tel Aviv: sifriat poelim, 1994); Isaac Bashevis Singer described his arrest (as Y. Varshavsky) in "*Fun der alter un nayer heym*" in the *Forverts* (published Sept. 21, 1963, to Sept. 11, 1965), Oct. 10, 1964. Hereafter cited as *Heym*.
42. Isaac Bashevis Singer (as Yitskhok Bashevis), "*Tsu der frage fun dikhtung un politik*" ("On the Question of Literature and Politics,") *Globus* 1: 3 (September 1932).
43. Fern Marja Eckman, "Daily Closeup: Interrupted Melody," *New York Post*, July 6, 1972.
44. *Love and Exile*, 186.

45. *Farayn* (Sept. 14, 1979): 3.
46. Isaac Bashevis Singer, *In My Father's Court*, (New York: Farrar, Straus & Giroux, 1966), 278. Hereafter cited as *Court*.
47. *Court*, 155.
48. Isaac Bashevis Singer (as Yitskhok Bashevis), *Der sotn in goray*, first serialized in *Globus* between Jan. 1933 and Sept. 1933. Published in book form by the Warsaw Yiddish Pen Club, 1935. First translated as *Satan in Goray*, (New York: Noonday, 1955). *Satan in Goray*, (New York: Fawcett Crest, 1980). Hereafter cited as *Satan in Goray*. Please note, however, that on several occasions, including the present citation, I have used my own translations to more clearly render the sense of the original.
49. *Satan in Goray*, 68–69.
50. *Satan in Goray*, 69.
51. *Satan in Goray*, 99.
52. Max Weinreich, *Bilder fun der yidisher literatur-geshikhte*, (*Pictures from Yiddish Literary History*), (Vilne: Farlag Tomor, 1928), 259–260.
53. Alma Singer, Interview, Dec. 19, 1992.
54. Isaac Bashevis Singer (as Yitskhok Bashevis), *"Tayves"* ("Passions"), originally appeared in *Goldene keyt* 87 (1975). Translated in *Passions*, (New York: Farrar, Straus & Giroux, 1975), 184.
55. Meirav Hen, Interview, February 12, 1993.

Chapter 4

1. *Love and Exile*, 183.
2. *Love and Exile*, Author's Note.
3. *Love and Exile*, 184.
4. *Love and Exile*, 223–224.
5. Elenore Lester, "At 71, Isaac Bashevis Singer Makes His Broadway Debut," *The New York Times* (Oct. 26, 1975): 1.
6. *Love and Exile*, 231.
7. *Love and Exile*, 237–238.
8. *Love and Exile*, 255–256.
9. *Love and Exile*, 258.
10. *Love and Exile*, 271, 325.
11. Isaac Bashevis Singer, "When the Old World Came to Sea Gate," *The New York Times* (Jan. 2, 1972): 1, 6. Hereafter cited as *Old World*.
12. *Love and Exile*, 254.
13. *Love and Exile*, 259.
14. Eric Pace, "An Unchanged Storyteller," *The New York Times*, Dec. 9, 1978 ("Man in the News").
15. *Love and Exile*, 272.
16. *Love and Exile*, 278.
17. *Old World*, 6.
18. Letters to Ravitch are in the Ravitch Archives, The Jewish National and University Library, The Hebrew University, Jerusalem. I thank the Bergner family for granting me permission to read the correspondence.

19. *Love and Exile*, 283, 284.
20. *Love and Exile*, 286, 287.
21. *Love and Exile*, 287.
22. Letter to Ravitch, April 1936.
23. Letter to Ravitch, Aug. 1936.
24. Letter to Ravitch, April 1936.
25. *Love and Exile*, 283.
26. *Love and Exile*, 284.
27. Philip Roth, "Roth and Singer on Bruno Schulz," *The New York Times Book Review* (Feb. 13, 1977): 20 (Transcript of an interview which took place in Nov. 1976).
28. Peter S. Prescott, "Singer the Magician," *Newsweek* (Oct. 16, 1978): 97.
29. Letter to Ravitch, April 1936.
30. *Love and Exile*, 261–262.
31. *Love and Exile*, 284.
32. *Love and Exile*, 296.
33. In another version of the story, Bashevis indicates that he made the trip to Canada alone. *Heym*, Jan. 8, 1965.
34. *Love and Exile*, 303.
35. *Love and Exile*, 312.
36. *Love and Exile*, 304–305.
37. *Love and Exile*, 336.
38. *Love and Exile*, 337.
39. *Love and Exile*, 348.

Chapter 5

1. From an unpublished memoir of which Mrs. Singer generously allowed me to use two chapters.
2. Walter Ruby, "Alma Singer," *The Jewish Monthly* (April 1982): 12. Hereafter cited as Ruby.
3. Sylvia Weber, Interview, June 28, 1992.
4. Elizabeth Shub, Interview, Dec. 6, 1992.
5. Cathy Lynn Grossman, "The Story of Isaac," *Miami Herald*, May 25, 1980.
6. *Heym*, April 24, 1965.
7. *Heym*, Jan. 23, 1965.
8. Alma Singer, Interview, Oct. 1992.
9. *Heym*, Jan. 30, 1965.
10. *Heym*, Feb. 20, 1965.
11. Lillian Silver, the daughter of Shimen and Sylvia Weber, recalls that Bashevis usually allowed her father to pay when the two couples went out together. Every so often, however, Bashevis would feel guilty and would invite the Webers for dinner at an Upper West Side coffee shop. "But then when they would start to order, he would say, 'Alma-le, I'm not very hungry, let's share some soup,' and then they would share pudding and then they would share coffee." The Webers felt pressured to be similarly frugal. Interview, Aug. 4, 1992.

12. Michael Weissner, "On This Desk I Will Write Great Things," *Forward* (October 8, 1993): 11. Hereafter cited as *Forward*.
13. Isaac Bashevis Singer, *Forward*.
14. Ruby, 13.
15. Mirra Ginsburg, Interview, April 24, 1993.
16. *Heym*, Feb. 26, 1965.
17. Isaac Bashevis Singer (as Y. Varshavsky), "*Farbrekhns vos froyen bageyen iber umgliklekhn familyen-lebn,*" *Forverts* (March 24, 1940): 2.
18. Isaac Bashevis Singer (as Y. Varshavsky), "*Mentshn, vos hobn lib tsu paynikn andere un mentshn, vos hobn 'plezhur' ven zey aleyn vern gepaynikt,*" *Forverts* (Aug. 4, 1940): 2–4.
19. Isaac Bashevis Singer (as Y. Varshavsky), "*Vos iz platonishe libe?,*" *Forverts* (February 25, 1940): 2, 4.
20. For a discussion of Bashevis's pseudonyms, see David Neal Miller, *Fear of Fiction: Narrative Strategies in the Works of Isaac Bashevis Singer,* (Albany: SUNY Press, 1985), especially 39–70.
21. *Heym*, March 13, 1965.
22. Isaac Bashevis Singer (as Yitskhok Bashevis), "*Arum der yidisher proze in poyln,*" *Di tsukunft* 48:8 (Aug. 1943): 468–475. Translated by Robert Wolf as "Concerning Yiddish Literature in Poland," in *Prooftexts: A Journal of Jewish Literary History,* 15:2 (1995). Hereafter cited as *Yiddish Literature*.
23. *Yiddish Literature*, 118, 119.
24. *Yiddish Literature*, 119.
25. *Yiddish Literature*, 120.
26. *Yiddish Literature*, 121.
27. *Yiddish Literature*, 127.
28. *Heym*, March 20, 1965.
29. Isaac Bashevis Singer (as Yitskhok Bashevis), "*Problemen fun der yidisher proze in amerike,*" in *Svive* 2 (March-April, 1943): 2–13. Translated as "Problems of Yiddish Prose in America (1943)," in *Prooftexts: A Journal of Jewish Literary History,* 9:1 (Jan. 1989): 5–12. Hereafter cited as *Yiddish Prose*. For an insightful understanding of Bashevis's struggles during this period, see David G. Roskies, *The Lost Art of Yiddish Storytelling* (Cambridge: Harvard University Press, 1995), 266–306.
30. *Yiddish Prose*, 7.
31. *Yiddish Prose*, 8.
32. *Yiddish Prose*, 10.
33. *Yiddish Prose*, 11.
34. *Yiddish Prose*, 10.
35. *Yiddish Prose*, 12.
36. *Heym*, March 26, 1965.

Chapter 6

1. David Neal Miller, *Bibliography of Isaac Bashevis Singer, 1924–1949,* (New York: Peter Lang Publishers, 1983), 165.
2. Isaac Bashevis Singer (as Yitskhok Bashevis), *Di familye mushkat* (*The Family*

Moskat), serialized in the *Forverts* between Nov. 17, 1945–May 1, 1948; published in English in a translation by A. H. Gross and Nancy Gross (New York: Alfred A. Knopf, 1950); reprinted by Farrar, Straus & Giroux; eighth printing, 1988, 6. Hereafter cited as *Moskat.*

3. *Moskat,* 25.
4. *Moskat,* 252.
5. *Moskat,* 462.
6. *Moskat,* 370.
7. *Moskat,* 315.
8. *Moskat,* 237.
9. *Moskat,* 601.
10. *Moskat,* 223.
11. *Moskat,* 21.
12. *Moskat,* 162.
13. *Moskat,* 47.
14. Eleanor Foa Dienstag, Interview, Nov. 1992. Hereafter cited as Dienstag.
15. *Moskat,* 157.
16. Dienstag.
17. *Moskat,* 537–538.
18. *Moskat,* 532.
19. *Moskat,* 474.
20. *Moskat,* 486.
21. *Moskat,* 487.
22. Isaac Bashevis Singer (as Y. Varshavsky), "*Eroplanen un vos m'hot oysgefunen vegn zey in di yorn fun der milkhome,*" *Forverts* (March 7, 1943): Sec. 2, 4.
23. Isaac Bashevis Singer (as Y. Varshavsky), "*Di daytshn hobn oyf alts a 'sistem' un di sistem vet zey avek–hargenen,*" *Forverts* (March 14, 1943): Sec. 2, 1,2.
24. Isaac Bashevis Singer (as Y. Varshavsky), "*Ven vet platsn di makht fun natsi-daytshland?,*" *Forverts* (March 23, 1943): Sec. 2, 1,2.
25. Isaac Bashevis Singer (as Y. Varshavsky), "*Vi azoy es vet forkumen di invazye fun eyrope,*" *Forverts* (March 28, 1943): Sec. 2, 1,2.
26. *Moskat,* 610.
27. *Moskat,* 398.
28. *Moskat,* 536.
29. Isaac Bashevis Singer (as Yitskhok Bashevis), "*Der kurtser fraytik,*" *Di tsukunft* 50: 1 (Jan. 1945): 19–23. Translated as "Short Friday" in *Short Friday and Other Stories,* (New York: Fawcett Crest, 1964); *The Collected Stories of Isaac Bashevis Singer,* (New York: Farrar, Straus & Giroux, 1953); eleventh printing, 1992. All future citations of this work refer to *The Collected Stories.*
30. Isaac Bashevis Singer (as Yitskhok Bashevis), "*Di kleyne shusterlekh: dertseylung,*" *Di tsukunft* 50: 4 (April 1945): 232–241. Translated as "The Little Shoemakers" in *Gimpel the Fool and Other Stories,* (New York: Knopf, 1950); Reprinted in *The Collected Stories of Isaac Bashevis Singer,* (New York: Farrar, Straus & Giroux, 1953); eleventh printing, 1992. All future citations of this work refer to *The Collected Stories.*
31. Isaac Bashevis Singer (as Yitskhok Bashevis), "*Gimpl tam,*" *Yidisher kemfer* 24: 593 (March 30, 1945): 17–20. Translated as "Gimpel the Fool" in *Gimpel the*

Fool and Other Stories, (New York: Knopf, 1950); Reprinted in *The Collected Stories of Isaac Bashevis Singer,* (New York: Farrar, Straus & Giroux, 1953); eleventh printing, 1992. All future citations of this work refer to *The Collected Stories.*

32. Lester Goran, *The Bright Streets of Surfside: The Memoir of a Friendship with Isaac Bashevis Singer,* (Kent, Ohio, and London, England: Kent State University Press, 1994), 61; *Heym,* Mar. 27, 1965.

33. "Little Shoemakers," 50.

34. "Little Shoemakers," 53–54.

35. "Little Shoemakers," 52,53.

36. "Little Shoemakers," 56.

37. "Gimpel the Fool," 7.

38. "Gimpel the Fool," 9.

39. "Gimpel the Fool," 14.

40. "Short Friday," 197.

Chapter 7

1. Alma Singer, Interview, May 22, 1994. Hereafter cited as Alma Singer.

2. Jerry Tallmer, "At Home With the Isaac Bashevis Singers," *New York Post* (Nov. 15, 1975): 13. Hereafter cited as Tallmer.

3. Courtesy, Singer Archives, University of Texas, Austin.

4. Isidore Haiblum, "The 'Hidden' Isaac Bashevis Singer," *Congress Bi-Weekly* (Dec. 25, 1970): 33–34.

5. Alma Singer.

6. Isaac Bashevis Singer, "What's In It For Me?," *Harper's Magazine* (Oct. 1965): 170. Hereafter cited as "What's In It For Me?"

7. *Heym,* April 24, 1965.

8. "What's In It For Me?," 173.

9. Saul Bellow, Interview, June 1995. Hereafter cited as Saul Bellow.

10. Nancy Gross was the daughter of A. Gross, the ill-fated translator of *The Family Moskat.*

11. *Heym,* April 24, 1965.

12. Saul Bellow.

13. After *The Family Moskat,* Bashevis published another huge, sweeping historical novel about Poland. Published in English as two novels, *The Manor* and *The Estate* did not appear in English until 1967 and 1969, even though they had been serialized in the *Forverts* between 1952 and 1955.

14. Isaac Bashevis Singer (as Yitskhok Bashevis), *Der kuntsnmakher fun lublin,* originally serialized in the *Forverts* in 1959. Published in book form in 1971 (Tel Aviv: ha-Menorah, 1971). Translated by Elaine Gottlieb and Joseph Singer (New York: Noonday Press, 1960).

15. Isaac Bashevis Singer (as Yitskhok Bashevis), *Der knekht,* originally serialized in the *Forverts,* 1960–1961. Appeared in book form (Tel Aviv: Farlag Y.L. Perets, 1967). Translated by I. B. Singer and Cecil Hemley (New York: Farrar, Straus & Cudahy, 1962).

16. Orville Prescott, "Books of the Times," *The New York Times,* July 6, 1962.

17. Personal communication, Rabbi William Cutter, June 29, 1994.
18. Janet Hadda, *Passionate Women, Passive Men: Suicide in Yiddish Literature,* (Albany: SUNY Press, 1988), 213.
19. Orville Prescott, "Demons, Devils and Others," *The New York Times,* "Books of the Times," Dec. 14, 1964. Hereafter cited as Prescott.
20. *Heym,* April 2, 1965.
21. Courtesy, Singer Archives, University of Texas, Austin.
22. Letter from Hinde Esther to Bashevis.
23. Personal correspondence from David Ellenberg, June 27, 1994.
24. *Heym,* April 9, 1965.
25. Masha, in *Enemies, A Love Story,* Dora, in "A Tale of two Sisters," Margit Levy, in "Neighbors," and Magda, in *The Magician of Lublin,* are just a few of the many passionate and unstable women Bashevis invented over the course of his long career.
26. *Heym,* April 9, 1965.
27. Prescott.
28. Richard Elman. "Singer of Warsaw," *The New York Times Book Review* (May 8, 1966): Sec. 7, 1.
29. Isaac Bashevis Singer quoted in *Morgn-frayhayt,* July 15, 1965.
30. Isaac Bashevis Singer (as Y. Varshavsky), *"Iz der roman a farelterte form in der literatur?"* ("Is the Novel an Obsolete Form in Literature?,") *Forverts,* Sept. 25, 1966.
31. Chaim Suler, *"In der yidisher prese,"* in *Morgn-frayhayt* (Sept. 22, 1966): 3. Hereafter cited as Suler.
32. B. Reynes in *Morgn-frayhayt* (Feb. 13, 1964): 6.
33. Ophra Alyagon, Interview, Sept. 1993.
34. Fern Marja Eckman, "Daily Closeup: Interrupted Melody," *New York Post,* July 6, 1972.
35. *Heym,* April 17, 1965.
36. Dorothea Straus, *Under the Canopy,* (New York: George Braziller, 1982), 19–20.
37. Richard Elman, "Bashevis," *TIKKUN* (Jan./Feb. 1994): 63.
38. Eric Pace, "An Unchanged Storyteller," *The New York Times,* Dec. 9, 1978 ("Man in the News").
39. Mark S. Golub, "A Shmues with Isaac Bashevis Singer," *Sh'ma: a Journal of Jewish Responsibility* (Nov. 24, 1978): 9. Hereafter cited as Golub.
40. Vegetarians often formulate their world around exclusions, rather than inclusions. They prefer less, rather than more, choice; they embrace less, rather than more. "Vegetarians can be defined by an act of rejection; they do not eat certain foods.... The negative self-definition of the vegetarian makes it easy to construct a boundary around the self—'this is what I do, and this is not me.'" Kurt W. Back and Margaret Glasgow, "Social Networks and Psychological Conditions in Diet Preferences: Gourmets and Vegetarians," *Basic and Applied Social Psychology* 2: 1 (1981): 3.
41. *Love and Exile,* 19.
42. Elenore Lester, "Singer's rise to literary heights as strange as any of his stories," *The Jewish Week–American Examiner,* (Oct. 15, 1978): 3.

43. Grace Farrell, ed., *Isaac Bashevis Singer: Conversations,* (Jackson and London: University Press of Mississippi, 1992), 230. Hereafter cited as Farrell.
44. Suler, 3.
45. Farrell, 29.
46. Herbert R. Lottman in Farrell, 120.
47. Mirra Ginsburg, Interview, April 24, 1993.
48. David Gelman and Beverly Kempton, "Isaac Singer on People, Demons & Dybbuks," *Manhattan Tribune,* Dec. 28, 1968.
49. Kenneth Turan in Farrell, 150.
50. I am grateful to Elizabeth Shub for drawing my attention to the significance of this story.
51. Isaac Bashevis Singer (as Yitskhok Bashevis), "*Toybn*" ("Pigeons"), first appeared in the *Forverts* on January 28, 1966. Published in book form in *Mayses fun hintern oyvn,* (Tel Aviv: ha-Menorah, 1971). First translated in *A Friend of Kafka,* (New York: Farrar, Straus & Giroux, 1970). Republished as *A Friend of Kafka,* (New York: Fawcett Crest, 1980). Hereafter cited as *Friend.*
52. *Friend,* 121.
53. Letters to Ravitch are in the Ravitch Archives, The Jewish National and University Library, The Hebrew University, Jerusalem. I thank the Bergner family for granting me permission to read the correspondence.
54. Alma Singer, Interview, April 29, 1993.
55. Tallmer, 13.
56. Ravitch.
57. Alma Singer, Interview, Dec. 19, 1992.
58. Elizabeth Shub, Interview, Nov. 1992.
59. Golub, 9.

Chapter 8

1. Israel Zamir, "The Meeting," *Moment* (April 1993): 78. Hereafter cited as *Moment.*
2. Israel Zamir, *Journey to My Father: Isaac Bashevis Singer,* (New York: Arcade Publishing, 1995), 25. Hereafter cited as *Journey.*
3. Israel Zamir, Interview, March 24, 1993. Hereafter cited as Zamir; *Journey,* 24–25.
4. Letter, Courtesy of Singer Archives, University of Texas, Austin, Oct. 4, 1945.
5. Eleanor Foa Dienstag, the daughter of Alma's sister, does not recall any mention of Israel Zamir while she was growing up.
6. *Journey,* 26.
7. Isaac Bashevis Singer (as Yitskhok Bashevis), "*Der zun,*" ("The Son"), first appeared in *Svive* 4 (1961), 17–33. First translated in *A Friend of Kafka,* (New York: Farrar, Straus & Giroux), 1970. Republished as *A Friend of Kafka,* (New York: Fawcett Crest, 1980), 257. Hereafter cited as "The Son."
8. "The Son," 258.
9. *Moment,* 76.
10. *Moment,* 77.

11. "The Son," 259–260.
12. *Moment*, 77.
13. Zamir.
14. Israel Shenker, "A Bit of Reality by I. B. Singer and Son," *The New York Times* (April 17, 1970): 44.
15. Zamir.
16. According to both Bashevis [Farrell, 208] and Elizabeth Shub [Interview, Nov. 1992. Hereafter cited as Shub], the idea to write for children came from her.
17. Shub.
18. Isaac Bashevis Singer, "Zlateh the Goat," in *Stories for Children*, (New York: Farrar, Straus & Giroux, 1984), 48. Originally published in book form by Harper & Row, 1966, as *Zlateh the Goat, and Other Stories*, translated by I. B. Singer and Elizabeth Shub.
19. Isaac Bashevis Singer (as Y. Varshavsky), *"Der palats"* ("The Palace"), first appeared in the *Forverts* (Sept. 14, 1967): 2,6. Published in English translation as "Menaseh's Dream," in *Stories for Children,* (New York: Farrar, Straus & Giroux, 1984), 321.
20. Isaac Bashevis Singer, "I See the Child as a Last Refuge," *The New York Times Book Review* (Nov. 9, 1969): 1, 66.
21. *The New York Times*, Dec. 11, 1978.
22. "Students Entertain Author (Turning the Tables)," *Long Island Press*, May 27, 1971.
23. Alma Singer, Interview, Oct. 18, 1992.
24. Zamir.
25. Shub.
26. Ophra Alyagon, Interview, March 24, 1993. Hereafter cited as Alyagon.
27. At the end of his life, Singer would tell his son, "I'm Herman, for good and for bad." *Journey*, 93.
28. *Journey*, 93.
29. *Journey*, 89.
30. Phone conversation, January, 1996. During the 1960s, Bashevis made several visits to the Menninger Clinic, where he spoke to psychiatric analytic residents. Aliza Shevrin recalls one incident involving Dobe: "Isaac held forth on his usual stuff and the students asked him questions. Someone asked him, 'What is the basic thing that a writer needs? What is it that makes a writer, that makes you know how to write?' And Isaac very seriously said, 'A writer needs roots.' And Dobe from some place piped up, 'Like a dentist.' And every head looked—dead silence. And she said, 'Well, a dentist needs roots.' And Isaac said, 'Dobe, I told you never to speak. Keep quiet!' She could care less."
31. *Journey*, 91; personal communication; Zamir erroneously refers to her as Dove Gruber.
32. Courtesy, Singer Archives, University of Texas, Austin: At least between 1977–1980, Singer was authorizing checks to both women.
33. Alyagon.
34. Sylvia Weber, Interview, June 23, 1992.
35. Richard Elman, "Bashevis," *TIKKUN* (Jan./Feb. 1994): 66,67.

36. Alma Singer, Interview, May 22, 1994; Eleanor Foa Dienstag, Interview, Nov. 1992.
37. *Journey*, 92.
38. Fern Marja Eckman, "Daily Closeup: Interrupted Melody," *New York Post*, July 6, 1972.

Chapter 9

1. Singer received his first National Book Award in 1970, for *A Day of Pleasure*. The prize, administered by the Association of American Publishers, was awarded annually in several categories.
2. Isaac Bashevis Singer, *Yiddish* 2:1 (Fall 1976): 9.
3. *The New York Times* was not publishing because of a strike that Autumn.
4. The *Los Angeles Times* also carried this paragraph from the *Times* Wire Service.
5. Joseph McLellan, "American 'Storyteller' in Yiddish Wins Nobel Prize for Literature," *The Washington Post*, Oct. 6, 1978.
6. Not recognizing that Sholom Aleichem was a pseudonym based on a greeting in Hebrew and Yiddish, the paper announced that: "Following in the tradition of Aleichem and Sholem Asch, Singer is often considered the last great writer in that tradition." The same wording, from the *Times* Wire Service, appeared in *The Washington Post*.
7. Lance Morrow, "The Spirited World of I. B. Singer," *Atlantic* (Jan. 1979): 39. Hereafter cited as Morrow; it is likely that Singer was blissfully ignorant of the error. According to Associated Press Writer, Amy Sabrin, who interviewed him in *The New York Times,* Oct. 17, 1978 (Supplementary Material from the *NYT News Service* and *The Associated Press*): "Singer does not watch television. He calls it a thing for half-children, or 'Schmatahs,' a Yiddish term translating roughly as nonsense." Sabrin may not have realized that the literal meaning of *shmate* is rag. Hereafter cited as Sabrin.
8. Roger Rosenblatt, "Isaac Stern: Like a Character of His Own," *The Washington Post* (Oct. 19, 1978): 23.
9. Robert Alter, "Singer's Nobel: Posthumous Recognition of the Yiddish World," *Los Angeles Times*, Oct. 8, 1978.
10. Peter S. Prescott, "Singer the Magician," *Newsweek* (Oct. 16, 1978): 97.
11. Ben Gallob, "Isaac Beshevis Singer [sic] First Yiddish Writer to Win the Nobel," *Chicago Sentinel* (Oct. 19, 1978): 10.
12. Morrow, 43.
13. Alfred Kazin, "Remembering Singer's Flights of Fancy," *Forverts,* Books Section, Nov. 1991.
14. *Times* Wire Service, "Jewish Writer Wins '78 Nobel Literature Prize," *Los Angeles Times* (Oct. 6, 1978): 12.
15. *New York Post*, Oct. 18, 1978.
16. Vida Goldgar, "Jews and the Nobel," *The Southern Israelite*, Oct. 13, 1978.
17. *The Associated Press*, "Singer Finds a Nobel That He Didn't Look For," *New York Post*, Oct. 6, 1978. Hereafter cited as "Finds Nobel."
18. Sabrin.

19. Donald Singleton, "I. B. Singer Wins a Nobel," *City News,* Oct. 6, 1978. Hereafter cited as Singleton.

20. Joseph McLellan, "American 'Storyteller' in Yiddish Wins Nobel Prize for Literature, *The Washington Post,* Oct. 6, 1978.

21. Singleton.

22. Mirra Ginsburg, Interview, April 24, 1993.

23. Alma Singer, Interview, Dec. 19, 1992. Hereafter cited as Alma Singer.

24. "How Singer's Kibbutznik Son Heard the News," *The Jerusalem Post,* Oct. 10, 1978.

25. Alma Singer.

26. Isaac Bashevis Singer (as Yitskhok Bashevis), *Sonim: di geshikhte fun a libe,* first serialized in the *Forverts* between Feb. 11, 1966, and Aug. 13, 1966, 2, every Friday and Saturday. First translated by Aliza Shevrin and Elizabeth Shub as *Enemies, A Love Story,* (New York: Farrar, Straus & Giroux, 1972). Republished as *Enemies, A Love Story,* (Greenwich: Fawcett Publications, 1973), 41. Hereafter cited as *Enemies.*

27. *Enemies,* 17.

28. Personal communication from David Brandes, Canadian filmmaker.

29. Shimen Weber, "An Honor for Yiddish Literature, Pride for the *Forverts,*" *Forverts* (Oct. 6, 1978): 1.

30. Isaac Bashevis Singer, "I Share my Nobel Prize With my Readers, Says Bashevis-Singer," *Forverts* (Oct. 8, 1978): 1.

31. "Nobel Prize for Bashevis Singer," *Morgn-frayhayt,* Oct. 8, 1978.

32. Ber Grin, "I. Bashevis Singer and the Nobel Prize," *Morgn-frayhayt* (Nov. 19, 1978): 10.

33. Aaron Lansky, *The Book Peddler* 16 (Winter 1991–92): 2.

34. *The New York Times Magazine,* Nov. 26 and Dec. 3, 1978; Press release, American Jewish Committee, Nov. 6, 1978.

35. Personalities Column, *The Washington Post,* Oct. 25, 1978.

36. Eleanor Foa Dienstag, Interview, Dec. 1992.

37. "A Great Day for Jewish Forward: Its Writer and Yiddish Honored," *The New York Times,* Dec. 9, 1978.

38. John Vinocur, "Singer, in his Nobel Lecture, Hails Yiddish," *The New York Times* (Dec. 9, 1978): 4. Hereafter cited as Vinocur.

39. Lars Gyllensten, "The Work of Isaac Bashevis Singer," *Forverts* (Dec. 24, 1978): 25. Hereafter cited as *Forverts.*

40. Israel Zamir, Interview, March 24, 1993.

41. The Yiddish term for Jewish quarter is *"di yidishe gas,"* the Jewish street. It is more accurate than *ghetto,* which refers to an area where freedom of entry and exit is forbidden. The term was first applied in sixteenth-century Venice, when Jews were required to live in a designated section of the city; later, during the Nazi years, it was again used to refer to the neighborhoods into which Jews were herded and where they were imprisoned.

42. From the text of Singer's Nobel lecture. Reprinted in *The New York Times* (Dec. 9, 1978): 4.

43. Vinocur, 4.

44. Saul Bellow, Interview, June 24, 1995.
45. "Nobel Winner Singer Tells: Why I Write in Yiddish," *New York Post*, Dec. 11, 1978.
46. Saul Bellow, Telephone communication, August 15, 1996.
47. *Forverts*, 14.
48. *Journey*, 57.
49. *Forverts*, 1.
50. *Forverts*, 1,2,4.
51. Richard Burgin, "Isaac Bashevis Singer Talks...About Everything," *The New York Times Magazine* (Nov. 26, 1978): 24.
52. "Finds Nobel."
53. Personal correspondence, Saul Bellow, July 12, 1995.
54. Tony Schwartz, "Has the Nobel Prize Changed Singer's Life?," *The New York Times* (Oct. 17, 1979): C21.

Chapter 10

1. "Finds Nobel."
2. Christopher Lehmann-Haupt, "Nobel Prize to I.B. Singer," *The New York Times*, Nov. 6, 1978.
3. Stephen M. Silverman, "I.B. Singer's 'Demon' Lands at the Atkinson," *New York Post*, Dec. 7, 1979. Hereafter cited as Silverman.
4. *Short Friday and Other Stories*, (New York: Fawcett Crest, 1964). Hereafter cited as *Short Friday*.
5. Elenore Lester, "At 71, Isaac Bashevis Singer Makes His Broadway Debut," *The New York Times* (October 26, 1975): 1. Hereafter cited as Lester.
6. Isaac Bashevis Singer, "Yiddish Theater Lives, Despite the Past," *The New York Times* (Jan. 20, 1985): Arts, 1.
7. Farrell, xxv.
8. In the headline of the review by Mel Gussow in *The New York Times* ("Issac Bashevis Singer's 'Mirror' Staged at Yale," Feb. 7, 1973), Singer is referred to as "Issac"—yet another indication of the difficulty the media had with him.
9. Farrell, xxvii. Isaac Bashevis Singer (as Y. Varshavsky), "*Di bord*" ("The Beard"), first appeared in the *Forverts*, May 15–16, 1970. Translated as "The Beard" in *A Crown of Feathers*, (New York: Farrar, Straus & Giroux, 1973).
10. *Journey*, 46.
11. Lester, 1. The Broadway version was cut from more than three hours to slightly over two.
12. Martin Gottfried, "Feldshuh as Yentl Is Overpowering," *New York Post* (Oct. 24, 1975): Theater Section, 21. Hereafter cited as Gottfried.
13. Mendel Kohansky, "A Lesbian Fable," *Jerusalem Post International* (Feb. 3–9, 1980): Theater. Hereafter cited as Kohansky.
14. Press release from *Present Tense: The Magazine of World Jewish Affairs*, Nov. 3, 1975. Hereafter cited as *Present Tense*.
15. Earl Wilson, "It Happened Last Night: Oh Boy, That's a Girl," *New York Post*, Dec. 1, 1975. Hereafter cited as Wilson.

16. Lester, 1.
17. Wilson.
18. Gottfried.
19. Kohansky.
20. Lester.
21. Elenore Lester, "Singer's play entertaining enough although wry humor is burlesqued," *Jewish Week*, Nov. 2, 1975.
22. Lester.
23. Isaac Bashevis Singer, "Once on Second Avenue There Lived a Yiddish Theater (Did It Really Die?)" *The New York Times* (Apr. 17, 1966); Seymour Rexite, President of the Hebrew Actors Union of America, angrily responded in "Hebrew Actors Union vs. Isaac Bashevis Singer," in *Jewish Currents*, July–Aug., 1966.
24. Martin Gottfried, "Who Would Not Be Thrilled," *New York Post* (Nov. 8, 1975): Entertainment, 2. The reviewers at *The New York Times,* however, were not so enthusiastic. Walter Kerr found the stage adaptation of Singer's story "irritating," complaining that "an idea has been stubbornly, perversely pursued far beyond its usefulness to the play," (Nov. 2, 1975), and Clive Barnes called "Yentl" "...the kind of play that melts in the mind." (Oct. 24, 1975).
25. Lester, 1.
26. *Present Tense.*
27. Wilson.
28. Originally published as *Taybele un hurmiza* in the literary journal *Svive* (Feb. 1962): 7–16, it appeared in English in Singer's collection *Short Friday*, translated by Mirra Ginsburg.
29. "Taibele and Her Demon," reprinted in *The Collected Stories of Isaac Bashevis Singer,* (New York: Farrar, Straus & Giroux, 1953), eleventh printing, 1992, 139.
30. Walter Kerr, "The Theater: 'Teibele and Her Demon,'" *The New York Times* (Dec. 17, 1979): C15.
31. Julius Novick, "Devil in the Flesh," *The Village Voice*, Dec. 24, 1979.
32. Eve Friedman, "'Let's Write a Play,' He Said (Why Argue With a Genius?)" *The New York Times* (Dec. 16, 1979): Theater, 6. Hereafter cited as Friedman.
33. Carol Lawson, "Singer Play Due on Broadway," *The New York Times* (Oct. 3, 1979): C22.
34. Silverman.
35. Lars Gyllensten, "The Works of Isaac Bashevis Singer," *Forverts* (Dec. 24, 1978): 25.
36. "What's In It for Me?," 173.
37. Irving S. White, Interview, Spring 1995.
38. "The Luck of Isaac Singer: His Life's Already a Movie," *Charlotte Observer,* Nov. 20, 1978. Hereafter cited as "Luck."
39. Janet Maslin, "Screen: Singer's 'Magician of Lublin' Transformed," *The New York Times* (Nov. 9, 1979): C6. Hereafter cited as Maslin.
40. J. Hoberman, *The Village Voice*, Nov. 19, 1979. Hereafter cited as Hoberman.
41. "Luck."

42. Maslin, C6.
43. Hoberman.
44. Israel Zamir, Interview, March 24, 1993.
45. Roger Simon, Interview, June 16, 1993. Hereafter cited as Simon.
46. Silverman, 6.
47. Alyagon's, written in longhand on Singer's letterhead and dated Oct. 10, 1968, empowered her "to deal with potential publishers and newspapers about translating and publishing my works from the Yiddish into Hebrew, except for the books which have already been published in Hebrew. This contract is valid until October 10, 1971, and will be prolonged then. My friend Ophra Alyagon will get the usual 10 percent for her efforts." Shulman's contract, dated Dec. 14, 1971, authorized him to dramatize "Teibele and her Demon," in collaboration with Singer, for which Shulman was to receive forty percent of any profits. Neither contract was witnessed or notarized. Alyagon's initial contract was later formalized. My thanks to Ophra Alyagon for allowing me to see her contract. Mr. Shulman's contract is reproduced in an unpublished memoir, which he was kind enough to let me read.
48. "Barbra Streisand's 'Yentl' Due for December Release," *The New York Times*, July 15, 1983.
49. Chris Chase, "At the Movies," *The New York Times*, Nov. 18, 1983.
50. Alma Singer, Interview, Oct. 18, 1992.
51. Isaac Bashevis Singer, "I. B. Singer Talks to I. B. Singer About the Movie 'Yentl,'" *The New York Times* (Jan. 29, 1984): 2A.
52. Saul J. Berman, "Kol 'Isha," *Rabbi Joseph Lookstein Memorial Volume*, ed. Leo Landsman, (New York: ktav, 1980): 45–66.
53. Richard Corliss, "Toot, Toot, Tootseleh," *Time Magazine* (Nov. 21, 1983): 93.
54. Mrs. Walter Matthau, Pacific Palisades, CA, "Debating I. B. Singer's View of 'Yentl,'" *The New York Times* (Feb. 12, 1984): Letters to the Editor.
55. Dina Nerenberg, "Yentl: The View From Behind the *Mechitzah*," *Jewish Press Features* (editorial project of Jewish Student Press Service) (Feb. 21, 1984): 2–3.
56. Divertimento, *Gimpel the Fool*. CD produced by Delos International, Inc.
57. Paul Mazursky, Interview, July 3, 1994. Hereafter cited as Mazursky.
58. Angelica Huston received an Academy Award nomination for best supporting actress; and Paul Mazursky and Roger Simon were nominated for best screenplay.
59. Simon.
60. Mazursky.
61. Stephen Holden, "The Fun of Thinking It's Adultery When It's Not," *The New York Times* (July 9, 1994): Theater Review, 11.
62. John Lahr, "Bring Back the Clowns," *The New Yorker* (July 11, 1994): Theater, 75. The Polish city of Chelm is famous in Eastern-European-Jewish humor as a town inhabited entirely by simpletons. The *khelemer naronim*, the fools of Chelm, are the subject of countless anecdotes, jokes, and tales in Yiddish. Far from inventing Chelm, Singer self-consciously set his story within a well-known context of tradition.

Chapter 11

1. Meirav Hen, Interview, Feb. 12, 1993.
2. Courtesy, Singer Archives, University of Texas, Austin.
3. Ophra Alyagon, Interview, Sept. 23, 1993.
4. Ed Reiter, "Hall of Fame Medal Honors a Nobel Laureate," *The New York Times* (July 15, 1984): 27–28.
5. Morris U. Schappes, "Handel Medallion to I. B. Singer," *Jewish Currents* (Sept. 1986): 19.
6. William Grimes, "Toni Morrison is '93 Winner of Nobel Prize in Literature," *The New York Times* (Oct. 8, 1993): 1.
7. Lester Goran, *The Bright Streets of Surfside,* (Kent, Ohio, and London, England: Kent State University Press, 1994), 67. Hereafter cited as Goran.
8. Courtesy, Singer Archives, University of Texas, Austin.
9. Dorothea Straus, Interview, Dec. 8, 1995. Hereafter cited as Straus.
10. Cathy Grossman Keller, "The Calls Kept Coming in Surfside," *The Washington Post,* Oct. 6, 1978.
11. Goran, 33.
12. Alma Singer, Interview, Oct. 18, 1992.
13. Straus.
14. *Journey,* 226.
15. *Journey,* 2.
16. *Journey,* 7.

Epilogue

1. My thanks to Ida Haendel for this description.

INDEX

237